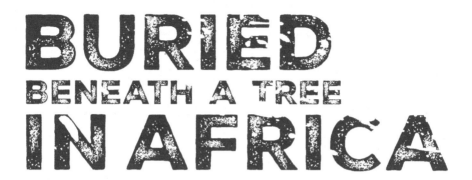

BURIED BENEATH A TREE IN AFRICA

The Journey to Investigate the Murder

of My Father in Uganda by Idi Amin

EDWARD SIEDLE

Buried Beneath A Tree In Africa

The Journey to Investigate the Murder of My Father in Uganda by Idi Amin

© 2023, Edward Siedle.

ISBN: 979-8-35092-435-0

THE REPUBLIC OF UGANDA

FOREWORD

In *Buried Beneath A Tree In Africa*, Edward Siedle, retraces the tragic events that led to the extra-judicial killing of his father. At the time of his death, in 1971, Robert Siedle was a lecturer and researcher at Makerere University.

The author's father, Robert Siedle, was captured while investigating the massacre of hundreds of Ugandan Army soldiers by Idi Amin's forces, in the garrison town of Mbarara. His body was never found. Robert Siedle suffered the fate of thousands of Ugandans, under Amin's bankrupt regime and the Obote dictatorship.

The people of Uganda, supported by our Pan-African Statesman, Mwalimu Julius Nyerere, were able to overthrow these dictatorial regimes. In 1986, we ushered in an era of peace, security and respect for human rights and property. After more than three decades of stability, under the NRM government, Uganda has become an anchor state, in the East African region and beyond.

I was not aware of Robert's efforts. Now that I am informed, I will also initiate my own inquiries into the criminal killings of the two friends of Uganda. Of course, I heard of the story around June – July, 1971. I had infiltrated back into Uganda from our external base of

THE REP. BLA OF UGANDA

Tanzania. While in Kampala, I got that additional terrible news from our network of Resistance fighters that included Kategaya, Rugunda, Akena Pajok and others. Unfortunately, many of the people who were involved in Amin's crimes are now dead.

I will read the book and find out how Robert interacted with Ali Fadhul. Ali Fadhul survived my AK-47 by a whisker on the 17th of September, 1972, when, hidden in a civilian Peugeot 504, drove through my column of 8 lorries full of soldiers at Mile 35 from Mbarara because I had forbidden soldiers from disturbing civilian vehicles.

I commend Mr. Edward Siedle's courageous attempt to retrace the last steps of his beloved father. The evil that was meted out against his innocent father was avenged by the Ugandan patriots. It is my hope that his book will inspire Ugandan survivors to tell their stories.

Y.K Museveni

PRESIDENT OF THE REPUBLIC OF UGANDA

4/10/2023

While I have spent decades writing bestselling books and educating millions of readers about finance and business, I have come to believe some things in life are far more important than money—such as the relationships between fathers and their sons. Ted Siedle's new book, *Buried Beneath A Tree in Africa*, is the true story of a son's journey to investigate the sudden disappearance and brutal murder of his father by President Idi Amin in Uganda in 1971. His expedition to Uganda, 26 years after the murder in search of answers about his father's work with the CIA and how he met his death, is gripping. The assistance he received from our and Uganda's governments, military, and intelligence communities, is miraculous. As Ted says, "The remarkable feature of life-affirming journeys is that you always encounter others who recognize the importance of what you're doing and will want to help you—as if the universe wants you to succeed and comes to your aid. You may feel yourself uplifted then passed over countless heads, floating on a sea of helping hands."

–Robert Kiyosaki, author of *Rich Dad Poor Dad*

"Mti umeangukia huko mbali, bali matawi joke yamefika hadi hapa."

("A tree has fallen far away, but the branches have reached here.")

– A Swahili saying for news of death.

Skulls found by local farmers remind Ugandans of thousands killed by former President Milton Obote and Idi Amin during their reign of terror. (Photo by John Tlumacki/The Boston Globe via Getty Images)

This book is dedicated to young people, everywhere, who find themselves in impossible situations—not of their own making and beyond their control. Situations which so haunt them that they must return as adults to the horrific scenes of the crimes. As adults, they can finally do what they needed to care for themselves when they were children, but couldn't. Blessed are they who survive to return.

Also, it is offered to all who have lost a loved one, their bodies never found and whose deaths remain a mystery. May you search and someday find the answers you need.

Lastly, this is a remembrance of my mother, Betty Zenobia Khan, whom I lost as a child of 3 and found thirty-five years later. And my father, Robert Louis Siedle who disappeared in Uganda, East Africa when I was 17 years old. Both parents found, returned to the heart.

CONTENTS

CHAPTER 1

A VISIT TO DEATH ROW

K nowing you can kill someone and walk away without consequences—morally blameless even—is very different from actually doing it. As I prepared to meet the man who either participated in the capture, torture and murder of my father, or at a minimum, covered-up the killing I wondered what would it cost to have him killed in his prison cell—maybe just a pack of Marlboro cigarettes?

In the Uganda, East Africa I had lived as a teenager, I learned anything could be accomplished for a small price. A single cigarette I offered to a "kondo" (thief or armed robber) at an impromptu tire-shredder roadblock in the bush late at night had once saved my life.

"What if he refuses to talk about what he did?" I asked. "Can we force him to tell me?"

The soldiers escorting me through the prison shook their heads dutifully, "Sorry, sir, torture is now prohibited under international law and Article 24 of the Ugandan Constitution."

"That's too bad," I said, "Can't we bring it back—*just this once*?" We all laughed nervously at my remark which was not entirely a joke.

After decades of human rights abuses, the Ugandan Army no longer engaged in torture. That was the official policy, but I knew better. Despite these laws, torture still happened in Uganda.

If I wanted it bad enough, I was certain I could bring the murderer's pathetic life to a quick, painful end.

Perhaps I would choose to have him killed.

If I made the choice—this day at this prison—to take his life in exchange for the life of my father he had taken decades earlier, I could live with it.

Luzira Maximum Security Prison, located in a suburb of Kampala, the bustling capital city of Uganda near the banks of Lake Victoria in East Africa, was built by the British in the 1920s—thirty years after the country had been made a British protectorate. In colonial days, the prison, which today houses both men and women, was less crowded but still inhumane: substandard living conditions, systematic humiliation and cruel discipline, including the use of punishment cells deliberately flooded with water to make them uninhabitable. The British used the prison to jail nationalists and political dissidents.

Post-colonial Uganda, after independence from the British in 1962, was even less humane to its prison population. Luzira is often mentioned in accounts of atrocities committed under the brutal regimes of former leaders General Idi Amin Dada and Dr. Apollo Milton Obote in the 1970s and 1980s. By the early 1990s, Luzira was ravaged by HIV and so poorly funded that less than a quarter of the inmates were supplied with basic necessities, such as blankets. Prisoners buried the dead in mass graves and grew vegetables on the same earth to keep the living fed. In 1993, a group of former soldiers started a two-day riot that required army intervention and left two prisoners dead and many injured.

While Luzira—the only maximum-security prison in Uganda—is hardly the most forbidding prison structure (at least compared with American correctional fortresses), conditions inside the Third World facility are notoriously harsh. Even today, the exact population of Luzira is unknown; however, it is the largest prison in Uganda. It was designed with a maximum capacity of 1,700, but often houses as many as 20,000—including about 500 men and women on the country's only death row.

Murderers have long been isolated from free society by confining them behind Luzira's high walls and huge gates. Unsurprisingly, this makes the prison an ideal place for committing murder.

In 2005, a key suspect in the murder of a lawyer and chairperson of Transparency International, a leading anti-corruption organization, was shot seven times in the head while in Luzira. He survived the initial attack, but later died while in medical care, despite being under tight security with three elite guards. Prison personnel suspected foul play, potentially poison, or suicide, but the real cause was never entirely clear.

It has long been easy for Uganda's ruling elite to slaughter their victims in the shadows of Luzira's walls—the only potential witnesses being convicted murderers, rapists, armed robbers, and kidnappers, locked in their cells along with many lost souls awaiting trial, often for years due to the glacially slow Ugandan court system. No one ever needed worry about any of these unfortunates talking.

Although I have visited prisons a few times as a pre-law college student studying criminal justice reform, prisons terrify me—even supposedly well-managed and adequately funded prisons in the United States.

Luzira Prisons Complex Main Security Gate

It was a bright, sunny day when we drove up to the prison. Inmates could be seen working outside on the grounds in crews without shackles and in the prison courtyard. The prisoners were dressed in a rainbow of color-coded jumpsuits. Remand prisoners awaiting trial, and those serving less than twenty years, wore pale yellow overalls; prisoners wearing more intense yellow were serving more than twenty years; psychiatric patients were in green. Inmates who wore a red stripe had tried to escape, and a blue stripe indicated seniority and privileges. Due to staff shortages, some inmates had been designated as regimental police who wore white arm bands, and they helped keep the peace. The inmates on death row lived separately from the main prison population and wore white overalls. The condemned convicts were not allowed to interact with the other prisoners and were let out just a few minutes a day to sit in the compound (under heavy guard) to take fresh air.

This day in 1997, I was escorted through Luzira's maze of hallways by Major Albert Kareba, who was in full military uniform—burgundy beret, olive green fatigues and spit-shined black combat boots. In his early thirties, tall, proud, physically fit, and handsome, he commanded respect from the demoralized prison guards and the clammy, flu-infected warden who was profoundly unenthusiastic about his assignment to the prison and hopeful the assistance he provided to us might offer him a way out.

My visit to Luzira Prison had been arranged by Major General Mugisha Muntuoyera, Commander of the Ugandan Peoples Defense Forces and commonly referred to as "General Muntu" by civilians and soldiers alike.

"Please be sure to tell General Muntu how helpful I have been," the sniffling warden pleaded. "Remind him, if you will, that I was originally only temporarily assigned to the prison and *that* was seven years ago. Has the General forgotten about me?" He coughed and then wiped his runny nose on the sleeve of his frayed uniform.

Major Kareba (or Albert, as I called him) and I were easy friends by now, having spent the week prior traveling together through remote regions of the country. Our destination had been the town of Mbarara—where my father was last seen alive. Mbarara was included in Robert Young Pelton's "indispensable handbook for the intrepid adventurer" entitled, *The World's Most Dangerous Places.* Concerned for my safety, I had read the chapter on Uganda closely in preparation for my journey. Pelton begins by ominously stating:

> "The pearl of Africa, the mountains of the moon promises a sense of Africa renewed, pristine, undiscovered and perhaps pure. What Uganda offers, though, is a mist-covered glimpse into hell.
>
> It is where Western tourist were ruthlessly hacked to death with machetes, a place where jails are stained with the brains of former inmates, where children are snatched and sold into slavery... Uganda is a fertile and deadly place, always has been."

With respect to Mbarara, Pelton said, "The maxim for most dangerous places is, don't go unless you have to."

Little did I imagine when I read Pelton's book I would soon be jogging, under guard, alongside killing fields in Mbarara where the bodies of hundreds of bludgeoned Ugandan Army soldiers had been heartlessly scattered decades earlier.

Albert's appearance reminded me he was one of the most promising officers in this impoverished army—a beleaguered force where soldiers who retire after a lifetime of service receive a seemingly paltry retirement benefit of $1,200, I was told.

"Do you mean $1,200 a month?" I asked. "I imagine a retired soldier could live very well indeed in Uganda on that amount."

"No, $1,200—period—a one-time, lump-sum payment," said Albert.

"How do you retire on that?" I asked.

"Easy," Albert explained. "It's enough money to buy a plot of land to farm and a small herd of cattle for milk and beef, which together, absent disaster, will produce a stream of income adequate to provide for a soldier's declining years."

Albert was the Army's Chief Protocol Officer, charged with handling all matters of etiquette—including the delicate task of escorting this son of an American who had disappeared in the custody of the Ugandan Army decades earlier during Idi Amin's murderous rule, on his journey to find answers.

As we approached the prison, Albert did not appear to be the relaxed tour guide he had been over the past week, dressed like a yuppie in his starched button-down collar Polo shirt, khaki slacks and loafers. He had always been so courteous and eager to please, as well as hear of life in the USA. As we turned the corner returning to the warden's office for the interrogation of a prisoner, I asked myself: "How can I persuade the man I am about to meet to tell me exactly how and why he murdered my father?"

I needed the details to finally come to terms with my father's death. With no picture of the murder in my mind and without his body as proof of death, I had never been able to fully accept he had been killed.

Could I reason with Lt. Col. Ali Fadhul, a distant relative of Amin's with a hair-trigger temper and reputation for savagery? Under Amin's military dictatorship, Fadhul, the commander of the Army's Simba battalion had once acted like a local warlord ruling Mbarara. Appearing before a tribunal investigating my father's murder in 1972, Fadhul's demeanor was preposterously arrogant as he testified—confusing facts and dates, and refusing to produce records, dressed in a Savile Row lounge suit, wearing two gold Rolex watches, one on each wrist.

The gold Rolexes were gifts from Amin's so-called "whiskey runs" to Stansted Airport in England, where planeloads of expensive Scotch whisky, transistor radios, and other luxury items were purchased for Amin to distribute among his loyal officers. Quoting an old African proverb, Amin justified lavishing his army with such treasures: "A dog with a bone in its mouth can't bite."

Now Fadhul was an inmate in this maximum-security prison on death row, having been found guilty in 1987 of only one of the hundreds, maybe thousands, of murders he had ordered or committed with his own hands— the grisly killing, in public view, fifteen years earlier, of a local government official in Mbarara who he forced into the trunk of his own car at gunpoint and later coolly shot in the head. Fadhul was one of very few Amin followers to be convicted for crimes committed from 1971–1979. The fortune he had amassed by exploiting his military and government positions and participating in illegal smuggling operations had been seized by the new government.

I wondered if he would fear confessing to another murder he had committed almost thirty years ago?

Justice David Jeffreys Jones, a distinguished judge of the High Court of Uganda who had presided over the Ugandan Commission of Inquiry investigating my father's disappearance in 1971, had warned the unknown murderers, in his published Report, that "Nemesis," the god of retribution, "will one day claim her pound of flesh." Was he merely expressing a longing as old as mankind—that justice will someday prevail? Was there not a hint of frustration in his words? After all, Justice Jones had been unable, or perhaps unwilling (due to presidential intimidation), to even name the killer(s) in his final Report. It seemed an empty threat to warn that someday this wrong would be addressed and those responsible would suffer. Jones had spoken of "the hand of God intervening on the side of justice," aiding him in his inquiry when he referred to remarkable coincidences that broke the sinister wall of silence initially surrounding the case. Retribution and justice—beliefs onto which the living victims, survivors of murdered loved ones cling—surely were long overdue.

Some never know where, when or how their loved ones were killed. How they grieve, I do not know. But for this son, who had initially drifted and then boldly passed from youth to manhood in East Africa with this father, the time had come to finally go back for him.

At age 42, still crippled by the fear that struck me upon his death and that had been unshakable since, I had chosen to travel back to the last home he and I would ever know. To end my suffering, I had elected to return to this land—hell on earth, as seen through the prism of my traumatic past. It had taken me 26 years to travel halfway around the world to finally say goodbye.

Robert Siedle

Edward Siedle

CHAPTER 2

THIS LAND OF BEAUTY AND ADVENTURE

I once knew Uganda well, having lived there alone with my father for two years before his death. When we first landed in the country on the day of my fifteen birthday, June 22, 1969, I was "mad as hell" (as my father would say) at him. Like so many times before, when we had moved from Trinidad to Venezuela, then Peru, then Panama, he had taken me from friends and societies I had grown comfortable with to a distant land to satisfy his curiosity about other races and cultures. Yet, by the time I left Uganda, days after my seventeenth birthday, I was a young man awakened to an exotic world my father had wished for me.

College professors and their children are blessed with especially great social mobility. Professors may not earn much money or live in the best neighborhoods. However, due to their richness of thought or learning, many doors are left open to them. Their children may go to the best schools on scholarship, they may travel more frequently, and they may be greatly respected in the community. Their financial condition need not limit their social status.

Our family never had much money. For most of my childhood, we lived in graduate student housing. We never owned a home, a washer or dryer and rarely a television. As renters, we never had to mow a lawn. Furniture we bought at the Salvation Army Thrift Store and sold whenever we moved, generally every couple of years. Our old, unfashionable and frequently unreliable family cars were usually a source of embarrassment to me. There were mornings we had to push the old faded-black Volvo sedan down the hill and pop the clutch to get it started. Yet we lived our lives with a richness money cannot buy and which the wealthy seldom experience. Forever curious and committed to learning, armed with our library of books, we travelled wherever our imaginations propelled us. And while I now know—from reading his diaries after he died—he privately worried about finances, I don't recall my father ever giving me reason to be fearful about money. Money was tight, but our needs would be met, he seemed to be saying. And there was never any shame in openly acknowledging our limited financial means and living frugally.

In Uganda, especially, finances did not define our social experience. This was the wealthiest time in my family's life. My father had completed his graduate studies, earning a doctorate in gerontology and now teaching at Makerere University. He was making more money than ever—enough to maintain the comfortable standard of living the European community in Uganda enjoyed, including employing a housekeeper/cook. We moved, my father and I, in social circles that included professors, researchers, diplomats, local government officials, development agency workers, intelligence operatives, and members of the international press.

Makerere University—then the only university in East Africa and dubbed the "Harvard of Africa"—was a meeting ground for those interested in exchanging information about the region. East Africa was an unsettled region during the Cold War: Israelis piloted the planes of the Ugandan Air Force and were involved in construction projects; Chinese were building a railroad for neighboring socialist Tanzania; the British still had a foothold from the colonial era; and America, Europe and Russia vied for the hearts of the people through their development programs.

Makerere University Main Administration Building

When we arrived, Makerere University itself was immersed in a very public controversy in connection with the scheduled dissolution of the University of East Africa. The UEA had been established by Britain in 1963 to maintain its influence in East Africa as the region exited colonialism and entered into the independence era.

Britain sought to use the UEA for the continued intellectual and ideological indoctrination of the regional elites it had started in 1949 following the establishment of Makerere in Uganda as an inter-territorial institution for all of East Africa. After July 1, 1970, the UEA would be split into three separate national universities established in Kenya, Uganda and Tanzania. President Obote appointed a Visitation Committee to conduct an investigation immediately prior to the UEA dissolution due, in part, to dissatisfaction regarding the high percentage of non-Ugandan staff teaching at Makerere. As my father observed:

"Many are white which is sometimes resented and the Americans and the British are distrusted because of their white "colonial" and "imperialistic" flavor. There is also fear voiced that an educated elite will develop in Uganda which holds itself above the "common man." Just about all African students at Makerere are paid by the state for attending school, both in cash, free room and board, and an allowance for books.

Inasmuch as students receive so much and live much better than the average laborer or farmer, this seems to be a valid fear."

Uganda was said to have the largest international intelligence community of all Africa. Unlike me and my father, American intelligence operatives generally lived within the American Embassy compound, separated by walls, guards and barbed wire from the people.

They gathered information about life in Uganda, as opposed to living it like we did.

In this land of beauty and adventure, remote and innocent, where rich, green forests teemed with scampering tree monkeys and noisy hippos woke me at night when camping alongside Lake Victoria, I had been granted the remarkable opportunity to freely pursue my own direction. In the absence of any obvious choice for my schooling, my father reluctantly permitted me to not attend—i.e., to drop out of secondary school. In the slowness of African evenings, unencumbered by any schedules or commitments, I listened to the voices of the African and Asian students at Makerere University, as well as Peace Corps, international development and diplomatic services workers and learned of vastly different worlds.

In America, we lead lives of endless, smoldering worry. We worry about our jobs, keeping up with the mortgage, whether we have adequate insurance to protect against every conceivable adverse outcome, whether we'll outlive our retirement savings. Yet, the more relentlessly we chase after ever greater, ever longer-term safety and security for ourselves, our children and their children—the more elusive these goals seem. The strife of life becomes joyless for many.

In Uganda, life is perilous. It is understood.

In Uganda, they pray. They pray that famine, disease and war will not overwhelm them. They pray that they will not lose their will to live, die of a broken heart or crushed spirit. The weight of human suffering seems unbearable, yet it is borne by these people. They have not lost their humanity or capacity for brief, splendid moments of heartfelt joy—joy that knows no past or future, only the moment.

In Uganda, fears are not imagined; they are forged on an anvil of hard reality.

Harsh conditions breed cruelty. Cruel leaders emerge—leaders who are even tougher than the worlds they destroy. Frightened soldiers, pawns in a desperate, deadly game, follow their leaders' orders—no matter how insane—for fear of their own lives. The poor, simple recruit manning an army roadblock at night who, perceiving insult from a would-be passerby, asserts his momentary supreme authority and in a flash of fury, kills. The gun he clutches being all that separates him from every other desperate night crawler.

In Uganda, they know the most dangerous man is the man who is afraid, the man who senses his mandate to rule is as tenuous as a thread. He is the lion who stalks the peaceful villagers—the wild animal heard pacing and grumbling in the night.

Such a leader was Idi Amin, an illiterate Army underling who following a military coup in 1971 declared himself president of the nation, dissolved the parliament, and amended the constitution to give himself absolute power. He gave himself the title "His Excellency President for Life Field Marshal Al Hadji Dr. Idi Amin, VC, DSO, MC, Lord of All the Beasts of the Earth and Fishes of the Sea, and Conqueror of the British Empire."

After assuming the role of commanding officer of the Army, he elevated many of his staunchest supporters, including uneducated and untrained civilians to command positions as his captains, majors and lieutenants.

His Excellency President for Life Field Marshal Al Hadji Dr. Idi
Amin, VC, DSO, MC, Lord of All the Beasts of the Earth and
Fishes of the Sea, and Conqueror of the British Empire.

Amin and his cronies even developed and used a special vocabulary
of killing and torture. "Giving the V.I.P. treatment" to someone meant to kill,
as did the instruction "Go with him to where he sleeps." "Giving tea" meant
whipping and dismemberment.

Over time, Amin's often inane utterances made him a buffoon in the
international community. He once said in a telegram to Tanzanian President
Julius Nyerere: "I want to assure you that I love you very much, and if you had
been a woman, I would have considered marrying you, although your head
is full of gray hairs." He also infuriated President Richard Nixon by sending
him a "get-well-soon from Watergate" telegram.

With his poorly disciplined Army by his side, the mercurial Amin ruled for eight years with a bloody hand, destroying Uganda's economy, expelling tens of thousands of Asians from the country, and murdering hundreds of thousands of men, women, and children. Popularly known as the "Butcher of Uganda," he is rightfully regarded one of the ten most evil men of the millennium.

CHAPTER 3

AMIN COUP
CHANGES EVERYTHING

On the morning of January 25, 1971, my father and I awoke to the sound of gunfire. Military troops swept about the Makerere University campus. We heard the Kiganda ululation—a whooping sound with the hand held over the mouth and then rapidly moving back and forth. All classes were cancelled.

At about 3:45 p.m., an announcement was made over Radio Uganda that President Milton Obote—who was in Singapore for two weeks to participate in the summit of the Commonwealth of Nations—had been overthrown by the armed forces of Uganda. About half an hour later, it was announced that the Army had given power to their fellow soldier, Major-General Idi Amin.

Before leaving for Singapore, Obote had written a memorandum to Amin demanding explanations about costs that had been discovered in the Army and about police suspicions Amin had been involved in murdering a senior Army officer whom Amin had seen as a rival. Amin viewed Obote's memorandum as a severe attack on his honor and a pretext to oust him from the Army. The coup was carried out seemingly without prior planning when one evening several Uganda military officers appeared at the gate of Amin's house and he feared they would arrest him. Amin decided Obote's absence gave him the opportunity to overthrow the unpopular regime and save himself.

The charismatic Amin, a former assistant Army cook and undefeated Army heavyweight boxing champion, was now a national hero. He rode through the streets of Kampala and was welcomed as a vibrant new leader who could bring prosperity and stability to Uganda after almost a decade of corruption and violence under Obote.

A few minutes later, my father walked down the hill from the campus to the city. He wrote in his journal:

> "The street was full of happy people in their cars, on scooters and bicycles, shouting. There were people carrying branches of trees and waving them from their cars. Cars passed with people on the roofs and in the open trunks; trucks were loaded with others yelling and waving. When military vehicles came into view, the crowds cheered wildly. People were proudly displaying pictures of the late Kabaka, the King of the Baganda tribe, yelling, "Kabaka Yeka" or "the Kabaka has risen." It's a crazy, carnival-like time. Everyone is happy to see Obote gone."

The day after Amin assumed power, he proudly—and falsely—declared the coup's only casualty was a single wounded soldier. And he pledged, "We all want only unity in Uganda and we do not want bloodshed. Everybody in Uganda knows that."

That day my father was at the Apollo Hotel—the best hotel in the city—when foreign news correspondents arrived on a special flight from Nairobi. He noted in his journal:

> "Some troops were stationed at the hotel and they searched the rooms for certain people they wanted to arrest. Minister of Internal Affairs Bataringaya, was badly beaten and then arrested by the soldiers. They drove off with him on the top of a tank. The desk manager, a member of the Kigala tribe, was beaten and marched off because he hadn't told the soldiers that Bataringaya was there."

All we knew for certain was that they were beaten and taken away. The next day, late at night, Radio Uganda announced the release of those detained by the military after the coup. Once again, the whole city seemed to be ululating and beating on tin pans for hours. Within a few days of the coup, however, unbeknownst to us, hundreds were imprisoned and killed.

Basil Kiiza Bataringaya, whom my father witnessed being beaten and arrested, was a prominent Ugandan politician in post-independence Uganda. He was the Leader of the Opposition at the beginning of the Obote government. Later, he changed parties and was appointed to the powerful role of Ugandan Minister of Internal Affairs. He was tortured and imprisoned in Makindye Prison, then dismembered alive outside the town of Mbarara. His severed head was placed on the end of a pole and paraded around the town until it was ultimately displayed in the Mbarara barracks. His wife, former head of the Uganda Council of Women, was executed in a later purge by Amin.

Basil Bataringaya Under Arrest

We did not know what we could not see.

My father noticed dozens of large hawks wheeling and soaring in updrafts over the city for several days a month later. He commented on their beauty.

"How graceful and free they seem floating effortlessly, hardly moving their wings."

That the hawks were drawn by decaying bodies, we never imagined. There were reports of isolated killings and the gunfire continued periodically. But Amin always had an explanation—that armed robbers or "kondos" had been apprehended by his troops and refused to surrender. By March, a series of mass killings in the armed forces began. But all we heard were rumors.

Soldiers in the Streets of Kampala
Following the Coup, Photograph by My Father

My father first met then-General Amin on Saturday night, May 9, 1970, less than a year before the coup. He was photographed talking with him and the Israeli ambassador at a Soviet Embassy reception to commemorate the 25th anniversary of the victory of the Red Army in Europe. He wrote:

> "I had a very pleasant and stimulating evening with a bunch of convivial Communists. I attended the reception with some Yugoslav friends and met the Ambassador, his wife, and many of the Russian staff. I also had a chat with General Amin, the commander-in-chief of the Uganda Army. He is over six feet tall, heavily built, a Madi by tribe, and a Muslim. He wore a sports jacket with the Uganda coat of arms on the breast pocket, and was accompanied by only one young man about a head shorter than he, who wore a bulky sweater which seemed incongruous in the more formally dressed crowd."

After his murder, this eerie photograph of Amin and my father together—murderer and victim—would be shown in magazines around the world.

My Father, Israeli Ambassador, Amin at Russian Embassy

He talked with Amin again, six months later on October 8, 1970, at the inauguration of Makerere University and the installation of then-President Obote as its first chancellor. From his journal:

> "He is a big, heavy fellow and I like him. It has been rumored that he was under arrest. There was an officer with him in the background. He didn't seem well. He appeared confused or at a minimum he had trouble understanding my English."

At this time, before becoming president of Uganda, Amin was appealing to the Western world, particularly Britain, Israel, and the United States. Speculation as to whether one, or more, of these countries may have assisted Amin in the coup continues to this day.

• British Involvement

Amin was well known to the British.

Despite his claims that he fought in World War II, Amin joined the King's African Rifles of the British colonial army in 1946—after the War was over—and took part in the British campaign to prevent the independence of Burma. Later he was deployed in Kenya as part of an infantry brigade against the Mau Mau rebellion targeting European settlers until 1949, when his unit was deployed in Somalia to fight the Shifta, who were raiding cattle. Amin was promoted to corporal in 1952 and to sergeant in 1953. The following year, he was made effendi (warrant officer), the highest rank possible for a Black African in the colonial British army.

Amin's willingness to follow orders without question, his sports abilities and his spotless boots brought him promotion. He was popular with his English officers, who appreciated his skill on the rugby field, obedience, and devotion to all things British.

"Not much grey matter, but a splendid chap to have about," said one British officer who knew him when he was in the King's African Rifles.

In the military, he was an ambitious sadist who threatened cattle rustlers by making them stand with their penises on a table while he held a machete aloft, and who raided villages, torturing and murdering their inhabitants. With independence from Great Britain in 1962, he promoted himself to field marshal and decorated his chest with a garden of combat medals he either had stolen or bought.

• Israeli Involvement

It was the British who first "invited" the Jews into Uganda, after Uganda became a protectorate of the British Empire. The British Colonial Secretary first proposed a plan in 1903, known as the British Uganda Programme, to give a portion of British East Africa (5,000 square miles of the Mau Plateau in what is today Kenya and Uganda) to the Jewish people of the world as a homeland.

More recently, Israel had forged a special relationship with Uganda since Ugandan independence. Israel sought strategic partnerships with states on the edge of the Arab world, including Uganda, Kenya, Iran, and Turkey, to counter the hostile nations on Israel's own borders. As part of what became known as the Peripheral Doctrine, Israel trained and equipped Uganda's military and carried out construction, agriculture, and other development projects.

In 1967, Israel sold Uganda weapons worth millions of dollars and two years later Israel began funneling weapons through Uganda into southern Sudan, where a rebel group had been fighting the Arab-dominated Sudanese government. Israel's purpose was to distract the Sudanese Army so that it would not join forces with Egypt, which was mobilizing to retaliate for the capture of the Sinai Peninsula. Uganda's President at the time, Obote—like most African leaders—condemned Israeli aggression against Egypt and wanted to cut off support to the rebels.

Increasingly unpopular at home, Obote announced a turn to the left on the closing day of the Uganda People's Congress party annual delegates' conference held at Lugogo Indoor Stadium, Kampala in late 1969. The conference lasted three days with presidents Julius Nyerere of Tanzania, Kenneth Kaunda of Zambia and Mobutu Sese Seko of Zaire gracing the opening day. Obote promised his government would "fight relentlessly" against "ignorance, disease, colonialism, neo-colonialism, imperialism, and apartheid." Private companies and freehold land would be nationalized, he threatened. As Obote was leaving the stadium, an assassin fired one shot at the president. The bullet struck Obote in the face, breaking two of his teeth and passing through his cheek. After the assassin's pistol jammed, a second assassin threw a grenade at the president but it failed to explode. While the first assassin was shot by Obote's bodyguards, both conspirators escaped in the ensuing chaos. Investigators arrested them within 24 hours, as well as several members of the Democratic Party—the leading opposition party—accusing former prime minister Benedicto Kiwanuka of orchestrating the plot. (Interestingly, when Obote was shot, top military and government officials initially suspected Amin was the would-be assassin because there had been bad blood between the two men since late 1968.)

Kiwanuka and the other suspects were incarcerated at Luzira Maximum Security Prison, where they remained until Amin released them following the 1971 coup.

Obote survived this assassination attempt, but he was then aware of internal threats to his Presidency.

On December 24, 1969, my father wrote of the incident:

"Friday night December 19th at about 10:30 President Milton Obote was shot in the jaw region after speaking at a mass meeting of the majority political party he heads at Lugogo stadium here in Kampala. That act set off a sort of mini reign of terror that night and in the days following it. At this point it seems that the shooting was the act of an individual without a larger plot. The man said to have done it is in jail, but there has been no word as to his identity or motives. As a result, there are many rumors. A state of emergency was declared for the whole country right after the shooting. Such a situation deprives all of basic civil rights and gives the police and army free reign. Starting right after the shooting the army troops beat up many civilians and killed some. Officially only seven have been reported killed as of Wednesday December 24. Sounds of gunfire could be heard in Kampala most of Friday night and it seems doubtful that all of the shots missed. If the troops were acting under orders, it would be even more alarming than if they were out of control of their officers. The terror continued into Saturday morning when Africans going to work in the industrial area were stopped, sometimes beaten, and their bicycles smashed. As in most cases such as this, it was safer to be a non-citizen, as foreigners were less often beaten and never killed. An Englishwoman returning home Friday night after the shooting saw the African man in the car in front of her beaten by troops to a bloody mess, apparently killed. President Obote is reported to be in good condition and reportedly returned home Wednesday December 24. Army troops were on duty in and around Mulago hospital where he was kept and were seen carrying their weapons in the corridors. I was at Mulago Hospital Tuesday and was stopped at one of the entry roads by a tall, dark, buck-toothed northern army man dressed in a camouflage uniform. He threatened me if I ever came on that road again. I told him I would report him to his commanding officer, but was happy to drive away. Opposition parties have been outlawed and their leaders arrested in some cases. The streets are almost empty in Kampala these nights. Christmas should be a quiet one, but the New Year should be interesting."

A few weeks later he wrote:

"Both supporters and those in opposition are pleased that the December 19th attempt on the life of President Obote failed and that he recovered quickly from a minor wound. It was felt that a takeover by those just under the President would have meant very harsh rule indeed. In spite of the violence on the part of the Army men directed at civilians right after the shooting, those military men guilty of such conduct were in the minority. Most were courteous in carrying out the searching of vehicles and persons. It is quiet here now and almost all of the roadblocks at which vehicles were stopped and searched are gone. Cars are usually waved on at the few remaining. Although many people have been jailed, rumors are still the only source of information as to who first fired the shots as there has been no official statement. Rumor says that whoever fired the shots dropped the gun, that it was picked up by a bystander, and that he was jailed."

As Obote's chief of staff, Amin had good relations with Israeli military officers stationed in Uganda and was considered a friend of Israel. He had briefly taken (but not completed) a paratroopers' course in Israel. The Israelis had given him the name Hagai Ne'emen, which means "reliable helmsman" and is a Hebrew translation of the Swahili name Idi Amin. As a member of the Kakwa tribe located near the border with Sudan, Amin supported the southern Sudanese rebels with whom he had an ethnic affinity. He shared Israel's interest in aiding the southern Sudanese rebellion. Obote, on the other hand, was more cautious and even requested that Israel end all assistance to the southern Sudanese through Uganda.

The close cooperation between Amin and the Israelis, along with Israel's displeasure with Obote, led some to believe Israel had helped Amin in his coup. Obote himself publicly accused Israel of doing so, while Israel rejected Obote's charge and claimed its military personnel in Uganda were solely advisers and had no connection with the coup. However, according to one Israeli military historian, Amin called Israel's military attache in Uganda months before the coup because he feared being arrested for the murder of an Obote ally. The military attache was eager to help Amin, who was serving Israel's interests in Sudan, and advised the Ugandan commander to form a battalion within the army to protect himself. The Israelis would train it. This unit, consisting of paratroopers, tanks, and armed jeeps, proved instrumental later during the coup.

According to one observer:

> "… there is no doubt that the Israelis were instrumental in planning the logistics for the coup, particularly in the deployment of the mechanized equipment and afterwards they had a high profile in the capital and its environs. They were to be seen everywhere. For example, they manned roadblocks in Kampala…"[1]

• American Involvement

Finally, there were rumors of American involvement—or acquiescence—in the coup, i.e., America "enjoyed" a direct relationship with the General before he came to power, as he had been a principal "asset" of the CIA for some time.

---

1.   Mutibwa, Phares (1992). *Uganda since Independence*. Trenton, New Jersey: Africa World Press. p. 89.

CHAPTER 4

MY FATHER AGREES TO HELP INVESTIGATE ARMY MASSACRE

Our second year in Uganda a fellow American, Nicholas Stroh, his wife and two young children, moved into a small house on the Makerere University campus up the hill overlooking ours. He and my father came from similarly privileged backgrounds, and they quickly became friends.

The reluctant heir to The Stroh Brewery Co., Nick was an adventurous spirit not content to remain in Grosse Pointe Farms in Michigan and assume the family legacy. He had pursued African studies at three American universities. After serving in the Marines, he became a reporter for the Detroit News where his bull-dog tactics got him booted out of a job. He then traveled to Liberia with the Peace Corps. An article he wrote while there so infuriated the Liberian government that he was hastily flown out of the country to save him from being killed. But his fascination with Africa lured him to the continent once again in 1970. He became a freelance reporter in Kampala, sending dispatches to U.S. and Canadian news organizations, especially Reuters and the Washington Star. "This will make me or break me," he told a friend as he set out to cover Africa, "but it is a lifetime dream." Once settled on the University campus, he quickly eased into the social and political scene, eventually befriending the egomaniacal Amin during pool-side cocktail hours. Amin courted Stroh because he needed an avenue to Western newspapers, which in turn allowed Stroh to become the only U.S. journalist to have access to a developing international story of considerable interest.

When Amin first came to power, he and Stroh laughed over a few beers:

"You didn't tell me you were a newspaper man," Amin said to Stroh, in a conversation later reported by Stroh's family.

"You didn't tell me you were going to take over Uganda," Stroh shot back with a smile.

Stroh began a series of articles in the spring of 1971 called "Misbehavior in the Uganda Army." They reported tales of rape, murder, and torture. Stroh's stories infuriated Amin.

Word filtered back to Stroh, but the reporter would not back off.

On June 5, 1971, Stroh telegrammed his boss Burton Hoffman, the assistant managing editor of the Washington Evening Star, a story about "certain problems of discipline among Ugandan Army troops stationed in Mbarara." According to Hoffman's testimony, "The story was cautiously worded. It was so cautious, in fact, that I did not feel the Star could print it. I thought more information was required." Hoffman's next testimonial statement reads like it was drafted by the Star's lawyers, shifting responsibility onto Stroh for his own death.

> "Apparently, Mr. Stroh also felt more information was necessary. On July 5th I received a cable from him warning me that he had additional reports of problems in the Army and telling me he was leaving Kampala to further investigate the reports. That was the last word I had from him."

Months later, after Stroh's disappearance, Amin would claim Stroh was his friend and that he had advised Stroh and other journalists not to visit the military barracks at Mbarara, as anti-government elements there knew the

President was a friend of Britain and the United States. Amin would maintain former President Obote had been responsible for the disappearances of my father and Stroh in an action designed to discredit Amin and his new government. On the other hand, later testimony would reveal Army officers in Mbarara had advance warning about Stroh's impending visit and Stroh himself told them, when he first appeared, he had obtained clearance from high-ranking officials at General Army Headquarters in Kampala before proceeding. That is, Amin had not discouraged visiting the military barracks—he had given Stroh a "green light" to travel there.

Stroh needed to go to Mbarara, some one hundred fifty miles outside of Kampala, to get firsthand additional information his editor had told him was needed to print the story about Army disciplinary problems. Being new to Uganda, Stroh knew he couldn't get the critical information from locals—military or civilian—on his own.

That's when he went to my father, a friend and neighbor with the necessary skills and local contacts, for help.

Like Nick, my father had come from a well-to-do family (also of Germanic ancestry) and was thoroughly disinterested in his family's successful real estate business, Siedle, Stevens & Walker, based in Rye, New York—a small, prosperous suburban city in Westchester County within easy commuting distance of Manhattan. After serving in the Army and while still attending Syracuse University, one summer he joined the Merchant Marine and worked his way across the Atlantic Ocean on a cargo ship to distant South Africa. There he stayed with wealthy, prominent Siedle relatives and did research on the urban "Native" problem, gathering material he later used in term papers.

> "I found the people of South Africa to be warm and friendly yet
> the plight of the Natives saddened me. I pitied too those cast in
> the role of their oppressors, the "Europeans." Here I experienced
> a land tormented by racial and cultural differences."

After graduation from college, his desire to travel and learn foreign languages led him to work for an oil company in Venezuela where he soon learned to speak Spanish fluently. Later he worked as a special field technician in sociology for a rural Credit, Health, Education and Soil Conservation Program where he talked before groups of farmers and fishermen (in Spanish) and conducted surveys of rural communities regarding the feasibility of starting maternal and child health centers.

> "Here I became aware of the condition of much of the world's population, witnessing the problems of chronic unemployment, poor diet, lack of basic sanitation, and gross inequalities in the distribution of wealth. I experienced what it is like to live under a dictatorship with military rule and the abuse of police power in an authoritarian state."

Then he did the unthinkable, as he wrote in his diary:

> "I fled the snobbish, rich society of Westchester County where I grew up and went to Venezuela. Still fighting with my very conservative father, I married a beautiful Moslem, East Indian girl from the island of Trinidad. How I shocked my family! When we went to visit, my mother called my 2-year-old son "black" and hit him. How I hated her!"[2]

---

2.   In the early 1950s, Indians and other non-Whites were considered "black" by most white Americans, including, tragically, my father's family. My mother and I were not welcome to visit the grandparents in Rye. Dining with them at the Westchester Country Club, to which they belonged, would have been unthinkable. Its first Black member was finally reportedly admitted in 1990, and in 2001 of the club's 975 members, only three were black—each admitted shortly after golf's governing bodies threatened to pull tournaments from country clubs that did not strive for integrated memberships.

Stroh knew my father, a sociologist/gerontologist had interviewed Catholic missionaries in various villages outside Kampala for a book he had recently finished writing about the care and housing of the elderly and, in so doing, had established a broad informal intelligence network. A distant relative, Bishop James Holmes-Siedle, of the Missionaries of Africa (White Fathers) in Kigoma, Tanzania had facilitated the missionary interviews. Stroh had reason to believe these missionaries might have some confirmation about whatever had transpired at the Army barracks in Mbarara. They wouldn't talk to Stroh, even if he could locate them. But they trusted my father.

My father agreed to accompany Stroh on the assignment. Through his contacts in the field, my father learned children living at the Army barracks had told the missionaries in Mbarara school had been canceled the day of the massacre (June 22, 1971, coincidentally my 17th birthday) because of an incident at the barracks. With this grain of information, Stroh's news sense told him he had a story, one that could win him headlines in every major newspaper in the world. After all, Amin's hold on power was becoming shaky—Great Britain and other nations, including Israel and the United States, were beginning to rethink their earlier approval of him after increasing reports of torture, executions, and Amin's clownish behavior—and a story about an Amin-instigated massacre could seal the dictator's fate in the international community. For my father, guiding Stroh was an unanticipated last chance to use his intelligence skills and network to expose Amin's brutality, in hopes of improving the plight of the Ugandan people before returning to the United States to assume a teaching position at the University of Virginia.

Their disappearance alerted the world for the first time that Amin, the friendly dictator so many governments—including the United States— had supported, was a monster whose regime would ultimately be responsible for the torture and murder of almost half a million people. My father and Stroh were the first Americans to die in Uganda by Amin's hands.

So, on a steamy summer morning over 50 years ago, they cranked up a battered pale blue Volkswagen station wagon (license plate UUA 133) with an infant car seat attached to the back seat and a hand-written "Press" sign stuck to the windshield and drove off into the tangled heartland of Uganda. My father had just celebrated his forty-sixth birthday, four days earlier. Stroh was thirty-three and around his neck wore a silver cross with the inscription, "I am a Catholic—please call a priest." On his left hand he wore a gold wedding ring and on his right a U.S. Marine Corps ring with red oval stones set in gold. A calendar wrist-watch he wore on a leopard skin band was inscribed with his initials—NWS 1957.

The two men confronted the changing reality in Uganda, and they walked into a nightmare. The Uganda where my father and Stroh were killed was not the same enchanting country that stirred my imagination, where I grew from boyhood to a young man. Uganda was changing from relative peacefulness to wild savagery—quickly, yet quietly.

Horrific changes usually come about slowly in a country, I believe. The horrors of Nazi Germany did not mushroom overnight. One monstrous act quietly follows another, a step at a time. As much as possible is done in secrecy. When secrecy is compromised, governments proffer explanations for their actions—defenses to make their atrocities seem less horrendous. People always, it seems, resist hideous thought. When we are told by our government, "no one was injured," or "the killing was justified," we believe. We believe because we want to believe our world is under control. We need order in our lives. To believe unspeakable acts happen daily around us, is outrageous. Then, we are only left with stark terror, helplessly alone in an electrified world of chaos with no one to trust. There is no social compact. We revert to an animal existence. Hunter or hunted, all are engaged in a fierce battle for survival.

How could we not have known what was happening in Uganda at this time? It seems so obvious today. What in the country's history, in its culture, allowed such evil plants as Amin and Obote not only to spring from Ugandan soil but to flourish?

Perhaps, an answer can be found in the African nation's ethnic heritage, which involves more than forty different groups.

The challenge that has always faced Uganda, as it has other countries in Africa and elsewhere in the world, is to find a way to build a nation from often conflicting ethnic groups and to ensure the successful assimilation of those groups.

Uganda was shaped by four kingdoms: Buganda, Bunyoro, Toro, and Ankole. The first Bantu-speaking people arrived from western Africa in what is now Uganda around 500 B.C. They settled mostly in the southern part of Uganda, and by the fourteenth century, had established various kingdoms, ruled by kabakas or kings. Meanwhile, others began migrating into the area—Lwo people from the Sudan and the Alur and Acholi ethnic groups. By the seventeenth century, Bantu predominated in the south, and the Nilotic languages—the languages of the Nile (which originates in Uganda)—were spoken in the north.

Today, most Ugandans speak one of the Bantu languages and belong to one of the main Bantu ethnic groups: Ganda, Soga, Ankole, Nyoro, Toro. English and Swahili are Uganda's two official languages.

British explorer John Hanning Speke, searching for the source of the Nile River, was one of the first Europeans to visit Uganda when he arrived in 1862. Soon, Protestant missionaries from England came, followed by Catholic missionaries from France. Around the same time, in the 1880s, Gandas were converting to Islam. Christians and Muslims used the ruling Kabaka to manipulate a power base, until 1889 when the Kabaka signed a treaty with Germany. England, not wanting to give up a strategic position along the Nile, signed another treaty with Germany allowing Great Britain total rights over Uganda, which became a British protectorate in 1894. Indians, Pakistanis, and Bangladeshis were brought to the country by the British, originally to help build the East African rail system. Uganda became independent on October 9, 1962 with Obote, a member of the Langi ethnic group and a Christian, as prime minister.

Obote abolished the kingships that had lasted for centuries, captured the Ganda palace in Mengo, and allowed the military to flourish. He chose Idi Amin, then a sergeant in the Kings Rifles, to head his ever-expanding army.

Should my father and I have known what was about to happen and, through knowing, have prevented the next terrible turn of events? Perhaps explaining resistance to "thinking the unthinkable" is impossible. But once you have lost your belief that the worst cannot happen, forever fearing it all-too-often becomes a way of life.

CHAPTER 5

THE RETURN JOURNEY BEGINS

The Rafiki Maji (Swahili for "water friend") was already an old boat when I bought and re-named her. A handsome 28-foot Carver cabin cruiser sporting a canvas-roofed upstairs fly bridge with generous seating, she was nevertheless in fine condition with less than 1,000 miles on each of her twin in-board gasoline engines. Neither sleek nor swift, she had a surprising amount of room for her size, sleeping up to six. There was plenty of room for entertaining guests onboard whether at my backyard dock, slowly navigating the "no wake" zones of the intercoastal waterway, or cruising out the Hillsboro Inlet into the open waters of the Atlantic Ocean.

As I sat on her deck watching a vivid orange sunset the evening before my departure, I felt strangely calm and prepared for my upcoming journey—even though I had no idea what to expect. The time for thinking and planning was long over—now was the time for action.

I left my waterfront home in Lighthouse Point, Florida, on May 10, 1997, to return to Uganda and learn as much as I could about how my father met his death. Hopefully, I would be able to locate, recover and bring his remains back to America. I wasn't sure what I would do with his remains, if found, or where I would relocate them. I wasn't thinking that far ahead. His Last Will and Testament, signed in June 1969—immediately before he and I left the United States for Uganda—simply stated:

"I direct that my body be cremated and that the ashes be disposed of in such manner as my survivors and my executrix may decide is appropriate. I direct that minimum funds be expended on my funeral and disposition of my remains."

Nevertheless, I had always felt a deep obligation to bring him home—to a peaceful place where he would have wanted to be laid to rest.

My back began to hurt as I settled into my coach seat for the long overnight flight from Miami to London. I couldn't sleep. I was carrying a ton of angry emotional and spiritual baggage with me.

My horoscope in the airline magazine seemed so poignant that I tore it out and stuffed it in my briefcase:

"Cancer: The amount of tears shed over children throughout human history could fill all the oceans a thousand times over. But loving anyone, child or adult, isn't an art. It's often a test that squeezes the last drop of blood out of your heart. To be healed, though, you need only raise your eyes heavenward. The comfort is there. The truth is there. You've gambled so much already. Why not gamble on that?"

With my father's disappearance in Uganda in 1971, my life had changed suddenly and dramatically. Ours was a single parent household and with Daddy gone, I had lost both my family and home. At 17, my new reality was that I was completely alone—orphaned and penniless—and if I didn't learn to take care of myself, I would perish. Terrified, I struggled with grief through my late teens and early twenties but eventually graduated at the top of my college class and went onto law school. Upon graduation, I landed in Washington, D.C., working for the United States Securities and Exchange Commission, the federal agency which regulates the nation's financial markets as a specialist in the highly secretive world of international money management.

A few years later, I left government service in Washington and went to Boston to work for a prestigious international investment firm, as its Legal Counsel and Director of Compliance. While there, I came face-to-face with the seamy side of the money management business. I uncovered longstanding illegal trading activity involving senior mutual fund portfolio managers which I forensically investigated and confidentially reported, as a "whistleblower," to the FBI and SEC—illegalities which remained secret for the next 15 years until I was subpoenaed by then-New York Attorney General Eliot Spitzer. When the wrongdoing was finally made public in 2003, there was a "run on the bank." My former firm's assets under management plummeted from $400 billion to $192 billion and the firm was fined $110 million—the largest fine in the history of the money management industry at that time. The firm has never recovered its once stellar reputation.

It's exceptionally rare for a whistleblower who exposes wrongdoing involving his employer to survive with his reputation intact. However, as a Confidential Informant to the government I was able, upon leaving the firm, to immediately raise start-up funding from corporations unaware of (and disinterested in) my prior investigative work to start two successful investment firms of my own.

But my career would continue to be defined by high-profile forensic investigations I was hired to conduct involving trillions of assets held in secretive pensions providing for the retirement security of millions of workers—investigations which I detailed in articles I wrote for Forbes magazine.

Forensic work—applying scientific methods and techniques to the investigation of investment fraud, proving that massive financial losses are often not due to unforeseeable market forces, but to greed and illegalities— came naturally to me. My father's murder had taught me to think like a forensic investigator at an early age—to connect-the-dots using evidence that was often publicly available, but not well understood, and expose investment scams. Even when I didn't go looking for wrongdoing, people would bring frauds to my attention because they knew I had the skills to investigate and they had good reason to believe no one else would help them. Regulators and law enforcement have always been notoriously slow to grasp and prosecute investment frauds of all varieties, including, most notably, the $65 billion Madoff fraud that went undetected for decades.

To be absolutely clear, had my father not been murdered, I would never have made the hard-nosed decision to go to law school and felt driven to pursue a career investigating financial crimes globally. I probably would have migrated toward the arts or music.

Flying back to Uganda, I now had the professional credibility, financial resources, as well as government and intelligence contacts to both provide for myself and forensically investigate my father's disappearance.

My father's murder had also thrown me into a complex world of international intrigue, which would have been difficult for anyone, at any age, to handle. He had been murdered along with a member of the international Press. The Press, beginning with *Newsweek* days after the disappearances, wrote countless articles initially pressing for their release and speculating what might have happened to the two men. Articles had been written saying they were captured, tortured, beaten to death, starved, their throats slashed, hacked to death with machetes, fed to crocodiles or tied over oil drums, shot and burned. Protecting one of their own, the Press had been both helpful and hurtful by reporting every sensational possibility.

Both my father and Stroh were rumored to have been involved with the Central Intelligence Agency and Amin's intelligence unit had reportedly been closely monitoring Stroh for espionage for quite some time.

A superficial investigation into their disappearances hastily undertaken by a Ugandan Army Board of Inquiry was, in response to international outcry, followed by a highly politicized, frequently disrupted, protracted civilian Commission of Inquiry into the Missing Americans Messrs. Stroh and Siedle conducted by a well-respected member of the Ugandan judiciary. An early attempt to "invite" President Amin to testify nearly provoked a major constitutional crisis which the judge was advised he could not win.

As the Commission of Inquiry dragged on month after month, the one-year statute of limitations applicable under Ugandan law for filing legal claims against the Government was rapidly approaching. Three alternative legal strategies were simultaneously pursued by the families and the U.S. Government:

1. A private lawsuit brought under domestic internal law against the Ugandan Government by the families;

2. A claim under international law for denial of justice brought by the U.S. Government; and

3. Negotiations for an "ex gratia" payment—a settlement without an admission of guilt by the Ugandan Government.

The likelihood of success with respect to any of these legal strategies, I was advised by both State Department officials and the lawyers I hired to represent me on a contingency basis, was extremely, extremely remote.

President Amin and his cronies in the executive branch of government and the Ugandan Army did everything possible to thwart the investigation by the judiciary including intimidating, hiding, and killing witnesses; lying under oath; withholding and destroying evidence, as well as threatening to kill the judge and lawyers involved. Amin regularly criticized, as well as sent notices and orders to, the judiciary through the media. As it became increasingly clear the judiciary would find the Government at fault, President Amin had even defiantly drafted a decree exonerating his Government from responsibility for any killings in connection with the takeover of the country from January 1971 to a date to be determined solely by him. Unsurprisingly, Amin extended the exoneration period "up to the end of July 1971"—the month of the disappearances of my father and Stroh. Never mind that the decree by the Executive branch violated the fundamental human rights provisions of the Ugandan constitution, prompting a second potential constitutional crisis related to the case.

Since my father and Stroh's bodies had not been found, a certificate of death could not be issued under Ugandan law unless an eyewitness had seen the body of either of the deceased. Otherwise, under applicable English Common Law, there was a waiting period of seven years before death could be presumed as a matter of law.

While Ugandan law initially appeared to tie the hands of the Attorney General absent any eyewitness testimony, it was the impression of the Department of State that, "Uganda is reluctant to issue certificates of death and may have looked for and found a convenient excuse."

A Presumptive Report of the Death of an American Citizen—which was issued in my father's name by the U.S. Department of State a month after his disappearance, on August 16, 1971—proved useless since it merely indicated he was "missing, believed to be dead, last known whereabouts, Mbarara, Uganda, July 9, 1971." American state courts would not accept the Presumptive Report as sufficient evidence of my father's death—even when accompanied with dozens of articles from major news services. As a result, his will could not be probated—Social Security benefits, life insurance, civil service retirement and G.I. insurance benefits could not to be paid.

PRESUMPTIVE

Form FS-192
11-19-51

DEPARTMENT OF STATE
FOREIGN SERVICE OF THE UNITED STATES OF AMERICA

REPORT OF THE DEATH OF AN AMERICAN CITIZEN

KAMPALA, UGANDA, AUG. 16, 1971
(Place and date)

Name in full ROBERT LOUIS SIEDLE   Occupation SOCIOLOGIST

Native or naturalized NATIVE _____ Last known address

in the United States HARRISON, NEW YORK

Date of death ON OR ABOUT JULY 10, 1971   Age 47
(Month) (Day) (Hour) (Minute) (Year)   (As nearly as can be ascertained)

Place of death _____
(Number and street) or (Hospital or hotel)   (City)   (Country)

Cause of death MISSING BELIEVED TO BE DEAD, LAST KNOW WHEREABOUTS MBARARA,
(Include authority for statement)
UGANDA, JULY 9, 1971.

Disposition of the remains _____

Local law as to disinterring remains _____

Disposition of the effects UNITED STATES CONSUL, KAMPALA, UGANDA, ASSUMING CUSTODY
Person or official responsible for custody of effects and accounting therefor _____
Informed by telegram: THROUGH DEPT OF STATE.

NAME	ADDRESS	RELATIONSHIP	DATE SENT
ANNE KATE SIEDLE	HARRISON, NEW YORK	SISTER	

Copy of this report sent to:

NAME	ADDRESS	RELATIONSHIP	DATE SENT
ANNE KATE SIEDLE			

Traveling or residing abroad with relatives or friends as follows:

NAME	ADDRESS	RELATIONSHIP
ALONE		

Other known relatives (not given above):

NAME	ADDRESS	RELATIONSHIP
EDWARD SIEDLE	HARRISON, NEW YORK	SON

This information and data concerning an inventory of the effects, accounts, etc., have been placed under File 234 in the correspondence of this office.

Remarks: PASSPORT # Z 1223788 IN CUSTODY EMBASSY, UGANDAN LAW DOES NOT RECOGNIZE PRESUMPTION OF DEATH IN CASE OF MISSING PERSON UNTIL SEVEN HAS ELAPSED

(Continue on reverse if necessary.)

Steve McDonald
American Consul

[SEAL]
No fee prescribed.

Consul

(Signature on all copies)
of the United States of America.

GPO 9 40513

However, in light of the obstacles I encountered in the effort to obtain my father's social security benefits, David Shinn, a Department of State Country Officer called the Washington headquarters of the Social Security Administration to discuss the situation. Then, in a letter to me dated January 28, 1972, he proposed a possible resolution. He had enclosed a completed Request for Reconsideration form which he recommended I send to my local Social Security office. He had filled in the section marked reasons for reconsideration with the following language:

> "Considerable information surrounding the disappearance in Uganda of Robert L. Siedle is in the possession of the Department of State in Washington. I request that an official with an appropriate security clearance from the Social Security Administration in Washington review this evidence in hopes that a determination can be made which will permit the issuance of Social Security benefits for this child of Mr. Siedle. In this regard, Mr. David Shinn, Uganda Desk Officer, Department of State has agreed to be of assistance."

Shinn's letter to me concluded:

> "I am hopeful that an officer from the Social Security Administration, after reviewing our files on the disappearance of your father, will be able to make a determination which will permit the issuance of benefits. Whether this effort fails or succeeds, I think it is worth a try."

Apparently, as a result of the State Department sharing sensitive information about my father's fate with the Social Security Administration (information which was not revealed to me), the Request for Reconsideration mercifully was granted. The Social Security Administration began to pay survivor benefits to me—prior to the issuance of any certificate of death.

Eventually the Stroh family and I did receive a settlement from the Ugandan government—reportedly, it was the largest compensation paid in the history of Uganda at that time "by a long shot." Not that the amount was particularly large; rather, the value of a human life in Uganda at the time was trifling and the Government rarely recognized an obligation to compensate anyone, whether foreigner or citizen, for harm it inflicted.

After the settlement under which the Ugandan Government acknowledged my father was dead, a certificate of death was finally issued enabling his entire estate to be probated.

Two long and painful years after his sudden disappearance, my father's death was finally established as a matter of law in 1973. Two decades later, questions related to who, how, when, where, and why he was murdered remained unanswered.

I had a hell of a lot to be angry about on this first leg of my journey back to Uganda. Grieving my father's disappearance and death, as well as shouldering the burden of the healing process, could not have been more complicated.

In 1997, upon entering my forties, I had begun to delve more deeply into the many lingering questions about my father's life and death. The limited efforts I had made over the preceding years, such as Freedom of Information Act requests of the CIA, FBI and Department of State had ended in frustration. I was provided a few complete documents; many others were released "subject to excisions" and most documents were denied in their entirety. The justification for all denied and excised material was "Classified under Executive Order 12356,[3] protected in the interest of national defense and international relations." Requests for

---

3.   Executive Order 12356 (April 2, 1982) prescribes a uniform system for classifying, declassifying, and safeguarding national security information. It recognizes that it is essential that the public be informed concerning the activities of its Government, but that the interests of the United States and its citizens require that certain information concerning the national defense and foreign relations be protected against unauthorized disclosure. Information may not be classified under this order unless its disclosure reasonably could be expected to cause damage to the national security.

appeal of these decisions were denied. With little assistance from these agencies of the U.S. government and limited resources, my efforts to learn more languished.

Declassified Documents with Internal Review Markings

I tried to locate the courageous Ugandan High Court Justice who conducted the investigation into their deaths and wrote the Report of the Commission of Inquiry, dated March 19, 1972, nine months after the disappearances. Justice David Jeffrey Jones had retired to England upon completing the Inquiry and had long since passed away.

I sent a letter to the Editor of the Ugandan newspaper, The New Vision, asking for his help. To my surprise, he published my letter in its entirety in the Sunday Vision, July 7, 1996, under the heading, *Help Me Trace the Murderers*. In response, I received a letter from a seemingly credible informant stating that Amin, believing the two men to be Jews on a spying mission, personally ordered their killings. He had dispatched members of his State Research Bureau from Kampala to butcher them at the barracks with bayonets.

Offering cash as a reward for new information proved fruitless.

It became increasingly obvious that to learn more, I would have to go to Uganda. I sensed that with my basic knowledge of Uganda, the rapport I had with its people, and the fact that I would be more relentlessly diligent in my investigation than anyone else due to my strong personal interest, going back myself was most likely to provide the answers I needed. Plus, I wanted to see, one last time, the world I had left behind with my childhood—a world to which I had never been able to return.

Travel to Uganda in 1997 was somewhat perilous. There were reports of on-going bloodshed in Uganda where the sanctity of life had little meaning. Stories spilled daily from frightened mouths: rebels in the west chopped off lips, ears, noses, feet, hands, and genitals of their enemies; an eleven-year-old girl related that she and another girl were forced to take an ax and sever the head and torso of another child—it was the rebels' way of teaching the children the fine art of killing so they would make better soldiers; bombs exploded on city streets, hospitals torched, crops destroyed, robberies and killings of tourists. It had become so dangerous for travelers that the government had closed some of the most distinctive tourist attractions, like the snow-capped Rwenzori range—the astounding "Mountains of the Moon" that lured climbers from around the world. Then in the north, where the Lord's Resistance Army set up camp, boys and girls hardly larger than the AK-47 assault rifles they shouldered scampered through the bush on terror attacks. An estimated 3,000 schoolchildren had been abducted in 1995 and 1996. In the first six months of 1997, the LRA was responsible for 400 deaths in the northern third of Uganda and the displacing of some 200,000 farmers.

My relatives and close friends understood my desire to go to Uganda but feared I would be risking the same fate as my father. Would this be a life-affirming or death-defying journey?

Peter Stroh, the Chairman of the Stroh Brewery, Nicholas' cousin, and I had begun sharing information over the past year about the murders. I told him I felt compelled to go to Uganda but had concerns regarding my personal safety. I asked if he could be helpful.

After graduating from Princeton University in 1951, Peter had been recruited by the Central Intelligence Agency. He spent a year in Washington waiting for security clearance. Three days after his final clearance was approved, Peter's legs were crushed by a truck in a Washington intersection. He spent a year in a hospital and limped for the rest of his life. Unable to join the CIA because of his injury, he returned to Detroit.

His 2002 obituary in The New York Times stated:

> "Mr. Stroh once said that he was "pampered" as a child. After he graduated from St. Paul's boarding school, he spent a year in a Navy training program and then waited in Detroit for a year as he worked his way up Princeton's waiting list.

> "I wanted to unload relief supplies in Yugoslavia. I wanted to work on a tramp steamer bound for Argentina, train polo ponies in Texas," he once told The Detroit News. "But I couldn't get my parents' permission.""[4]

Within days of the disappearance of Nicholas, his cousin Peter had rushed to Uganda to be of assistance to Nicholas's wife and children and make inquiries. When he arrived, he told me, there were rumors the two men were still alive. Then, a Makerere University senior administrator with connections in the Army told him the two men had been killed and for his own safety and the family's, they should leave the country *immediately*. He and the family left Kampala for Michigan on July 29th.

---

4.   https://www.nytimes.com/2002/09/19/business/peter-w-stroh-74-ex-chairman-of-brewery.html

In an interview Peter and Nicholas's wife gave to the Detroit News in 1977, entitled "*Family Is Convinced Amin Ordered Death of Nicholas Stroh,*" he was quoted as saying, "There is no question that Amin ordered his death. I learned that from some of the people who had left Uganda soon after the incident." The article went on to state that Peter quoted Uganda sources as saying that "either Ali or Juma had called Kampala and checked in with Amin and he had indicated that they should be done in."

I suspect that, after his first and only trip to Uganda, Peter never believed he had done all he could have or should have. He immediately understood why I had to go back. I sensed that if he'd been able, he would have taken a second journey back. Instead, I would go this time and tell him what I found.

Peter referred me to Ambassador David Miller, then a lawyer and consultant in Washington, D.C. who had served as the U.S. Ambassador to Tanzania from 1981-1984 and to Zimbabwe from 1984-1986. He was also Special Assistant to the President for National Security Affairs in the National Security Council staff at the White House from 1989-1990. He founded and serves as the Chairman of the Special Operations Fund, which provides scholarships for widows and children of deceased members of special operations military units. Miller knew both East Africa and the intelligence community. He seemed ideally suited to introduce me to people whose assistance would be critical once I landed in Uganda.

When I called Miller and indicated I wanted to leave for Uganda within a few days, he and his staff were immediately responsive. He asked that I put together a short letter stating the purpose of my trip which he would fax to the U.S. Ambassador in Uganda and the Ugandan Ambassador to the U.S. in Washington. Contrary to the dire warnings I had heard, Miller assured me travel to Uganda was safe. The purpose of my letter was to solicit assistance from our embassy in Uganda and the Ugandan Government. Early one morning, approximately two days later, I received a call from U.S. Ambassador Southwick in Uganda. He too assured me it would be safe to travel. While these reassurances were somewhat comforting, I wasn't about to believe my safety was guaranteed.

Southwick recalled having heard of the disappearance of my father and Stroh in 1971, when he had been working in Rwanda.

It had taken 26 years for me to get to the point of even considering travel back to Uganda. For the first 15 years after the murders, it had been impossible. Uganda had been one of the most dangerous countries in the world. The Amin and subsequent Obote regimes had brought about a prolonged bloodbath with a reported death toll of over one million. Then the AIDS epidemic hit Uganda, killing more than 100,000 people each year in the 1990s, or about 50% of adults in some areas of the country.

For anyone, travel to Uganda might have been high-risk. For me, having lived the "worst case scenario," it had been out of the question. By 1997, however, the widespread killing had stopped and the country was slowly rebuilding. There were still many risks, but those could be reduced through careful planning and the assistance of the American and Uganda governments, intelligence and military. I was determined that my journey would be no reckless gamble.

The time was ripe to act. Within days of arriving at my decision and gaining vital assistance of others to develop a plan, I was on my way to begin my expedition. What had been unthinkable for my entire adult life was now suddenly possible, in no small part due to the assistance of near strangers. Though they did not know me, they immediately understood the significance of my quest.

CHAPTER 6

TRAVELING BACK IN TIME

L anding in England, exhausted after a sleepless overnight flight with only thirty-six hours before my second overnighter to Uganda, I needed a quiet room to crash.

My Forte Creste Hotel room, connected to Gatwick Airport, was fashioned like a prison cell—with soundproofed walls and windows to muffle airplane noise, and gray walls, gray carpeting and gray furniture to dull the visual senses. I had a box fan brought in by housekeeping that would create "white noise" to mask any outside hallway, or room next door clatter and chose a room that did not face the runway. I wrote in my journal:

> "Here I sit in an insulated gray hotel room, writing about horrific events that happened decades years ago which I am still struggling with. Wow, I have really done a great job of surviving."

Cocooned safely in silence, I fell into a deep sleep.

When I awoke, the back pain that had begun on the flight from Miami had grown far worse—I could hardly stand. Could I continue with the trip? My body was screaming "Go no further!" Unless I could keep my fears about my health from snowballing, the journey would be over before it started.

But back pain in times of severe stress was familiar to me, so I knew what I had to do. I took a taxi to the nearest National Health Service clinic where an Indian doctor prescribed a muscle relaxant. My fears calmed, I returned to my hotel room and fell into another long sleep.

When it was time to leave the room for my flight to Nairobi and then onto nearby Uganda, I was fully rested and the back pain was gone. Thanks to the timely medical intervention, I was ready to continue the journey.

As I leisurely ate dinner in the terminal restaurant before departure, I watched two teenagers at a nearby table, perhaps brother and sister, who were passengers on my flight. They seemed comfortable flying together—unaccompanied by any parents—between distant international destinations. Dressed in smartly casual clothing, they were enjoying their journey, seemingly unaware of just how remarkable it was to have the opportunity to explore the world freely at their age. I had once felt like they looked to me—confidently traveling on my own at age 16, from Uganda to England, then Egypt, and finally Norway.

I grew up flying around the world with my father, moving smoothly between races, cultures, and languages. It was only after my father's murder, when I was forced to settle in suburban America, that I came to realize how exceptionally rich my global upbringing had been. Yet after his murder—and until my 30s—I was afraid of overseas travel which had been so easy for me in my youth.

As I sat in the restaurant watching these kids, I longed, not for a return to my youth, but for a life of unhesitant adventure free of fear or dread—without the need for extreme protection from extreme threats that kills the joy in living.

Before boarding my flight, I bought a cassette tape at the music shop in the airport of Dionne Warwick singing the songs of Burt Bacharach and Hal Davis. This was the music of the time I spent in Uganda, and it seemed fitting to listen again to the same tunes on my Sony Walkman as I returned. One song which captured the heartbreak of saying goodbye was special to me: "I Say a Little Prayer for You."

Once, when my friends and I converged at Entebbe Airport to bid farewell to a Canadian YMCA volunteer, the American girlfriend he was leaving played the song for him on a small portable cassette player, as she cried. He reluctantly returned to the sedate life in Canada he had left behind. We would miss him as our African adventures continued.

Flying from Nairobi over Lake Victoria, I gazed out the plane window and saw the morning mist draped over lush green treetops of the Ugandan countryside. Through the haze, I could barely make out the drifting clusters of delicate lavender flowers and thick mat of curling, lily pad shaped, waxy leaves floating on the surface of the lake. Water hyacinths—one of the world's most noxious invasive weeds. Native to the tropics of South America, the plant was introduced in Africa over a century ago and somehow established itself on the continent's largest lake. Their thickly tangled roots choked pumping stations and blocked the flow of water to the mighty electric turbines at Owens Fall Dam in Jinja, where the Nile River begins.

During Amin's bloody reign, so many were murdered that burial was impractical. Instead, the corpses were dumped into the Nile to be eaten by crocodiles. At times, remains of the bodies blocked these same intake ducts at the hydroelectric plant.

I could almost smell the wood-burning aroma from breakfast fires as families began another hard day. People here still lived perilously close to nature.

"Hyenas go for the face," my father had told me, "that's why they're so feared by people."

He had seen the mauled faces of their victims in the African countryside or "bush," as it was called then. On safari together, he introduced me to an elderly white missionary who had been in Africa for over fifty years. "Look closely at his forehead," he whispered, "and you can see where his scalp was stitched back to his head after a lion in a tree above leapt upon him and clawed it away."

The dusty, red clay roads snaking across the savannahs were now coming into view. Memories of another lifetime were flooding my mind: the enormous baobab trees on hot African savannahs that may live to be 3,000 years old; the rough brownish-orange "bark cloth" made by stripping, scraping, and beating the inner bark of certain trees in Uganda that covered the sofa pillows in our simple earthy living room; the sisal carpets, straw baskets and leather-beaded gourds handmade from the calabash tree by the Maasai people to store mixed milk and cow's blood, believed to provide strength and nutrition for hunting or fighting, that furnished our apartment; the elephant hair bracelets, passion fruit, and Kitange cloth we bought at the local outdoor market. The structure of the Swahili language with syllables typically ending in a vowel and the unusual implosive sound of consonants produced by air being inhaled, rather than exhaled from the lungs. Swahili had been easy for me to learn from a borrowed Peace Corps handbook and fun to speak from the first day—when I learned "jambo," the word for "hello," and "kiberiti," the word for matches.

Our journey to Uganda was entirely my father's idea and made perfect sense for his career. He had pursued a doctorate in sociology specializing in gerontology because his study of population demographics led him to understand America's population was rapidly aging. The nation, which had always celebrated youth, was not prepared to deal with its graying masses. A study of how the aged were treated in African traditional societies could provide insights to the European world, he reasoned. He secured funding from the Ugandan Government to teach sociology to graduate students and conduct groundbreaking research into elder issues that would advance his standing in academia. He was looking to learn as much as he taught while in Uganda.

Less researched, less clear was whether the country might offer any opportunities to his teenage son. Ultimately, Uganda would provide the excuse for me to completely break free of regimented, institutional learning.

Makerere University Guest House

The first few days after we arrived in the country, I was so angry at my father that I refused to get out of my bed in our room at the Makerere University Guest House—our temporary accommodations—except for meals. He cagily found a young Indian medical student willing to come, stand at the foot of my bed, shake his head and reprimand me:

"If you don't get up and use your muscles, they will waste away or atrophy," he warned. "You will lose your strength and become permanently bedridden."

"Can that really happen—atrophy?" I asked in shocked disbelief as I envisioned my muscles wasting away and a horrific death.

"Yes, that could really happen," he said with seeming conviction.

The dire warning worked and soon I was back on my feet. But since there was no American school in the country (and I was unwilling to attend a Ugandan school which followed a British colonial curriculum unfamiliar to me), my father initially enrolled me in a University of Nebraska high school correspondence course which I could complete from home. As that absurdly unimaginative program—worse still, pursued in isolation—failed to capture my interest, he eventually agreed to let me to explore the country with the new friends I made at the university and follow my developing interests. Still, as a college professor with a profound love of books and learning, it was difficult for my father to accept my discontent and apparent aimlessness.

From his diary:

"On education in France, I read, "There, they still believe that education is a matter of the student's acquiring knowledge rather than of his telling the world all that he, without learning, knows." How this and the following could be applied to Teddy who I love so much and want to help!"

"He who goes steadily, step by step, finds everything easy; he who suddenly attempts, after squandering years, to make up lost time by frantic effort, finds everything impossible. The mind, like the heart, is formed early and many of us remain all our lives what our childhood made us." How I hope and pray I can work out a program for Ted."

He worried so much about my lack of direction that he occasionally asked his colleagues in intelligence and academia for advice. They too shared his deep concern for my uncertain future.

"Send the boy to trade school, so he can at least earn a living as a plumber, carpenter or electrician" said one of his friends in intelligence.

The Head of the Department of Social Work and Social Administration at the university included commentary about me at the end of her January 1970 written evaluation of his work—after only seven months on the job.

"There is no questioning his academic knowledge, it is probably the best of any we have in the Department. He impressed our colleagues in the Sociology Department especially in the field of sociological theory… However, it is necessary for me to make some reference to his off-duty life as it reflects on the Department. He is a divorcee and is generally known among colleagues who have been frank enough to express opinions to me, and by teenagers as a "kooky individual" always chasing after skirts. I find this a rather unsavory situation to handle, in addition to which the problem of his teenage son is not helped by it."

Already, his supervisor was recommending against renewal of his two-year contract which expired in July 1971—in part supposedly due to my behavior. His supervisor—who had no idea about my father's work for American intelligence—was partially right in her assessment.

As a single man, he did, indeed, chase a lot of skirts and an undated yellowed article he saved from the Associated Press entitled, "To Do Oddball Work, You Need Oddballs" by an anonymous CIA Operative X, suggests that he believed himself to be an oddball among oddballs in intelligence. Said the article:

"…the idea that all employees of high-powered security and intelligence outfits should have been captains of their high school football teams and should remain, unswerving in devotion to blueberry pie, tidy lawns and Indian wrestling is absurd. Oddball work demands, after all, a certain number of oddballs. It is not likely to attract exclusively organization men, grown from all-American boys."

My father had no aspirations to be an organizational all-American. He relished leaving the conventions of his privileged upbringing behind and had no regrets.

In his last letter to his sister on June 24, 1971—weeks before his disappearance—he wrote:

"Teddy just had his 17th birthday and we went with friends, a British couple, to dinner at a Chinese restaurant. He is much better now, just about human. What a hell of a relief that is, now if he would show some interest in school."

My father feared I would never graduate from high school.

Ironically, I never did.

Instead, I got accepted to college early—before completing 11th grade.

And he never did "work out a program" for my education in Uganda, as he had hoped and prayed.

Instead of an education that forced me to sit in a room with others my age and acquire certain "knowledge" prescribed by him or American society, he allowed me to define my course of learning and pursue it on my own terms. Thankfully, my years in Africa, although at times lonely and aimless, were not "squandered." And while there were certain gaps in my education I had to make up for later, no frantic effort was required. When you commit to learning throughout your lifetime, there is ample time to address deficiencies from your youth.

What my father did in Uganda was the scariest task of all for parents: He recognized he could no longer force me to do his bidding and had to trust (or at least hope) that I would eventually get it right—despite making, what seemed at the time to be "all the wrong moves."

My life—like, I suspect, many others—would not proceed "steadily, step-by step." There would be quantum leaps forward followed by significant setbacks—rollercoaster moments, as well as extended periods when life seemed to be standing dreadfully still. And while it may be true that "the mind, like the heart, is formed early," many of us change over time to enjoy lives far beyond our childhood dreams. I certainly have.

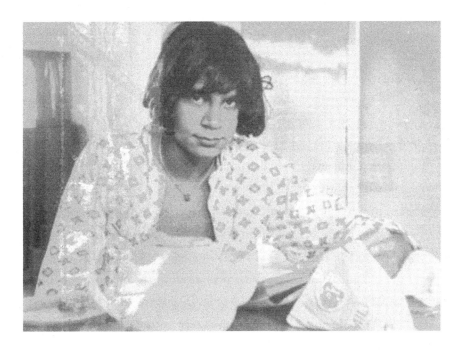

Author at Breakfast, Photograph by Father

My father and I arrived in Uganda just in time to experience an invasion of locusts, which the locals gathered to roast or fry, like the heaps of brown ants sold in the market. The locusts were caught by holding white sheets by the corners and flapping them under the city street lamps at night. The locust is drawn to the light and falls on the sheet, where its feet get stuck. Pluck the large insect which looks like a grasshopper from the cloth, cook and then munch.

My first few weeks in Uganda, I would walk alone up the hill from our apartment to the Makerere University Canteen in the evenings, eager to talk to any student who would talk to me.

In July 1969, America had accomplished the unthinkable: We had put a man on the moon!

The African students, to my amazement, were not remotely impressed, but genuinely confused as they watched Apollo 11's first-ever moon landing on the small black and white television screen in the Canteen.

"Why does your country not spend its money to end world hunger and sickness?" they asked. "With so much human suffering on earth, why are rich countries spending millions in a pointless race to the moon?"

I had all the time in the world to listen to the voices around me. Time had stopped for me—no homework, no early bedtime for school or any scheduled obligations. There were no distractions. In this strange new environment, I would learn to see the world through different eyes. No doubt being a teenager with mental flexibility made it easier for me to let go of the American mindset and become immersed in a radically different society.

The world of these poor students who had worked so hard to earn their place at the only university in East Africa was altogether different from my own. They had come from small villages where there was no running water or flushing toilets. At home, they had grown up squatting over holes dug in the ground out in the open. Moving into the new university dormitories with plumbing, many first squatted with their feet on top of the toilet seats before they were taught by fellow students to sit on the seats with their feet on the ground.

I befriended a huge broad-shouldered student of Arab descent from Zanzibar named Terik. This tough, yet gentle young man had been an Army bodyguard to Zanzibar's President before becoming, of all things, a Fine Arts major. He was rumored to have killed in his bodyguard days, but never spoke of that time in his life. Instead, he told me stories about growing up in a fishing village where he swam lazily with sharks that he considered harmless. Terik couldn't imagine why anyone would be afraid of sharks. At a European party one night, I teased my powerful friend as he struggled to slice some food with a large dull cooking knife. Then I felt deeply ashamed when I saw the hurt look on his face as he confessed he had never before seen this strange but tasty substance we called "cheese" and honestly did not know how to cut it.

I remembered the evenings on safari camping with my closest friends, Makerere Fine Art students, on the sandy beach at Lake Nabugabo, a shallow freshwater lake separated from Lake Victoria by a sand bar. We laughed at the sound of a hippopotamus blowing water through his nostrils in the darkness, and were annoyed to be woken by dozens of small tree monkeys rattling our pots, pans and utensils at dawn. I also thought about the times we rented dugout canoes from natives and paddled to the middle of the lake where we read Winnie-the-Pooh by lanternlight. I had been touched by Uganda's many beauties—from elephants, lions, leopards, rhinos and gorillas to Kingfisher and Crested Crane birds—and chilled by its many horrors.

As the plane began its descent into Entebbe and the mist exploded into pellets of rain, I wrote in my journal:

> "My heart hurts but I am going to the source of my hurt now so I have a sense of well-being. I believe I am going to find the answers I have been looking for. All I have asked for is the chance to go back and be there for my father—to let him know I always loved him. I am sorry it has taken me so long, Daddy. Please forgive me. I have never forgotten you."

I always called him Daddy.

It may seem odd that a 17-year-old boy would still call his father "Daddy," but I always did. No matter how much I asserted my independence and challenged my father in my teens, I never felt comfortable calling him just "Dad." "Dad" seems a distant term reserved for children who take their father's presence for granted. I loved him always, though I hated him sometimes—but I never took his presence for granted. Having lost my mother at age 3, Daddy was all I had.

I thanked God for the opportunity to be able to make the trip and for getting me through my fears of the last two days. The seatbelt sign flashed and I buckled up as the plane bobbed in an air pocket. I closed my eyes, took a deep breath.

Then I listened to the words of "I Say a Little Prayer for You":

> Forever and ever, you'll stay in my heart
> And I will love you.

CHAPTER 7

A LAND FULL OF SPIES AND SOLDIERS

The plane bounced once before I heard the muted screech of wet tires on a slick runway. My British Airways flight landed in Uganda on time at about 11:30 a.m. The sky was gray, and it was raining heavily as I walked down the metal stairs off the plane with the other passengers onto the tarmac runway. I had flown 20 hours altogether and spent probably another 10 hours getting in and out of airports.

I had finally made it back to the very last place I ever saw my father alive 26 years ago, Entebbe Airport.

As he wrote in his journal:

"June 30 Wed. – Ted's last day, and I shall miss him, but there's so much to be done and so little time before I too leave Uganda. His East African Airways flight should have left at 12:50 a.m. (July 1), but was about two hours late."

At 3:00 that morning, we hugged and said a quick good-bye. I would fly to London and then onto Oslo to spend a month with my Norwegian girlfriend Lise's family touring the fjord region. He would meet me in London in a month. *That* was the plan.

The next day was the last entry in his journal. Approximately a week later, he disappeared.

I overheard a fellow passenger on the flight say the shell of an airplane that had been destroyed during Operation Thunderbolt, when 100-200 commandos of the Israel Defense Forces carried out one of the world's most daring and risky counter-terrorist rescue missions in July, 1976, would be still sitting on the runway.

It wasn't.

Someone else said the plane had finally been removed six months ago—20 years after the nighttime attack which killed 3 hostages, 1 Israeli soldier, 45 Ugandan soldiers and all 7 of the airplane hijackers. Eleven Soviet-built MiG fighters supplied by the Russians to the Uganda Air Force were destroyed when Israel, in response to the hijacking, sent four Hercules C-130H cargo planes escorted by Phantom jet fighters.

Amin's attempt to establish ties with the Popular Front for the Liberation of Palestine by offering the Palestinian and Red Army Faction (a West Germany radical leftist group) hijackers of Air France Flight 139 from Tel Aviv, carrying 258 passengers, a protected base at the old airport in Entebbe—from which to press their demands for the release of 53 Palestinian terrorists from Israeli prisons in exchange for the release of the Israeli hostages—had ended disastrously for him. The dramatic successful rescue of the hostages by Israeli commandos was a severe blow.

Since Kenyan sources supported Israel, Amin issued orders to retaliate and slaughter several hundred Kenyans then present in Uganda in the aftermath of the operation. 245 Kenyans were killed and 3,000 fled the country.

The Entebbe airport terminal I walked into, this day, didn't look familiar. It was not the same building I had been inside so many times, either flying myself or saying goodbye to my wide international circle of friends. There were no bullet holes in its exterior revealing a bloody past. The old terminal that held the hostages and witnessed some of the most dramatic moments during Amin's reign had been demolished, I learned. There were plans to turn the site into a museum someday. Had spirits haunting the old building caused it to be abandoned? Had so many people been killed, so much pain inflicted that it had to be shuttered? But the defunct, bullet-scarred control tower was still standing.

Operation Thunderbolt, Entebbe Airport 1976

As I sat on the shuttle bus waiting to be taken to the Sheraton Hotel in the capital city of Kampala, I eavesdropped on my fellow passengers. Seated immediately behind me was Megan, a 40-ish pale Canadian doctor with a pixie haircut working on a project with the World Health Organization. She had last been in Uganda 10 years ago—at a time when she and another passenger, a French electronic salesman, agreed the country was at its worst. They were convinced Uganda was now one of the most pleasant places in Africa to do business. It was an up-and-coming country. A well-dressed, gray-haired distinguished British traveler sat further behind who boasted he was in Uganda to plan a military conference. Evidently, countries were still playing spy or military games in Uganda.

Many, many times over the years since my father's disappearance the question of whether he and/or Stroh were in the CIA had arisen and I had tried to find answers. I had listened to many theories and stories about the two men and their involvement in international espionage. The picture of my father with Amin and the Israeli Ambassador at a Soviet Embassy cocktail reception raised lots of questions in my mind.

Why had the ex-gratia monetary settlement, that I eventually received from Amin's government, originally been proposed to Amin by the Israeli ambassador, as declassified U.S. Department of State documents revealed?

Why did the governments of the United States and Israel work together on the matter, initially at least? What was the Israeli interest in the murders? The Israelis had large building projects in Uganda at the time and were working closely with Amin. The Israelis were even engaged in a building project at the Mbarara barracks where my father and Stroh were last seen alive. There was testimony that my father and Stroh were killed because they were thought to be "spies for the Jews."

Regardless of how the Israelis came to be involved in preliminary settlement negotiations regarding my father's murder in 1971, any perceived benefit of working through them quickly disappeared as relations between Israel and Amin deteriorated over the next year. In the words of the American Ambassador to Uganda:

> "As to the matter of the ex-gratia settlement being originally presented by the Israeli Ambassador, if the Israeli taint is as bad as it has appeared in other matters, e.g., General Amin's reaction to Israeli interests elsewhere, it may very well be that the entire settlement will have to be worked out again."

A few months later Amin sent a cable to United Nations' Secretary-General Kurt Waldheim saying, "Hitler was right about the Jews, because the Israelis are not working in the interests of the people of the world, and that is why they burned the Israelis alive with gas in the soil of Germany." In the same message, he congratulated the Black September terrorists who had murdered members of the Israel Olympics team in Munich. When fighting flared up again in the Middle East a year later, Amin's postscript to this remark was, "People all over the world now agree with me that the Israelis are criminals. Hitler was right to burn six million Jews during the Second World War."

Although Israel had previously supplied Uganda with arms, in 1972, Amin, enraged over Israel's refusal to supply Uganda with jets for a war with neighboring Tanzania, expelled Israeli military advisers and turned to Libya and the Soviet Union for support.

Declassified State Department documents indicate Amin believed our Peace Corps was "full of spies," Israeli agents were penetrating Uganda disguised as American tourists, and that other U.S. tourists were agents of the CIA. He was similarly obsessed with other foreign "spies," especially Israelis.

"Amin apparently believes that all Jews are Israelis and has implied that he might not want American Jews to visit Uganda."

While I was still in law school in Boston, I arranged to meet Clyde Ferguson for a drink in Cambridge near Harvard Law School where he was teaching. Ferguson, who was African American, had been appointed Ambassador Extraordinary and Plenipotentiary to Uganda in 1970 by President Nixon. Five months after Ferguson assumed his ambassadorship, Amin took control. According to The New York Times, Ferguson's abilities as a diplomat were wasted in the chaos that followed the coup. He informed Nixon that American involvement in Uganda had to be limited to developmental and humanitarian aid and protection for Americans in the nation.

He returned to the U.S. from Uganda in 1972. Ferguson was in Uganda when my father and Stroh disappeared and knew them personally.

Ferguson told me he had reason to believe Stroh and my father were involved with the CIA. He confided Uganda had been the second largest CIA base in Africa—second only to South Africa. I should also be aware, said Ferguson, of American corporate involvement in Uganda at the time, especially what he referred to as the "Coffee Connection."

While President Carter stated that Amin's actions "disgusted the whole world," his administration opposed the imposition of economic sanctions against Uganda and tried to downplay any American support for Amin. In fact, American coffee companies provided Amin with a staggering percentage of Uganda's foreign capital earnings (from 53 percent in 1971, up to 93 percent by 1977). Since Ugandan coffee was the only coffee in the world which withstood the then-popular freeze-drying process, Ferguson told me, America was the largest buyer and certain U.S. food conglomerates opposed restricting trade with Uganda. While the coffee companies publicly deplored reported conditions in Uganda and were eager to avoid negative publicity, they maintained that any decision to boycott Ugandan coffee should be made by the government and not any individual company.

One of these corporations (which he named) importing vast amounts of Ugandan coffee was represented by the very same Washington D.C. law firm which would initially represent me in my lawsuit against the Ugandan Government. This law firm, Ferguson told me, was subject to a conflict of interest in that it had been more interested representing the interests of that large American corporate client of the firm than me. (As a result, the firm subsequently referred me to another lawyer for representation.) In addition, other American companies supplied Amin's jets, a telecommunications satellite system, and pilot training.

Ferguson suggested I file a Freedom of Information Act request with the CIA and State Department regarding my father's death.

My head was spinning after our meeting, swirling with theories of global conspiracies, capitalism run amuck, sinister conflicts of interest and clashes between judiciary and executive branches of government in a nascent, struggling democracy—all which had been kept secret from me but which determined, or even undermined, the investigation of my father's murder and outcome of my lawsuit against the Ugandan Government. Ferguson had dumped a massive legal research project on me before I had even graduated from law school. It was as if he was challenging me, "This is your legacy. I've helped you all I can. The next step of the journey is in your hands. Go forward and figure it out."

Ferguson died of a heart attack at age 59 in 1983—the very year I graduated from law school. He had given me intriguing information about how American intelligence, multinational corporations and international law firms operate—matters which I felt helpless to prove—but nothing he told me had brought me any closer to understanding what had actually happened to my father. Everybody, it seemed, had theories which were thrilling and added to the excitement surrounding, as well as significance of, my father's life and death. But, more than anything, they added to my sense of helplessness. If central to my father's death was a global conspiracy, what chance was there that I would be able to unravel it?

The information Ferguson gave me reminded me of one important lesson I had learned as a young man: a U.S. citizen whose family member disappears, or is killed in a foreign country has two governments to fight with—the other country and his own.

After graduation, when I was a young attorney working at the Securities and Exchange Commission in Washington, a colleague arranged for me to meet a few CIA agents he knew for lunch. They were older agents—nearing retirement—who had initially joined a forerunner to the CIA, the Office of Strategic Services ("OSS"). The OSS was the first centralized intelligence agency in American history established to collect and analyze strategic information, as well as conduct unconventional and paramilitary operations during World War II.

They were intelligence-gathering (clandestine) sorts who drank and laughed a lot, obliquely referencing outrageously illegal exploits from their days of spying overseas—call it "gallows humor." My friend, a fellow SEC attorney who was well-connected in Washington, asked these jocular chaps whether they might be helpful in finding out what happened to my father and clarifying his involvement with "the company."

After some heavy lunchtime drinking, a member of the group asked, "What would you do if we could tell you who killed your father?"

What would I do? That was a question I pondered often over the years but was surprised to be asked so early in our discussion. But I suppose the question they needed answered before they answered mine was: Why do you want to know?

The group went silent as they awaited my response. I had no idea what to say. It was likely some kind of test—which I apparently failed—because they never did come through with any new information and did not recruit me to the Agency—not at that time.

When an opportunity to join the CIA was presented to me a few years later, I seriously considered but ultimately declined the offer. An old friend of my father visiting from England at the time, who had retired from intelligence work, warned me against it. "If you get involved, you'll never know who to trust and never be able to get out," he said.

Six years after my informal CIA luncheon, I met Jack Anderson, the nationally syndicated American newspaper columnist and Pulitzer Prize winner considered one of the fathers of modern investigative journalism. He was the keynote speaker at a government pension convention I attended in San Diego. Anderson had written several stories about Amin's regime. Anderson revealed in 1977 that Ugandan police pilots were receiving "advanced flight training and pilot ground school at the Bell Helicopter Company, Fort Worth, Texas," after which they would receive further training at Oak Grove Flight

School (also in Fort Worth) for approximately six weeks. Anderson concluded that these pilots "could never have been admitted into this country without quiet State Department assistance."

He also wrote about my father and Stroh's murder, most notably a lengthy September 12, 1976 article in Sunday Parade Magazine, *The Sinister End of Two Americans in Uganda* which included the picture of my father having cocktails with Amin shortly before his murder and a sequel in November 6, 1977, *Idi Amin's Reign of Terror, Witnesses Tell How Two Americans Were Killed*. I approached Anderson at the podium after his speech, introduced myself and thanked him for the stories he had written. He had been helpful, years after the murders, telling the world what the families—surviving victims of this international incident—had endured.

Anderson asked, "So, what was the final outcome?" I told him that despite years of searching for answers, I still knew little of the facts surrounding my father's murder. I shared with his office my correspondence with the various U.S. government agencies. I told him of my bizarre lunch with the group of CIA agents. He wrote a short follow-up article entitled, *Disappearance in Uganda Still A Mystery*, which told of my struggle to gain access to government documents related to my father's death, as well as described the strange world I was exposed to whenever I, as a young man, attempted to learn more about what happened to my father.

> "When his father vanished in Uganda in 1971, Ted Siedle, who was 17 years old at the time, had no idea that nearly two decades would pass and he still would not know for sure how, or even if, his father had died. Today the U.S. government refuses to tell Siedle the truth."[5]

---

5.   https://www.washingtonpost.com/archive/local/1990/11/09/disappearance-in-uganda-still-a-mystery/5513433e-e75a-47eb-bbf9-d2f748c74f68/

One thing had grown clearer to me over the years: my father was, at a minimum, involved in intelligence gathering. How deeply he was involved in spying and for how long were secrets he took to his death. For supposed national security reasons, our government was not going to tell me—*ever*, not even 50 years after his death.

In my experience, there are those who work for intelligence agencies, those who assist in intelligence gathering, and from time-to-time the lines blur. The world of spying is all about blurred lines.

After the last passengers straggled onto the shuttle bus with their bags, the driver closed the doors and we lurched onto the road to Kampala—thankfully cutting short the well-groomed Brit sitting behind me droning on about his military conference plans. Having finally made it back Uganda, I had *zero interest* in military so-called "conferences" or any other clandestine dealings I suspected he was orchestrating.

I already knew far, far too much about that world.

CHAPTER 8

WELCOME BACK

Megan and I talked as the shuttle bus slowly made its way to Kampala in the rain.

"What brings you to Uganda?" she asked. At first, I was hesitant to reveal the dark nature of my journey, i.e., that I was searching for my father's murderers and remains. She listened intently as I told her of my teenage years in the country, my father's disappearance and murder, and the fears for my personal safety that had kept me from returning for decades. She immediately grasped the significance of my quest; however, she did not view Uganda through the same lens of trauma.

Megan told me she had first been in Uganda 10 years earlier.

"Things were really horrible then. The country had just come through 15 years of Amin's bloody regime and the return of Obote for a second time. Over a million of the country's population of, say, 17 million had been killed. The country was devastated. As a doctor, I was shown the effects on people's health of 15 years of brutality and then the outbreak of AIDS. It was awful then. Life here is so much better now," she concluded.

The Sheraton Kampala Hotel—where both Megan and I would be staying while in the million-plus densely populated capital—stands 15 stories tall on the grassy slopes of Nakasero Hill, the highest of the seven hills upon which the city was built. The hotel opened in 1967 as the Apollo Hotel, named after then-President Apollo Milton Obote.

"Great ivory tusks formed a parenthesis through which guests entered the lobby, where the stuffed magnificent heads of Cape buffalo gazed dully over carefully tanned lion and zebra hides," said The New York Times.[6] The view from the room balconies was of manicured lawns with the name "Apollo" spelled out in bursting blossoms. The hotel was only two years old when I lived in Uganda. As a teenager yearning to hear the latest music of the Western world, I would dauntlessly walk to the roundabout at the bottom of the hill outside the gates of Makerere University, hail a taxi, and make my way alone to the hotel. Then I would take the elevator to the disco upstairs—aptly named the Leopard's Lair—which opened onto an expansive rooftop patio overseeing the city.

When Amin overthrew Obote in 1971, his conquering Army made this poshest of hotels, renamed the Kampala International Hotel, a command post, raiding its million-dollar wine cellar, its silverware, a few hides and tusks. Following the overthrow of Amin by Tanzanian forces, who made the hotel their headquarters (and tore it apart), and the Uganda National Liberation Army in 1979, and the return to power of Obote in 1980, the hotel reverted to the Apollo Hotel name. Later, Middle Eastern investors secured the rights to lease and manage the hotel from the government of Uganda and the hotel was renamed the Sheraton Kampala Hotel in 1991. The hotel then underwent extensive renovations.

Now redone in granite and mahogany, the hotel looked like any other Sheraton in the world I had ever checked into and nothing like the Apollo I once knew. Gone were the massive ivory tusks, Cape buffalo heads, lion and zebra skins. How many poor souls had been murdered in its rooms, I wondered, before the blood-stained furnishings had to be replaced and the walls repainted?

---

6.   https://www.nytimes.com/1981/04/20/world/a-stylish-hotel-lives-to-mirror-uganda-s-fate.html

Yet the neighboring downtown area had changed little. The ugly giant Marabou storks with their long grey legs and massive ten-foot wingspan were still everywhere—including nesting in the trees outside the Sheraton. Most of the nearby downtown buildings were older, neglected over the decades and showing signs of unrest—such as bullet holes.

There was little new construction.

After I settled into my room, I called the U.S. Embassy and made an appointment to see the Deputy Ambassador the next morning. It was early afternoon but exhausted from my overnight flight, I quickly fell asleep.

When I awoke, I went down to the hotel lobby and asked about popular dining spots. This first night, I wanted to see the European society of Kampala of today and compare it to the European society of my time, but also view these folks as an adult, not as a teenager. Who was there and why? What brought foreigners to Uganda these days and how were they different in their values, dreams, desires and priorities from Americans I was surrounded by in my current life? I was searching for the sort of society that had been lost to me forever after my father's death—people who love to travel, for whom money is not the greatest motivation or an obsession—people who are comfortable moving between different cultures, languages and races.

A couple of Africans in the lobby recommended the Half London Bar. That was the night club where the muzungu (whites) go I was told. What wasn't said was that it was a place to catch the "women of the night" chasing after white men. The name of the bar was initially hard to understand both because of the heavy Ugandan accent and its nonsensical nature. The explanation of the name was that the bar represented an environment halfway between London and Uganda. I called Megan's room and invited her to go with me.

While I had traveled the streets of Kampala by taxi at night alone without a care at age 15, this night—decades later—the ride was frightening, unlike during the day. There were no streetlights. The small fires burning and lack of electrical lighting in the bars, shops and homes along the road made the country look that much more primitive. The Kampala I knew, decades earlier, had ample electricity. Now there was darkness and quiet. No rhythmic booming of music from roadside bars like in other Third World countries, or the Uganda I had known. As we drove through the streets, I commented to Megan about the changes I observed.

Soon the taxi driver and I were drawn into a conversation as I recalled life in the city decades earlier. I asked him what happened to this old restaurant and that nightclub, and in so doing, revealed I was no tourist. I was someone who had roots here, who knew the country when it was at its best and spoke kindly of its glory days. I remembered the joy, prosperity, liveliness, hope, and optimism of the people and of the time. We shared memories, like two brothers talking about their childhood.

"Whatever happened to the Susanna?" I asked, surprising myself that I still remembered its name.

The Susanna Night Club was Kampala's most notorious nitery at the height of Obote's political career in the late 1960s and briefly in the Amin years. It featured the best live bands, dance floor, and attractive, available women. As a result, it was the favorite of many politicians, European aid workers, and Makerere students.

"The Susanna is now a church," the driver said.

It seemed fitting that as the swinging '60s morphed into the troubled '70s, followed by years of war—as conditions in Uganda worsened—the people might have needed a church more than a bar. Comfort, safety, caring, a reason to carry on—hope for a better tomorrow—were more important than music, booze and sexual depravity.

The Half London Bar was virtually empty and quiet. There was a pool table, a small dance floor, lots of beers but no band or music. It was a Tuesday night, after all. There were a couple of young African women at the bar slowly sipping their drinks, who appeared to be waiting for someone, or interested in quickly making new friends. Prostitution has long been illegal in Uganda but is widespread due to poverty and lack of other opportunities. A study of Kampala teachers in 2008 showed that they were turning to prostitution to increase their incomes since sex workers can earn in a month as much as the yearly wage for a secondary school teacher. Worse still, Uganda has one of the highest rates of HIV in the world, ranking in the top ten.

The prospect of eating at the Half London wasn't appealing, but since we had come so far, Megan and I decided to sit and have a couple of beers. Megan told me about herself and her family. She was a doctor in a rural part of Canada, working with First Nation peoples in a general practice.

"We Canadian doctors don't make the kind of money American doctors do, believe me. I sure don't make a lot of money and I'm the breadwinner in my family. My husband is the primary homemaker. These overseas assignments as an independent contractor with the World Health Organization pay pretty well and while they take me far from home for extended periods of time, they are fascinating. There was one project I did in Bangladesh which I didn't get paid for because the project ultimately wasn't approved by W.H.O. but, thankfully, that's only happened once."

Megan had two troublesome teenage kids back at home. She confessed she'd been a wild, promiscuous kid herself and ran away from home at an early age. Her mother had been an alcoholic who she tried to save. Megan became a doctor helping others but had failed to save her mother. And while she didn't come out and say it, she suggested her husband was having an affair—with a man. Clearly, there were reasons Megan might have wanted, as an adult, to, once again, run away from home.

Ours was a bare-knuckled conversation with no time for pretense, only brutal honesty.

Then I spoke about my guilt—about how badly I'd always felt for not having done more to save my father. I had not been there to protect, or watch over, him and had not gone back to Uganda as soon as I received news of his disappearance. I had never found definite answers to my questions about what happened to him.

"Are you always so intense?" Megan asked.

What a stupid question, I thought. Having finally journeyed halfway around the world back to the scene of the crime decades after my father's murder, surely, I now had permission—for the first time—to delve into my feelings of guilt, not bury them for another 26 years. I wanted to feel bad—really bad—to feel the full force of my grief and survivor's guilt and leave no stone unturned as I questioned whether I was in any way to blame.

"Do you think your father would have wanted you to go back to Uganda to try and save him?" she asked.

"What do you think you could have possibly done at age 17?" she pressed further. "What do you think would have happened to you had you returned immediately after learning of his disappearance?"

Megan was trying to help me make sense of the impossible situation I confronted in my youth—to see the obvious with her rapid-fire leading questions, even as she sensed my pain.

Yes, had I tried to save my father, I, too, most likely would have been killed. That was the truth.

But maybe that's exactly what should have happened to me, I thought but didn't say out loud. Maybe I deserved to die for not protecting him. Dying would have been so much easier than spending the succeeding decades riddled with guilt.

After our second beer, we grabbed a taxi back to the Sheraton. As we drove past Kampala Bat Valley where tens of thousands of fruit bats live in the city, I asked the driver if Makerere University—where I had lived—was on our way back. I *did not* intend for him to take us there but within minutes the taxi pulled up at the gates of the University.

"What should we do now?" I asked Megan.

"Well, since we're here, we may as well go on through," she said, by now fully engaged with my mission and eager to help me.

I told the driver to proceed and we made our way in the darkness onto the campus. There were no streetlights; trees and bushes grew onto the narrow, poorly paved streets. Nevertheless, I could make out where we were.

"Turn right, here," I said and then pointed, "There's the university swimming pool I used to go to every day. Go straight through the round-about, then turn left up the hill."

Some of the roads were completely washed-out, no pavement remained—only deep tire trenches in the red earth. The once-manicured campus had been decimated: classroom buildings were in complete disrepair; apartments that had once housed international faculty were now in worse condition than the servants' quarters accompanying each building had been when I lived on the campus. Neglect, erosion, deterioration, destruction was evident everywhere. Then our taxi crept down the steep road with a deep trench carved in the middle by heavy rains, to the Livingstone Flats apartment building where I once lived with my father.

Megan sat with the taxi driver in the small empty parking lot, engine running and lights shining into pitch blackness as I got out and looked around. The asphalt pavement had crumbled and washed away long ago. Now the parking area was only dirt. The apartment building was so degraded that it was only recognizable by its unique three-spoke form. The walls were stained with dirt and mildew. Most of the window openings were glassless or boarded. There were bullet holes in the wall near the entry. We could hear the voices of children whispering in the dark from one of the apartments on the ground floor. The whispers were, no doubt, about us.

"Why are the mzungu here? What do they want?"

No adults emerged. I could see in an upstairs apartment a bare light bulb shining through a thin sheet hanging over a glassless window opening. None of the apartments had curtains—just pieces of cloth tacked over windows or openings. The front door into the building had been removed. An abandoned gas stove stood inside the entryway.

"Should I knock on the door of my old apartment?" I asked Megan.

"Probably not a great idea," she said, "A stranger calling late at night would probably scare the hell out of the kids who seem to have been left alone."

She was right. This was neither the time nor place to ask to be invited into my old home which was now someone else's. I got back into the taxi, vowing to come back another day—in daylight.

This return to the world of my childhood was like a frightening nightmare that kept getting uglier and more painful. All that remained of the home I remembered—where I had once lived, laughed, loved, eaten, and slept—was ruins.

We drove back to the hotel in the darkness and then walked down Nakasero hill to an Indian restaurant in the nearby Speke Hotel for a late dinner.

Later, as I lay in my hotel bed alone in the darkness, the impact of all I had seen my first evening in Uganda caught up with me. I now finally had a better picture of what happened to Uganda after I left in 1971. The savage regimes of Amin and Obote had decimated the rational social order and left in its place madness and devastation. Wreckage from the massive destruction of the physical environment—an infrastructure that had taken decades to build—was everywhere.

The murder of my father and Stroh had not been an isolated act of violence in an otherwise stable country. The year 1971 marked the end of sanity in Uganda for the next 15 years. The loss of my father had destroyed my world but Amin, Obote and their henchmen had destroyed the lives of millions of their fellow countrymen.

How bad had what happened in Uganda truly been?

Many died, virtually everyone else suffered and progress that had taken decades to achieve had been virtually erased. I not only lost my family and home, but was swept off to a distant shore, forced to begin a new life with strangers and without a moment to grieve my loss.

That is how bad what happened in Uganda was—for me.

CHAPTER 9

A LITTLE HELP FROM AMERICA

The next morning, I put on the only business suit I had brought, grabbed my briefcase and took a taxi the short distance to the United States Embassy. Security at the Embassy was tight—with guards both inside and outside the gate. The guards went through my briefcase and told me—offering no explanation—I would have to leave my Sony Walkman behind. Perhaps they mistakenly thought it was a recording device.

A line of Ugandans seeking visas to enter the U.S. stood outside the Embassy. While I waited inside for my meeting, I listened to the young Embassy employee question each applicant, searching for a reason to issue a quick apologetic denial.

A clean-cut balding young white man in his early thirties wearing wire rim glasses, a starched white shirt, a tie, and suspenders introduced himself as Mark Smith. He looked like he belonged on Wall Street or at a law firm in the 1980s, not in East Africa.

"The Deputy Ambassador is running a little late," he said, "but we can talk in my office while he concludes his meeting if you'll follow me."

We passed through a corridor with several security doors, one with a combination lock and then into his office. Mark explained he was the CIA Chief in Uganda. He had seen a copy of the letter I had written to Ambassador David Miller in which I explained why I wanted to travel to Uganda and what

I hoped to accomplish. As I elaborated on the contents of my letter, at one point my voice embarrassingly broke.

I didn't want that to happen—not here and not with him. I knew when I decided to make this trip that I would come into contact with government and intelligence types who would judge whether I was emotionally damaged, or had questionable motives. I was determined to present the appearance of a successful, intelligent, strong independent businessman who was engaged in an inquiry because he loved his father—which was natural, understandable and even commendable. I was a strong survivor who was reaching back from a position of strength to bring a sense of order and completeness to a tragic event from my past. I was not a lost soul, crippled by a tragedy returning to pitifully beg for assistance. Sure, I wanted assistance uncovering what had happened but I would handle everything from that point on. Tell me what happened to my father and I will be able to deal with it.

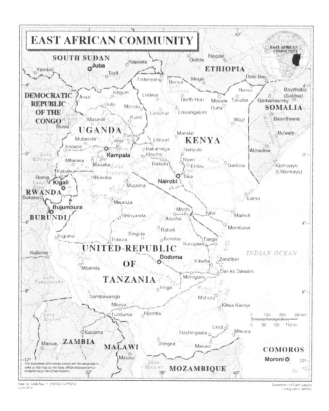

On the wall was a large map of Uganda. Mark pointed to the areas of the country where there was current fighting: the borders of Zaire (today known as the Democratic Republic of Congo), Sudan and Burundi. He also explained the nature of the conflict in each area and the political and economic conditions in each bordering country. I was surprised to learn that Uganda was now generally regarded as the most stable country in East Africa and getting better all the time. Tanzania, where Mark was stationed for several years previously, had never experienced any substantial economic development largely due to its socialist orientation, he said. Kenya, which had long been regarded as the most promising East African country and which had had such success in tourism and economic development was rapidly deteriorating. Sudan and Zaire were always a mess, although Zaire was by far the wealthiest nation in the region due to its substantial natural resources. The government of Uganda was wholly capitalist and its President was committed to weaning the country off its dependence on developmental assistance.

Mark talked about the President of Uganda, Yoweri Kaguta Museveni, as if he knew him personally. Whether he did or not, I don't know, but I doubt he had ever had extensive political and economic discussions with the leader. More likely, he was speaking based upon information he had from intelligence sources, public statements of the President and from reading Museveni's recently published autobiography, *Sowing the Mustard Seed: The Struggle for Freedom and Democracy in Uganda (1997),* which was an apparent bestseller in plain view everywhere I went in Uganda—including on Mark's desk.

When I remarked that I was shocked to see conditions in Uganda had so deteriorated, Mark was surprised. He found the country to be a delightful place to live with his family. Tanzania had been a hellhole; Uganda, by comparison, was well-developed, he said. The kid has no idea what this country used to be like, I thought.

Winston Churchill famously praised Uganda in 1907 while just a young Member of Parliament, saying:

"The kingdom of Uganda is a fairy-tale. You climb up ... and at the end there is a wonderful new world. The scenery is different, the vegetation is different, the climate is different, and, most of all, the people are different from anything elsewhere to be seen in the whole range of Africa ... I say: 'Concentrate on Uganda.' For magnificence, for variety of form and colour, for profusion of brilliant life – bird, insect, reptile, beast – for vast scale — Uganda is truly the pearl of Africa."

To this day, Uganda is still referred to as the "Pearl of Africa."

Many other explorers from the west (including Henry Morton Stanley, John Hanning Speke, and Frederick John D. Lugard), described the wonders of Uganda, including mountain gorillas, chimpanzees, the source of the Nile River, Murchison Falls, the Rwenzori Mountains, the 'Big Five' wild animals (lions, buffaloes, elephants, rhino and leopard) living in its ten national parks, using praising terms.

Moreover, Mark had no idea what this country could have been. In the late 1960s and 1970s there was such a sense of adventurous excitement and optimism. Visiting professors and their families came from all over the world to live and teach at Makerere University. Western curiosity regarding African history, traditional cultures and practices was at its apex and related research soared. What the Western world could learn from Uganda was as important as what the Western world could teach the Ugandan people.

Healthcare and economic development workers from England, Germany, Denmark, Norway, Canada, South Korea and the U.S. traveled out into the remote regions of the country attacking age-old problems such as infant mortality, family planning, nutrition and sanitation. This was an exchange of ideas that benefited all. Fifteen years of natural erosion, neglect and human destruction, followed by ten years of only modest rebuilding, had all but erased evidence of prior massive progress.

Mark said as long as I stayed away from the border conflicts, I should be perfectly safe. The road to Mbarara, the town where my father was killed, was a major thoroughfare which he regularly traveled. He would talk to his counterparts in Uganda internal intelligence, the equivalent of our FBI, to ask for their support for my mission.

At the risk of losing the support he had graciously offered, I asked:

"Do you know, or have reason to believe, my father or Stroh was involved with the CIA? I have repeatedly been told they were."

"I doubt they were. Historically, the CIA has only had a limited presence in Uganda," he said.

This was, of course, a lie—contradicting Ambassador Clyde Ferguson's statement to me years earlier in Cambridge, Massachusetts that the country was the CIA's second largest base in Africa. In the words of another commentator:

"The Americans and Israelis worked in very close co-operation in Uganda, particularly through their respective intelligence agencies, the CIA and Mossad. Washington provided some development aid while Israeli troops trained the Ugandan army and air force. The British economic and political presence was always predominant…"

The New York Times had even reported in 1986 that the CIA delivered bombs and other military equipment to Amin and took part in military operations for the Ugandan ruler in the 1970s.[7]

And, of course, Amin himself often decried the significant CIA presence in Uganda.

---

7.   https://www.nytimes.com/1986/12/17/world/paper-cites-cia-aid-to-amin-s-army-in-70-s.html

What answer did I expect? A spy, such as Mark, could hardly be expected to be entirely truthful about anything. It was a stupid question to ask.

"Unfortunately, my Freedom of Information Act requests for information about the murders from the CIA have been denied for national security reasons as recently as 1988," I confided.

"You should consider resubmitting those requests," he said. "I don't know if you're aware but the FOIA rules have been relaxed in recent years, so you might get more documents now. I have to tell you in my experience the CIA is pretty forthcoming on FOIA requests—much to the chagrin of my colleagues. Often our ability to do our jobs effectively is undermined by the threat of public disclosure."

Truth be known, the federal spy agency has regularly been challenged over the decades to re-examine its broad interpretation of its nondisclosure prerogatives under FOIA—to allow the public and the media to obtain information, as well as gain insight into how the agency conducts its business. If the public requests information from the CIA that has nothing to do with secret intelligence operations—as opposed to information which is justifiably classified on intelligence sources and methods, or is specifically about personnel and personnel records—the public should be able to get it.

Information that is not specifically protected under the Freedom of Information Act or the CIA Act should be released. Congress never intended for intelligence agencies to have a carte blanche, blanket exemption from FOIA. The CIA has often sought to apply an overly broad interpretation of federal laws that comes dangerously close to exempting from disclosure any information at all about anything the CIA does.

Only recently, a mere 59 years after the assassination of President John F. Kennedy and more than five years after the documents were originally required to be publicly disclosed, thousands of secret government files—largely from the CIA—were finally released.

"Pretty forthcoming," in short, has hardly been the CIA's modus operandi with respect to public records requests.

I assured Mark that my personal and professional background had led me to be sympathetic to the agendas of intelligence, regulatory and law enforcement organizations.

"I'm no investigative reporter looking to expose anyone. All I want to know is what happened to my father," I said. "And to know that, it would help to know what he was doing and for whom."

The few field research reports written by my father that I was able to retrieve revealed an intriguing mix of sociological, medical and military observations which raised as many questions about his motives as they answered. In the report below, he was able to travel across the country—including volatile border regions—under the auspices of the Uganda Red Cross; freely enter into hospitals, missions, infant care centers, and leper settlements; meet and interview missionaries, doctors, medical personnel, foreign development workers and soldiers; and even observe surgeries. It is difficult to imagine any single intelligence operative garnering as much diverse information and effectively weaving together his findings, without drawing attention to himself.

"On Monday morning, 14 September 1970 we left Kampala in a VW beetle marked on both doors with the sign "Uganda Red Cross Society- Donated from the German Red Cross- Bonn." We followed the smooth tarmac road which unites northern and southern Uganda beneath a blue African sky full of fantastic cloud effects. Somehow in this part of Africa the sky seems vaster and the clouds more beautiful. After a couple of hours, we crossed the Victoria Nile by bridge. Here the river follows a narrow deep channel and its flow is so swift that it leaps, foams and forms whirlpools. What potential it must have for production of power. We stopped for a few minutes to watch this untamed torrent battling its way toward Cairo hundreds of miles away.

We reached the rather flat northern town of Gulu around noon, passing no towns of any size or hardly any other cars on the more than 200-mile stretch between Kampala and Gulu. Nevertheless, we passed many people walking, usually women and children. Many carried cans of water on their heads. As we drove further north, we began to see bare breasted women which we had never seen near Kampala. Whenever we passed a stream or water-filled ditch, we saw people bathing and washing clothes.

After eating lunch at an Indian hotel in Gulu, baking in the hot afternoon sun we drove on and came upon a large giraffe by the road. He galloped off a little distance with strange grace, his muscles rippling under his skin like snakes. He turned to look at us and wiggled his ears. Soon we noticed an enormous elephant. We started downhill, approaching the calm Albert Nile where we took a little two-car barge-ferry across the wide and smooth river. Following a climbing dirt road, we reached the capital of Madi district, Moyo, before dark and got rooms at the government rest house. It had electricity and water, and was plain but clean and comfortable with mosquito nets for the beds, but no meals. The refrigerator had been out of order for quite some time.

We met the smiling, friendly district medical officer, who was Korean, who lives next door to the rest house who invited us for a Korean-style supper. We found there were no restaurants in the whole town and Father Bertuzzi of the Moyo Mission invited us to take our meals with him and the elderly brother who works and lives at the mission with him. The Verona Father's Mission at Moyo has an impressive church built by them, a babies' home serving

55 infants whose mothers have died, several primary schools, a convent of about 50 Sudanese nuns who fled from nearby Juba in the Sudan, due to the fighting. The schools at the mission founded by the Fathers were taken over by the Uganda government in 1964 and are no longer run by the Fathers.

We were within four miles of the Sudanese border but were not allowed to go closer as the area is occupied by the Uganda Army. This is because a guerilla war is still being fought by the Southern Sudanese Africans (Christian and Pagan) against the Northern Arab Muslim government. Over the past several years many have been killed and thousands of Southern Sudanese have fled to Uganda, Congo and Ethiopia. In 1968, some Sudanese (presumably northern) troops came to Moyo and were involved in shooting with Uganda forces. Some were killed, and, since then, troops have occupied the border area. Rumors abound.

The Southern forces, called Anya-Nya (meaning "snake poison" in Madi) are said to be supplied with arms from Israel. An unlighted plane flies over Moyo about every night, headed toward the Sudan. It is said that car travel in the Southern Sudan is only by armed convoy because of ambushes. Although the new Sudanese government has been encouraging refugees to return, few will go. One who did, returned nine months later. A captain of the Anya-Nya guerilla forces came to a missionary hospital to be fitted for glasses with a letter in correct English from his colonel requesting treatment. He returned to duty in the Sudan. Little is reported about what really goes on here.

Later we visited a crowded and poorly equipped Moyo government hospital. We watched an operation, the reduction of a fracture of the right arm of a child. Because the hospital was so crowded, and to save the only sterile operating room for serious cases, the patient was wheeled out of doors to a shaded area on the lawn under the water tank where he cried and screamed a few minutes while the Asian doctor and African anesthetist pulled on his arm to set it. Nearby a modern hospital with X-ray equipment is being built and will be finished in a few months. I visited a babies' home at the Moyo mission and dozens of tiny African children crowded around me holding my hands. There were 55 in all. This is the only babies' home in the whole northern area of Uganda. As there is a high maternal mortality rate, there are many children here. The Madi believe that a woman who cares for a dead woman's child will be barren, hence, in traditional Madi society many of these babies would die. Once the baby is able to feed himself many families are willing to take them back.

We showed Red Cross films at several schools. One school has mud benches and mud desks with blackboards for writing on and murals painted on the walls by students with mottos written on them in Madi. The students modeled animals in local clay and made iron-tipped arrows on an outdoor forge. Speaking of arrows, when we visited the hospital, we saw a woman who had been shot by an arrow through the breast and side of the chest. She had gotten up at night to relieve herself and no one knew who shot her or why. Leaving Moyo we stopped at a leper settlement and visited the school there with 65 leprous children. In Arua, I visited Kuluva Hospital for lepers. Although leprosy is still common, it appears to be decreasing. However, bilharzia is increasingly common and the cause of much loss of time from work. The snails that carry this organism seem to be spreading in the area called West Nile.

Heading back to Kampala, we passed a herd of about 15 elephants eating grass near the river. Returning through Masindi, we spent the night and enjoyed a party given by some friendly Norwegian aid workers. Driving through so many miles of Uganda and often waving to friendly people by the road, we thought about an unusual phenomenon of Ugandan driving. Drivers are instructed not to stop if they hit a pedestrian. The reason for this is, that if a driver stops, he would be beaten by a mob and probably killed. However much one may want to help, one must step on the gas and then report the accident at the nearest police station. African and European alike will probably be killed if they stop. It doesn't matter at all if the accident was the driver's fault or not."

Wayne Bush, the Deputy Ambassador, with whom I next met—like his CIA counterpart—also appeared to be in his early thirties. He was friendly, relaxed and unguarded.

How ironic, I thought. These two men were probably the same age as bureaucrats I considered "old" when I pleaded for help as a kid of 17 initially at the American Embassy in Oslo, Norway and later at the State Department in Washington, D.C. Now they seemed so young and inexperienced, as I was older and more experienced than either of them. I couldn't imagine these two having any meaningful first-hand knowledge of what went on in the remote regions of Uganda, much less being capable of investigating crimes. Like most American government officials I had known in my youth, they probably rarely ventured beyond the Embassy compound where they were protected by gates and guards from the local population. They certainly didn't speak any of the native languages. They weren't the adventurous types who could move through a Third World country undetected, or at least not arousing undue attention and suspicions. They were nice white boys—fine examples of the American way of life, well-versed in agency procedures who could be trusted by their bureaucratic bosses back home—but they would never be men of action who could get things done in Africa playing by local rules.

At 17, I probably had a better understanding of Ugandan life than these two ever would, I told myself.

The Deputy Ambassador asked how I knew former Ambassador David Miller in Washington. I told him I really didn't—Peter Stroh had introduced me to him. Judging by the Navy memorabilia, Bush had a military background. He and Mark operated independently, he said. He was on the diplomatic side; Mark was with intelligence. He didn't know what assistance Mark had offered but he would help me with his contacts.

As a lawyer well-versed in the failures of so-called "Chinese Walls" established to keep fellow-workers at Wall Street firms from sharing sensitive corporate financial information, I wasn't buying the bullshit of how the two operated independently for one second. I suspected they would compare notes the moment I left the building.

The Deputy Ambassador thought he could be most helpful by introducing me to the Commander of the Uganda Peoples Defense Forces, whom he referred to as "General Muntu." He picked up the phone and called the General, managing to get me a meeting with him that afternoon at 4:45.

"I'd caution you not to expect too much from Muntu. He's intelligent and will listen to you but probably not say much. He's not likely to give you a clear sense of what he's thinking. That's just the way he is. His reticence should not be construed as indifference. Now, if Muntu offers to have an officer accompany you to Mbarara—and I'm not saying he will—you should say you're willing to pay to rent a car for the trip. The Army does not have many resources available. They probably don't have a car to spare."

I thanked Bush for his help and promised to tell him the result of my meeting, as he had asked. I think he was genuinely curious how I would be received by the General. Would Muntu want to help me find the truth about my father's murder, or hide it from me?

CHAPTER 10

NO PREMONITIONS

There were no premonitions. No extrasensory perceptions. No dreams foretelling disaster. No visitations by ghosts. To say I had an inkling of what had happened to my father would be a lie. Over the years, I have searched my memory for any sense of impending doom. There was none.

Approximately a year after his disappearance, the contents of our apartment in Uganda, which had been packed into a single massive wooden crate under the supervision of U.S. Embassy staff and then shipped to me, finally arrived. The crate had been held by Ugandan Customs for months as the Commission of Inquiry proceeded. According to declassified State Department telegrams, "everything related to the Inquiry was extremely sensitive within the Ugandan Government and no one in authority could take any action without risking arousing the wrath of Amin and his military cohorts."

Packed carefully in a small box loosely tumbling about inside the enormous crate was a valuable 24-carat solid gold belt buckle. My father had it made for himself by a jeweler, years earlier, when we lived in Panama. While my father owned no jewelry (other than a Timex watch) and was never prone to extravagance, he explained to me that since the cost of having the buckle made in Panama was so little, it really wasn't a luxury purchase—more an opportunity to buy a luxury item at a significantly discounted price. His ornate initials "RLS" were skillfully carved into the heavy gold buckle by a master craftsman. Over the past fifty-plus years, I have realized the buckle finding its way back to me was truly remarkable for two reasons. First, since my father always wore this buckle with his belt, why was it not with him when he disappeared? Did he, sensing danger, intentionally leave it behind at our apartment? Second, the workers hired by the Embassy to pack our belongings would surely have recognized its value. Anyone could have easily pilfered it—no inventory or packing list accompanied the wooden crate. The story of the miraculously returned gold belt buckle is known by all my family. This buckle, framed in my office under glass today, is bequeathed to my son.

Also, included in the crate were all of my father's personal journals—dozens of volumes dating back to the 1940s. In the past year, prior to my return to Uganda, I finally unpacked, dusted off, and read them all. Searching his diaries, I found nothing in the months preceding his murder to suggest he foresaw his own death.

He had made a notation on a blank page six months into the future, "I wonder where I'll be working at this time?"

Likewise, my 1971 diary began with an entry in pencil, "When I look in this diary, I wonder what I will be doing this time next year. Better or worse?" Months later, in pen, I had written, "I never imagined things would turn out as they have so far. My world this time last year was completely different from today. I liked it then."

As opposed to foreseeing his death in his diary, a few months earlier he thanked God for watching over him. On safari, March 6th he wrote:

"Bright stars and a pale moon in a tremendously high, cloudless sky. It is so very quiet here tonight. People must be about nearby, dust-covered, unwashed, malnourished and hungry. Yet they do not know of the severity of their condition. They live according to custom, each as deprived as the next. A little boy was carrying a dry, wrinkled piece of paper in his arms. For fuel? For toilet paper? Every discarded thing is scavenged. A tall old tribesman was squatting on the ground on a vacant lot alongside a little Asian Indian tailor shop. The tailor had thrown out small patches of cloth and short pieces of thread. The old man was picking them up. The Karamojan will pose for pictures but only if you pay them. Around the missions, you can usually photograph them without paying.

Most people seem to be living largely on the posho (maize) flour. The missions give them a bowl a week. They say the population of Karamoja has increased greatly in the past few years, creating many more mouths to feed. It is said the posho flour that is given to the old people by the missions, is often taken away by their families. In a drought or famine, the older people and invalids will be given the least of what there is to eat, or encouraged to go off and die. I wonder how true this is. It is dry, parched and dusty here. The landscape is nothing but dust, dust, and dust.

We drove 70 miles north to Kotido and saw about 30 elderly Karamojan tribesmen. On the drive back our Land Rover skidded and bounced from side to side across the red dirt road. I was scared and thought we'd had it. I grabbed the dashboard and the door. The car came to a stop with the rear wheels in a shallow ditch. No one was hurt and the car was alright. We were down to our last drop of petrol and about 2 miles from the town of Morota when the left rear tire blew. We changed it and borrowed a gallon of petrol from a kind tribesman who stopped to help. We got to Moroto, got petrol first, then bought shampoo and had hot baths. What a blessing! My hair was so thick with dust I couldn't run a comb through it. Someone up there must have been watching over us this day."

There are stories of miraculous "awarenesses." We are comforted to hear of instances where the bond between loved ones extended over time and space. Those cases are the exception I am told. It is not reasonable to expect to know, sense, or feel danger about to strike a loved one. Premonitions and extrasensory perception are the exception, not the rule. But rational explanations do not make the guilt go away. We who survive the murder of a loved one feel we should have known and, if we didn't, it was because we didn't love enough. Had we held them closer, tighter—loved them more—perhaps we would have heard the warnings, sensed the imminent danger. Wasn't there something we could have done, we ask ourselves as we replay the incident in our minds over and over again, year after year.

I wasn't in Uganda when my father disappeared. I was in Kvietseid, a hamlet in the Norwegian countryside, lodged between mountains still snow-capped in summer and crystal clear, icy lakes fed by the melting snow. The entire month of July, I was vacationing with my girlfriend, Lise, and her family whom I had met in Uganda. Each sunny morning, we ate breakfast at a table set out in a field that we cleared of tall grass by scythe, adjoining the family's rough summer cottage. There was no running water, telephone or electricity. The mornings were spent on chores, and the afternoons swimming, hiking for berries and climbing up waterfalls. At night we sketched pictures, wrote, sang, drank and talked.

I remember hearing the musical chimes of the mailman's bicycle bell as he peddled up the rocky mountain road that morning. Lise's father was on a ladder painting the outside of the cottage when the mailman stepped up the first two rungs to hand him an envelope. Her father read its contents first as it was addressed to him. Then he climbed down and handed it to me.

The telegram—which I still possess—was from Les Essex, a British fellow faculty member at Makerere University and close family friend. Dated July 17th it simply read:

"Ted don't worry daddy ok, Les."

My stomach tightened and I was filled with a sickening feeling. I imagined the worst: My father was hurt or possibly even dying. In Africa, I knew when something goes wrong, it can go very wrong. There were no hospital emergency rooms to rush to in case of injury. A traffic accident seemed unlikely. An illness would be serious. My father was alone in a remote, untamed land. Something very ugly had happened. Lise's father had served as the head of the Norwegian Agency for Development Cooperation in Uganda, bringing the family with him for his three-year assignment before they all returned to Norway. We all had lived in Uganda long enough to know we should be worried. But no one speculated aloud as to what might have happened. We knew it would take time for more information to arrive from Uganda and let the matter lie.

Two days later, just as I had quelled my initial panic, a telegram dated July 15th arrived which read:

"Attention—stop—Bob Siedle delayed—stop—keep Ted in Norway—stop—letter follows."

The two telegrams had been delivered in reverse order. The second was sent two days earlier and was supposed to have arrived first, but didn't. Not that it really mattered. The messages still would have been confusing: worry—don't worry.

I remember sitting on the crude wooden built-in top bunk in one of the small cabin bedrooms one quiet evening after the telegrams had arrived as Lise stitched the inside pocket of my black silk jacket. Our relationship had changed with the arrival of the telegrams. In the past, she had been the thin, long-haired blonde, pretty girl who wore the shortest skirts simply made from African Kitange cloth folded over, stitched on each side with a hole cut for her head and neck. She knew how to get the attention of men and boys. I chased her and she enjoyed being chased. Now she had effortlessly, at age 16, become a caregiver.

"Lise, sometimes I feel glad my father may be finally out of my life," I confessed. "How can I think like that? What's wrong with me?"

"Ted, there's probably not a teenager in the world that wouldn't have that thought. I know I would if my parents suddenly disappeared. I'd feel free to finally live my life on my own terms."

There was no need to feel guilty, Lise assured me, I was just thinking like a normal teenager fighting to establish his independence. Except the deepest, darkest wish of this teenager—to live a life free of his parents—had seemingly come true.

And I had often said hurtful things to my father. As he wrote in his diary a year earlier on August 22, 1970:

"Ted continues often rude, self-centered and talking badly to me. God, I hope I haven't raised a problem. The questions arise, "Will he change this behavior?" "Is it my fault?" "How should I handle him?" "What did I do wrong?" All sort of doubts and discomforts.

In the early evening, as I was giving him a ride to Lise's house, he got angry and said several times that he hated me and that he wished I was dead. This annoyed me and made me unhappy, but I am rather used to such outbursts from him and so didn't lose my cool very much."

How could I have said I hated him and wished him dead—neither of which were true? My remarks had made him doubt his ability as a father, he had written.

I would remain in Norway for another few weeks, feeling numb, then afraid for my father, then equally afraid for myself and the unknown future I faced. What would happen to me? Where would I live? Who would take care of me?

Once we were back in Oslo, a long letter arrived from Les. The letter dated July 19th was intended to provide a lengthier account of events than telegrams permitted. Les explained my father and Stroh had gone on a trip to Mbarara about 10 days ago, were due back within two days, but were now long overdue. He and his wife had called the U.S. Embassy and learned nothing. He had also contacted a Reuters News correspondent in Kampala who said the two men were being held as prisoners by the Army at the Mbarara barracks. The Sunday Nation newspaper told the same story. Another paper, the Uganda Argus, printed an editorial comment concerning "foreign journalists who were making up stories about Uganda." While no names were mentioned, Les speculated it clearly was referring to Stroh.

Les was confident my father would be released soon. But no one knew for certain where my father was being held or when he would be released. Straining to remain optimistic, Les ended his letter joking, "Your father has now probably achieved the fame he deserved but not the fame he would like—as a jailbird." He promised to save my father a piece of his birthday cake.

The next day Lise and I went by train to the American Embassy in Oslo to ask for their assistance.

"I received these two telegrams and this letter about my father from a family friend in Uganda," I told an older female Embassy staffer, as I presented her with the documents.

"I'm really worried something may have happened to him. Can you look into whether he's okay? Something bad may have happened and I can't get any more information from Uganda. Can the Embassy do... something?"

"Well, there really isn't anything we can do," she said dismissively. "I'm sure your father is fine and will show up back at the university in a couple of days."

This woman knows nothing about conditions in Uganda, I thought. He won't simply casually resurface. That's not how things go down in Uganda. When someone disappears, it's serious, I knew.

"The most we can do is send an "interested person" telegram but that would cost you $50," she said.

"$50! Are you kidding me," I said. "An American is missing in a dangerous part of the world and you're telling me there's nothing you can do? You have an obligation to your citizens to look out for them. I am an American citizen and I have certain rights."

To this day it infuriates me that the Embassy staffers initially refused to offer any help. Incredibly, they had no sympathy for me—a teenage boy, frightened and alone in a foreign country, whose father had disappeared in Africa. They felt no obligation to even inquire as to my father's whereabouts. They wanted me to go away and not create additional work for them.

And the Embassy staff was hardly overwhelmed.

There was no global humanitarian crisis at their doorstep at this time, no masses of desperate refugees huddled in hallways. This was one-off situation involving one single, solitary American.

I cannot help but wonder whether my mixed-race brown skin and shoulder-length dark brown hair had a great deal to do with the treatment I received from the Embassy. Had I been a blonde haired, southern California Beach Boy—a thoroughly white "American" looking sort—I suspect I would have been treated far better. And, if I had had any indicia of wealth, notoriety or influence, no doubt the Embassy would have put its resources readily at my disposal. I would learn time and again in the months and years that followed, that who you are, all-too-often determines the treatment you receive from governments, agencies, lawyers and the press.

Finally, after completing an impassioned speech about the rights of American citizens and the duty of the Embassy to help Americans abroad in distress, the Embassy agreed to send, at no cost to me—after I told them I did not have $50—an "interested person" telegram to the Embassy in Kampala.

Apparently, if I was American enough to articulate a "rights of American citizens" argument, the Embassy—reminded of its duty—would treat me like an American citizen was supposed to be treated by his government.

In that moment at the Embassy, in the recesses of my soul, a decision had been made: Someday I would become a lawyer.

CHAPTER 11

A SUMMER NIGHT SKY
FULL OF STARS IN NORWAY

A day later, I received a call from the Embassy instructing me to come by its offices that evening to pick up from the Marine color guard outside the entrance, the response they had received from Uganda.

It was a clear, crisp, summer night under a sky full of sparkling stars when I was handed a plain white envelope by a white-gloved, impeccably attired Marine standing at the front gate of the Embassy in his dress blue uniform. The teletype message, which I immediately opened read:

"Robert Siedle departed Kampala July 7th for Mbarara in Uganda 160 miles southwest of Kampala, with Nicholas W. Stroh, Free-Lance correspondent for several American papers. Siedle and Stroh intended to return on evening of July 8th. Stroh went to Mbarara in search of news concerning situation along Tanzanian-Ugandan border and to investigate reports of intra-army fighting. Siedle apparently went along as company. When both men did not return Kampala by July 10th, Embassy Kampala began vigorous efforts to enlist aid of Uganda police and foreign ministry in attempts to locate them. Embassy consular officer and President of Uganda, General Idi Amin, ultimately visited Mbarara. Every feasible effort has been and is continuing to be made to trace Siedle and Stroh.

Neither Government of Uganda nor Embassy has been able to positively establish whereabouts Siedle or Stroh. In view of the long passage of time since men were last seen and unsettled conditions in Uganda at time of disappearance, we hold out only slight hope men are still alive. General Amin has ordered that court of inquiry begin July 29 in Mbarara in order to attempt ascertain what happened."

We two teenagers then slowly made our way back to Lise's home, with the words "In view of the long passage of time… we hold out only slight hope men are still alive," etched in our minds. Those were the very words I did not want to hear.

I remember thinking: Take care, thoughtless bureaucrats, that your sharp words not rob those who love the missing of their last thread of hope.

I wrote in my diary:

"Well, if the information the Embassy has given me is correct, my father, Robert Louis Siedle, Sr., died sometime between the 8th and I suppose the 11th, when he was due back in Kampala. The Embassy said today they believed Daddy was dead. They can't find him or Nick Stroh. If he's dead, then I wonder how he died. Was it a horrible death? It sort of scares me when I think about it. If he is alive—where the hell is he? I think he's dead. I'm sorry I think that but I do. I suppose it's wrong of me to think that way. I really don't know what to think or do or feel. I mean I'm not sure what I feel. I think I don't believe it yet. I feel a bit out of touch—perhaps it's shock. I feel I must know exactly how and when Daddy died. There I go assuming that Daddy's dead. When I stop to think about what has happened, everything is very still and quiet. I wonder how many people who knew Daddy have heard the news. I hate not knowing for sure what happened."

I do not recall being impressed or consoled that the Embassy counselor officer and the President of Uganda himself had already visited Mbarara engaged in the search for my father. Perhaps I should have been encouraged by the serious, high–level attention the matter was receiving. But I knew the American Embassy people in Uganda. They lived their lives behind the compound's walls, cruising about in conspicuous motorcades of black, oversized American cars with American flags flying on the front fenders, when they ventured through the streets of the city of Kampala. Rarely did they ever get out into the remote areas outside Kampala. How the hell would they find out what happened? All I could think about was how, if I were still there, I could hitch a ride to Mbarara and find my father. I had been there before and spent the night at the only government Rest House in the town—where my father most likely would have recently stayed.

But at age 17, what could I do? I had no money for a return ticket to Uganda and, even if I did, there was no way of knowing what I'd encounter once there. It was a journey I was ill-equipped to make, yet which I felt compelled to undertake. I was thousands of miles away from my father, helpless to save him. Worst still, my hopes for his safe return were dependent upon inept bureaucrats who neither knew, nor particularly cared, about my father.

A week later another letter came from Les Essex.

"Things have gotten much worse here. It is no longer likely your father is being held unharmed by the Army. The Army is now saying they know nothing about your father or Stroh. So, it seems as if they were arrested but now no one is saying where they are and this is most worrisome for us all. The British Sunday newspaper, *The Observer*, in its Sunday edition has a report about Uganda, which also mentions the disappearances and was most discouraging. We are all hoping to see them soon, but we are very worried."

Hope the two men were still alive was very slim now. Les knew at this point, they were almost certainly dead. But he did not want to come out and say it—not to me.

I flew back to the United States on August 1, 1971—alone—using the return ticket my father had purchased for me.[8] On the flight to New York I first heard the song, *Fire and Rain* by James Taylor, the words of which spoke to the sudden dramatic change in my life, my deep sadness and regret.

I've seen fire and I've seen rain
I've seen sunny days that I thought would never end
I've seen lonely times when I could not find a friend
But I always thought that I'd see you again

I always thought I would see my father again.

The next day *Newsweek* magazine printed the first article I had seen about the disappearances.

The article appeared in the section of the magazine dealing with "The Media," and was entitled, "End of a Dream." It was a tribute to Stroh, the newsman and spoke of his "abiding love of Africa," as well as his "expert knowledge of African life."

Remarkable considering the man had only lived in Uganda for a few months.

The only mention of my father in the article was his name, his overt occupation (college professor) and that he had accompanied Stroh—approximately 15 words. My father's knowledge of Africa, the articles and book he had written about missionaries caring for the elderly in the bush and that he

---

8.   Declassified State Department documents indicate "Norwegian friends of Edward
      Siedle associated with Oslo headquarters of Norwegian AID to Uganda were
      interested in receiving any information on the case that could be passed onto them."

had served as Stroh's guide, introducing Stroh to the informal intelligence network he had cultivated, were not mentioned—perhaps intentionally. Stroh's picture captioned, "Stroh: A job too well done," accompanied the article. On the one hand, I was proud my father had finally achieved some fame. He wanted recognition for his expertise as a sociologist but also to play a role in furthering global justice, as he had in opposing the Vietnam War and racial discrimination. He would have been proud to expose Amin's brutality to the world, in hopes of an international intervention to end Ugandan suffering. It was sad though that the degree of international notoriety he would have welcomed was only achieved in death. Even then, he was merely a footnote in another man's story. His intelligence-gathering activity remained hidden from the world.

According to the article, *Newsweek* reporter, Andrew Jaffe had travelled to Mbarara and traced my father and Stroh's movements. Jaffe was said to be the first foreign reporter to enter the area since the two men had disappeared. Jaffe said the first night the two had spent in Mbarara, Stroh had managed to meet secretly with Army soldiers who told him they had seen some bodies carried away by trucks following a mass execution. Jaffe was told that the two Americans had been arrested by the Commanding Officer, Lt. Col. Ali Fadhul. Barracks rumor had it that the two men were killed within a few days of their arrest.

A few days after reading the *Newsweek* article, I flew from New York to Washington, D.C. to be "de-briefed" by an official at the State Department, who wanted to know all I knew about my father and conditions in Uganda. This was the first time I met David Shinn, who would be so helpful over the next two years. I was accompanied by a young lawyer from a prestigious Washington international law firm which had agreed to initially represent me in the developing matter. I remember being uncomfortable when he did not offer to pay for the taxi ride. The young lawyer clearly had a lot to learn about taking care of an orphaned minor in distress—who happened to be his penniless client. By this date, newspaper articles were being published worldwide about the murders. The Washington Star, the newspaper with which Stroh was most closely affiliated, ran daily articles. With every new article came new conflicting accounts of how my father and Stroh had been killed.

One eyewitness claimed they had been stabbed to death. Another soldier said they were strapped to oil drums and then shot and burned.

"How could the State Department tell the reporter who wrote this article that my father and Stroh had been tortured with knives without telling the families first?" I said to Shinn raising my voice over the phone a few days later.

"We didn't say that to the reporter," Shinn responded sympathetically, "the State Department spokesman only stated—in response to a question that was asked—the possibility of torture could not be ruled out."

In a later interview Shinn spoke of this time in 1971:

"Uganda was a very busy place because Idi Amin was running the country. This was the beginning of his regime and we were trying to figure out whether he was as crazy as he appeared to be. We ultimately concluded that he really was.

The main issue during my year on the desk was the kidnaping and ultimate assassination of two Americans. One was a freelance newspaper reporter by the name of Strow [sic], a member of the prominent brewing family. I dealt with his father [sic], Peter. He was a person with considerable political clout in the U.S. I had frequent conversations with him during 1971-72. The other person who died was a school teacher [sic] in Kampala. The reporter had gone to Mbarara in southern Uganda to write a story on dissident activities. He obviously found out too much; he was killed by the local military as was the school teacher [sic]. The perpetrators burned both bodies. It took the embassy a long time to trace them and discover the horrible truth. Finally, when we did get enough proof, we informed the families who naturally were very distressed. The best that could be said about this episode was that we were able to find out what had happened. This incident took up an enormous amount of time during that year; it started soon after I arrived on the desk and was not completed until shortly before I left…

… Our embassy saw Amin regularly. That was not easy. On the one hand, he was very much in charge of a country with which we wanted good relations. It had a bright economic future; there was a certain amount of American business interest in the country. On the other hand, Amin was a very, very difficult person who became increasingly so with each year he remained in power."[9]

Since I was having headaches, as well as trouble sleeping, a doctor prescribed a low dose of Valium, as needed. Despite my initial resistance, in the weeks to come, I would use every bit of the little Valium I had been given.

9.   https://tile.loc.gov/storage-services/service/mss/mfdip/2007/2007shi02/2007shi02.pdf

CHAPTER 12

GENERAL MUNTU, THE UGANDAN ARMY LEND A HAND

General Muntu's offices were within walking distance of the Kampala Sheraton in a building adjacent to the President's house and offices. As I entered through the gate a half-dozen soldiers in camouflage fatigues toting machine guns were casually milling about the courtyard. The sentry at the gate asked who I was there to see but security was relaxed—at least compared to the U.S. Embassy. No one inspected my briefcase and no one seemed fearful or threatened.

While I was comforted by the soldiers' easygoing demeanor, I did not enjoy being surrounded by so many guns. It was a sunny day but dark as I entered the building. Directly ahead was a large room sparsely furnished with only a couple of dilapidated, soiled velour-covered French provincial style sofas. An attendant escorted me around the corner where a number of young armed soldiers were gathered around a doorway. This was the General's office and, the attendant explained to the soldiers in Swahili that I had an appointment to see him. The soldiers allowed me to pass.

General Muntu, a surprisingly young man of 38, quickly rose from his desk to greet me. He motioned for me to be seated on the sectional sofa to the side of his desk and conference table. His office was large—furnished with dated furniture, with the exception of the sectional sofa and coffee table which were more modern.

Muntu's background was truly exceptional for a Ugandan soldier. Since his father was a government official and a close friend of former leader Milton Obote, he'd had an affluent childhood. He graduated with a major in political science from Makerere University, where he was deputy president of the students union. He joined the guerrilla National Resistance Army (NRA) of Yoweri Museveni the day he completed his university exams, to the chagrin of his family and President Obote, who reportedly considered him a son. Early into the rebellion he was shot in the chest but survived after receiving treatment in Kampala. Later he emerged as the head of Military Intelligence after the NRA victory in 1986. He underwent further military training in Russia before rising to the rank of Major General and then Commander of the Uganda Peoples Defense Forces (UPDF). Many attributed his rapid ascension to the pinnacle of the NRA/UPDF to his reputation as an incorruptible and loyal officer to the President of Uganda. Many of the less-educated officers in the military resented his affluence, superior education and integrity.

Major General Mugisha Muntuoyera,
Commander of the Ugandan Peoples Defense Forces

I told the General about my father's death and that I was hoping for his assistance in learning exactly what had happened to my father—i.e., how he had been killed. I was not really interested in who had killed him. I already knew who gave the orders. I did not want anyone with information to offer to be afraid to come forward. This was a personal matter, not an official inquiry. No one should be concerned what they said might be used against them—even if they were to admit actual participation in the killings. The murders had occurred decades ago—under Amin's orders—and I believed the soldiers involved probably were just following orders.

General Muntu was very solemn as he listened to me closely. He seemed to appreciate the sanctity of my mission more than my fellow countrymen at the American Embassy. Mine was a deeply personal journey, the fulfillment of a sacred obligation between son and father. When a father is murdered a son has an obligation to learn whether he suffered, to care enough to find out how he met his death. A sense of justice is imbedded in the sacred obligation. However, I had never felt a strong desire to avenge his death.

The conversation between the General and I had moved into the realm of the sacred where timeless notions of justice, religion, obligation and duty are all that matter.

After listening for a lengthy period, the General began to speak *very quietly*. (Time and again, I have observed that when people who have witnessed, or endured extreme brutality talk about such acts they naturally lower their voices. My sense is that this is partially out of reverence for the victims, as well as perhaps a sense of shame for not having prevented the harm.)

"Over a million people were killed in Uganda during the fifteen-year period when Amin was in power and when Obote returned, following Amin, a second time. Obote's second regime was actually far more brutal than Amin's. It was a horrible time in Uganda's history. I and many other young Ugandans were forced to flee to Tanzania where we lived for several years. We were trained by the Tanzanians to fight and returned to Uganda, once trained, to live in the bush and fight the Ugandan Army under the control of Amin and then Obote."

He then told me about the fighting that was ongoing in Uganda. Rebels ransacked villages and attacked and murdered people on the streets. Joseph Kony, leader of the Lord's Resistance Army, governed his flock according to his own interpretation of the Ten Commandments. There were strict rules: no bicycle riding, no eating pigs. A man was once pulled from his bike and killed in front of his wife by rebels, who severed his feet and forced the woman to eat a foot or to be killed.

Uganda in 1997 was still a treacherous place where unimaginable cruelty was commonplace, said Muntu, contradicting assurances I had received from American officials.

I told him it was good to finally talk to someone who knew of the violence of which I was a surviving victim, and to be in the country where the killings happened. Every Ugandan is most likely a victim, a perpetrator, or both, of the abominations that occurred, I observed, and the General agreed.

"Had anyone written a history of the years of brutality endured by the Ugandan people?" I asked. "Were there any photographic or art exhibitions focusing on the fighting? Had any thought been given to establishing a national museum, like the Holocaust museums that were established in Israel, German or the U.S.? Or a Truth and Reconciliation Commission to provide a public forum for the private grief of the millions of perpetrators and victims of violence, like in South Africa?"

In Uganda, nothing had been done, the General told me. However, I would learn—much later—this statement was far, far from the truth.

First, as a result of strong public pressure for an inquiry into disappearances occurring in the early years of his government, in June 1974, President Amin established a Commission of Inquiry into the Disappearances of People in Uganda from January 25, 1971 (date of the coup) until 1974. This first truth commission operated for six months. Comprised of four members, it was chaired by an expatriate Pakistani judge, and included two Ugandan police superintendents and a Ugandan army officer. Although most hearings were open to the public, a report of the commission's findings was never published. A confidential copy was handed over to Amin. Three hundred and eight cases of disappearance were presented to the commission. The commission concluded that the Public Security Unit and the National Investigation Bureau, both of which had been set up by Amin, bore the main responsibility for the disappearances. The commission recommended reforming the police and the armed forces. It suggested that law enforcement officials be trained in human rights standards. The commission's findings had no impact, as brutality continued throughout Amin's eight-year rule. Rather, the four commissioners were targeted by the state in reprisal for their work. Included in Part V: Closing Appendices of the findings is a lengthy discussion of the Commission of Inquiry into my father's death, therein referred to as "the Jones Inquiry." As the commissioners noted:

> "In 1973 the government finally admitted responsibility for the killings and paid compensation to the relatives of the two men in the United States. Yet, to date, no action has been taken nor further investigation made into the evidence uncovered by Judge Jones' inquiry."

Also:

> "The Jones Inquiry is perhaps the most extensive official investigation of violence in Uganda in the past three years. The problems it encountered, as later described in Judge Jones' detailed report, are illustrative of some of the difficulties that plague the judicial process and make serious criminal investigation virtually impossible in Uganda."[10]

---

10. https://www.usip.org/sites/default/files/resources/collections/truth_commissions/
Uganda74-Report/Uganda74-Report_sec5.pdf

Second, twelve years later—shortly after Museveni's government came into power in May, 1986—it set up a Commission of Inquiry into Violations of Human Rights. This commission was empowered to look into the period between October 9, 1962 (the date of Uganda's independence) and January 25, 1986 (when the National Resistance Army marched into Kampala), investigating "the causes and circumstances surrounding the mass murder and all acts or omissions resulting into the arbitrary deprivation of human rights committed in various parts of Uganda."

There was some suspicion about this commission's charge since it only covered atrocities committed up to the time when Museveni's government took over. Over the course of the commission's lengthy (8-year) proceedings, accusations of murder and torture began surfacing against the new regime—notably from Amnesty International—which in 1989 complained that at least 3,000 political prisoners were being detained without trial. There were also reports that government soldiers in the north, where rebel activity continued, had burned civilians alive in the process of torching suspected rebel hide-outs.

Commissioners reviewed evidence about a wide range of issues including, arbitrary arrests and imprisonment; detention without trial; torture, cruel, inhuman and degrading treatment; the massive displacement and expulsion of people including Uganda citizens from Uganda and the consequent disappearance or presumed death of some of them; and the subjection to discriminatory treatment by virtue of race, tribe, place of origin, political opinion, creed, or sex. The commission was chaired by Arthur Oder, justice of the Supreme Court and its six members included a law professor, a medical doctor, a professor of history and a practicing lawyer.

It was important to create a historical record wrote Justice Oder:

"Ugandans should not think that the incidence which concerns them happened so long ago that it is useless to raise [them] now. They may say "What is the use of digging up the past"? Ugandans should not let by gone be by gone. ... I would like people to be positive and to come forward and talk about their human rights because that is the only way to prevent the possible violation of human rights again...If any individual comes to give evidence, he will encourage others not only now, but in the future to defend their human rights."

As a fellow Commissioner observed in his opening comments:

"...just after we came in the building, I saw an old man sitting there, led in by his grandson. That to me is the image I shall carry with me in the months to come. An old man who, by the Grace of whatever, escaped the fate of so many of these comrades and staggered through this Chamber this morning to hear what is going on, to tell us about what happened, brought in by his grandson who will remember long after these matters have ended, I am sure long after some of us have gone, what was done today until the time comes. An old man and his grandson and we must not fail them. We must find the culprits, get the evidence and send the culprits to their just punishment."

While Justice Oder initially hoped to have foreign governments extradite former presidents Amin and Obote to Uganda—both of whom were living in exile in Saudi Arabia and Zambia, respectively—on charges of violating human rights, nothing came of his request. When Amin, who had been living in exile in Saudi Arabia since 1979, visited Zaire in 1989, he was arrested upon his arrival at Kinshasa airport for using a false name and a stolen Zairean passport. An attempt was made to have him extradited to Uganda, but it failed because there was no extradition treaty between the countries.

Thousands of Ugandans completed questionnaires for the commission about their recollections of atrocities. Hearings were held throughout the country, and 608 people gave oral evidence. The hearings caught the nation's attention and accounts of the testimony featured prominently in the local newspapers. For some period of time, Ugandans with access to television could watch a 40-minute tape of highlights of the week's proceedings on Sunday evenings. The commission reportedly operated under many physical and official limitations, including perennial shortages of paper, ink and stencils. As a result, its staff of 15 secretaries struggled to transcribe the estimated tens of thousands of pages of testimony elicited from witnesses.

The final written record of the testimony filled eighteen large volumes and included graphic and oftentimes horrifying descriptions of violence committed against Ugandan people by agents of the governments of Amin and Obote.[11]

A highlight of the hearings was when Paulo Muwanga, chief of state during Obote's second term as president, was called as the 154th witness in 1988 to answer charges of complicity in atrocities. The allegations against him included that he had ordered a 20-year-old woman, a suspected rebel, tied to a seatless chair over a flaming plastic pail. Her breasts were cut off, and she was impaled on a hot poker. Another victim had been so mutilated that Muwanga allegedly ordered: "We can't let her out of here like this. Finish her off."

The Report of the Commission of Inquiry into Violations of Human Rights was publicly released in 1994, but attracted almost no attention. When I met with General Muntu three years later—in 1997—apparently even he was unaware of this commission's recently released voluminous findings. The report was not widely available until 2022.

In conclusion, two substantial inquiries into brutalities committed during the Amin-Obote years—hearing evidence from nearly a thousand witnesses—were commissioned and completed. Despite the tremendous governmental effort involved, the findings of these inquiries were never broadly distributed to the Ugandan peoples. All of which begs the question:

---

11.   Scans of the Oder Commission reports can be found at https://derekrpeterson.com/archive-materials/

why bother to elaborately document human rights abuses, only to continue to conceal them from the public?

General Muntu explained that the composition of the Army changed under Amin. By 1978, it had grown to over 25,000 personnel, almost twice the 1971 level. Amin killed many of its more experienced officers and imprisoned others for plotting to weaken or overthrow him. Some fled the country to escape the mounting danger. Amin also increased the number of military recruits from other countries. Eventually the Army was largely a mercenary force, half Sudanese, 26% Congolese, and only 24% Ugandan (mostly Muslim), exacerbating problems of communication, training, and discipline. Some units were barely controlled by the Army. A few, like the Simba Battalion barracks in Mbarara, became quasi-independent garrisons headed by violent warlords who lived off the community by brutalizing the local population.

The Ugandan Army of today, said Muntu, consisted of soldiers who had fought to overthrow the previous regimes of Obote and Amin and those older soldiers of the Obote and Amin eras who, based upon their good character, were allowed to remain in the service. The worst characters of past regimes, he said, had either died in the fighting, fled to the bush or were convicted of serious crimes by the civil authorities.

Following the call from the U.S. Embassy earlier in the day, the General told me he had inquired as to the whereabouts of any soldiers who may have witnessed or been involved in the murders of my father and Stroh. The commanding officer of the Mbarara barracks, the notorious Major Ali Fadhul was now in prison, on death row. Lt. Silver Tibihika, a soldier who had been at the barracks at the time of the killings who subsequently fled to Tanzania, the General knew had returned to Uganda. Silver was now living in retirement a short distance from the barracks. Unbeknownst to Muntu, Silver was the one person who had come forward and submitted testimony to the Commission of Inquiry investigating my father and Stroh's death. Had it not been for Silver, the Commission would have been unable to come to any conclusions about what happened to the two men. I was eager to learn more by talking to Silver, Ali Fadhul and any other soldiers General Muntu had arranged for me to meet with.

I showed the General a copy of the printed and bound Commission of Inquiry into my father and Stroh's deaths which I had received from the State Department in 1972 and brought with me in my briefcase. He recalled the highly publicized case from when he was a young boy. His keen interest in reading the Report surprised me, since I assumed that anyone who had wanted to read it could have. The Report had been printed in Uganda by the Government Printer Entebbe and offered for sale to the public for the price of ten shillings in 1972, according to its cover. The General said he certainly had never seen the Report and doubted it had ever been made widely available in the country. He read a few pages of the report closely, turning each yellowed page carefully as if it were a rare manuscript.

I told General Muntu that, in my opinion, the Report represented a proud moment in the history of Uganda when the judiciary stood up and challenged Amin's dictatorship in as articulate and heartfelt defense of democracy as has ever been written. I read to him some of my favorite passages which I had read again in the past year. I told him that, as a lawyer, it was the most inspiring legal opinion I had ever read. In his Report, a lone judge had told the President of a country—putting his own life at extreme risk—that he could not get away with murder. I wondered aloud how many American judges would risk their own lives for justice.

General Muntu's aide, Major Kabijamu, had entered the office about half-way through our discussion and had been listening intently from a table in the distance behind us as we had our remarkable, hour-plus long talk. The General instructed Kabijamu to arrange transportation and an escort for me to Mbarara. I told the General I deeply appreciated his assistance and the opportunity we had to speak. General Muntu and I shook hands as the Major escorted me out of the office.

Kabijamu had indeed listened closely to our conversation and, once outside Muntu's office, told the other officers gathered in the hallway that I was the son of one of the Americans who had been killed in 1971. The soldiers now looked sympathetically at me. They easily understood that as the son of someone who had been killed in Uganda—whose body had never been found—I would have to come back. I was not just a foreigner passing through on business or holiday. I was here because my personal history—my life—was forever tied to Uganda.

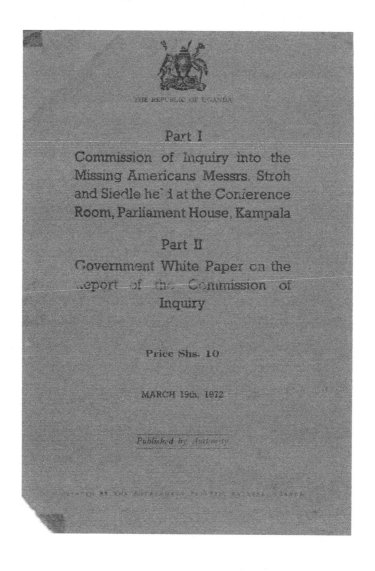

THE REPUBLIC OF UGANDA

Part I
Commission of Inquiry into the Missing Americans Messrs. Stroh and Siedle held at the Conference Room, Parliament House, Kampala

Part II
Government White Paper on the Report of the Commission of Inquiry

Price Shs. 10

MARCH 19th, 1972

Published by Authority

CHAPTER 13

THE COMMISSIONER'S REPORT

On September 10, 1971, David Jeffreys Jones, a judge of the High Court of Uganda was appointed by the Government of Uganda and the President, General Idi Amin Dada, to head a Commission of Inquiry into all aspects of the disappearance of my father and Stroh, who had not been heard from since the 9th day of July, 1971.

The disappearance of the two Americans was followed by strong rumors they had been killed and their bodies disposed by the Army. These stories, in turn, fed increasing rumors of the Government's inability to discipline members of the Army. This situation prompted the Government to appoint an Army Board of Inquiry to examine the possibilities of involvement, if any, of members of the Army in the men's disappearance. Throughout this period the Ugandan Government maintained the view that the men were not dead, but instead had left the country—this despite pleas from our families and pressure from the United States representatives to have them declared dead so that their estates could be settled and life insurance benefits paid out. The U.S. government also pressed for a more obviously independent inquiry, in addition to the Army inquiry. In response to these varied pressures, both within and without Uganda, the Government invoked the unusual constitutional device of a Commission of Inquiry.

The idea of the Commission of Inquiry was exported to the former British colonies in Africa by the Imperial British Government and since their independence from England has become an accepted part of their constitutional practice. In this exceptional case, a High Court judge and member of the judicial branch of the government was asked by President Amin to conduct an independent investigation, in a politically-charged atmosphere, to determine whether any of the various branches of Government, including the Army and the Executive, were involved in the disappearance and murder of the two Americans. It was said that Jones' appointment as Commissioner was interesting in view of "the healthy robustness of his criticisms of the behavior of the police and security forces of the former Obote regime."

This case would ultimately involve a clash between the judiciary and these other branches of Government, to determine whether the independence of the judiciary would be preserved, as established in the Ugandan Constitution and whether or not the country would continue to be ruled by its laws.

The following is a summary of the Jones Report published in 1972.[12]

"Following my swearing in as the Commissioner of the Inquiry, a meeting was held in my Chambers in the High Court. During the meeting, I expressed my concern about a recent article in *The London Times* which suggested the inquiry would have to probe the affairs of the Simba Battalion of the Armed Forces of Uganda based in Mbarara. I said the Army would appear to be "on trial." I also pointed out that the inquiry involved the relationship between two friendly States, and lastly, but not least, the World press would be keenly interested as it concerned one of their members.

The Attorney General of Uganda assured me that apart from all that, the Government was concerned at getting at the truth. I accepted that assurance. I suggested to him, however, that due to the delicate situations that could arise, I would like an independent investigator appointed to make inquiries.

---

12. Commission of Inquiry into the Missing Americans Messrs. Stroh and Siedle held at the Conference Room, Parliament House, Kampala, March 19, 1972.

I was also told at that meeting that the evidence the Army Board of Inquiry had already collected would be made available to me and a competent police force was at our disposal. *I could see clearly rocks ahead.*

I was disappointed that I never received a response to my request for an independent investigator, particularly since another Commission running at the same time had the services of an ex-Uganda Assistant Commissioner of Police, together with a world class accountant, for the best part of a year to investigate and assist in the inquiries into the affairs of a corporation set up by the former regime of Milton Obote. A strong team of police investigators was also at their disposal. We had *no one*.

Between October and December 1971, the Commission of Inquiry met on two or three occasions, but it made little progress. In spite of the fact that my appointment and oath-taking had been highly-publicized, no one seemed anxious to come forward to assist. I had, however, received one anonymous letter dated October 10, 1971. The writer advised me that I might be "wasting" my time looking for the two Americans because they were "frustrated with their conditions in Uganda" and had "decided to go to a neighboring country" and ask for asylum. As a result of one of our meetings, a letter was sent to the Attorney General indicating some sort of investigation into the disappearance of the two Americans ought to be conducted by the civilian or military police.

In December, we decided to make another appeal through the press and the radio for people to come forward and assist the Commission.

Nothing took place as a result of those announcements. I did receive a letter from His Grace the Archbishop of Uganda which included a letter received by him from a sister of one of the missing Americans, a Mrs. Carol Fishkin. In her letter, Mrs. Fishkin described the financial difficulties the young son of Mr. Siedle was encountering as a result of being unable to access the monies in his father's estate due to the fact that he had not been declared "dead."

The Commission officially opened to an unpromising start on March 15, 1972. Apart from the press, the Inquiry attracted little notice or attention. Over the course of 25 days, we heard evidence and addresses from 37 witnesses, and made two visits, one to Mbarara and one to Fort Portal.

Our first witness was the Mbarara Rest House keeper at the time the two Americans stayed there, i.e., the 7th, 8th, and 9th of July. When the proceedings adjourned at 4 p.m. that day, it was decided to go to the Simba Barracks, Mbarara on the following day to have a look at the place so that we would have some idea of what was being referred to in later stages in the proceedings. Our secretary made the arrangements.

On the morning of the 17th of March—approximately eight months after the disappearance of the two Americans—the members of the Commission, accompanied by our secretaries and two military policemen as escorts left for Mbarara. I went first to the Rest House where the two Americans had last stayed and then to one or two other places before joining the rest of our party for lunch at the Agip Motel.

After lunch, we went to the barracks where we had to wait for about three quarters of an hour. We had, to say the least, a frigid reception, which was understandable given that our staff had made arrangements for us to visit the barracks at 11 a.m., which we did not know. After explanations were offered and apologies made, the atmosphere thawed and we were shown the lay-out of the barracks. We visited the quarter guard, and the administrative block where the adjutant, chief clerk, orderly officer, intelligence officer, the Commanding Officer and second in command of the battalion were housed. The hospital, Motor Transport sections, the other ranks' quarters, and the Officers' Mess were pointed out to us. They were all located quite near each other, and we left with a pretty clear picture of the barracks buildings and lay-out.

After leaving the barracks, we returned to the town of Mbarara, where we visited the Ministry of Works Yard, the Police Station and the Revenue

Office. We also inspected the books of the Rest House and the book relating to the Mbarara air strip.

Our inspection of the Rest House book led us to summon two more of the Rest House staff, who produced the register of guests kept by the Rest House keeper.

As far as the Police and the Revenue Office were concerned, we drew blanks. The police seemed unwilling or frightened—possibly both—to assist. As for the Revenue or Licensing Office, we found that no black Zephyr car,[13] which will figure later in the report, had been registered in Mbarara. There were three other Zephyrs on the Register but of different colors.

We returned to Kampala that evening, and we resumed the hearing on the following morning.

The first witness called had worked at the Rest House as a cook/attendant. He was shown the photographs of Siedle and Stroh, both of whom he recognized as having been guests of the Rest House in July, 1971. He said they had arrived together in a Volkswagen estate[14] car ("dual tone") but he did not remember its number. He testified that they stayed two nights. On the morning of July 9th, they left. Stroh went away alone in his car before 10 a.m. leaving Robert (he obviously meant Mr. Siedle) behind in the Rest House, reading.

When Siedle left, he called to the witness who saw him leave with an African wearing a "Special Force shirt." He departed shortly after 12:00 on the morning of July 9th in a black Zephyr. There were four men in the car—three Africans, all dressed in the same kind of shirt, and Siedle who sat in the back with two of the men. The third African drove. The witness testified Siedle appeared to be happy when he was being driven away.

The next witness was Mrs. Hoyle, a part-owner of the Agip Motel in Mbarara who manages it with her husband. She was shown the pictures

---

13. The Ford Zephyr is a car that was manufactured by Ford of Britain from 1950 to 1972.

14. An "estate car" is a British term for a station wagon.

but couldn't identify either of the two men. She did however remember a Father You of the Mbarara Catholic Mission having lunch with two men at their Motel on July 8th. The restaurant was very busy, so she couldn't identify the two men as those in the pictures she had been shown. On that day, His Excellency the President was visiting the area and the restaurant was full of Government Ministers who had lunch there. Amongst the people present were Lt. Silver Tibihika and Capt. Musaka, Acting Adjutant of the Simba Battalion. The latter was organizing lunch for the Ministers. Mrs. Hoyle said that Capt. Musaka seemed to have recognized one of the two guests who were with Father You and spoke to him.

Some days later she heard about the missing Americans. In fact, she seemed to have been inundated with phone calls about them. Apart from what Father You told her that the Americans were his guests, or he theirs, on July 8th, she could not find out any information about them. When her inquiries were met with some hostility, she became frightened, gave up, and left it to the police to make any further inquiries, if they wanted to.

The present Rest House keeper at Mbarara was the next witness. He produced the Guest Register. The book was not accurate as both Siedle and Stroh were booked in and out on the 7th of July. He confirmed, however, that the two booked in on the 7th, and departed on the 9th from the Rest House.

The Rest House keeper at the time the two Americans stayed there was recalled. He denied that he had told the previous witness that he had seen military officers talking to one of the "Europeans." Apart from saying that he knew the two intended to leave on the 9th, he had little to say. I do not think this witness told the Commission all he knew.

After the Rest House employees had given their story, we heard evidence from two Roman Catholic Fathers, Father You and Seit. They were determined not to be enmeshed in anything appertaining to this Inquiry. Father You identified both Siedle and Stroh, stating they had come to say "Hello" and see what was going on in Ankole. Stroh had introduced himself as a journalist who intended to write an article on what was happening on the border between Tanzania and Uganda. Father You said he had heard of Siedle from his writings regarding Catholic missionaries who cared for the aged in Uganda. He described how he met Siedle on the 8th, and had lunch with Stroh and Siedle at Mrs. Hoyle's Agip Motel. Apart from informing him that they were leaving on the 9th, they seem to have said little or nothing to him. For inquisitive and inquiring Americans (one a journalist and one a lecturer in social subjects seeking information) they appeared to have been singularly reticent!!

Father You said that he last saw them at 6 p.m. on the 8th. The other Father, named Seit, said he met Siedle on the 7th of July at the Mission Social Centre, when he walked in and introduced himself. He identified both men when shown their pictures. Stroh was introduced by Siedle as a journalist who was there to investigate "trouble in the barracks," and was obviously seeking information. Seit was equally as eager as Father You to tell what he knew about the two Americans, but he did say there had been trouble in the barracks in June. He referred to one particular day, the 22nd of June, when, on visiting Christian homes in the vicinity, he found that children who normally went to a school *inside* the barracks were at home that day due to trouble there. I am not suggesting for one moment that the two Fathers lied, but one thing I am certain of, and that is that they did not tell the Commission all they knew.

The next witness was a Deputy Superintendent of Police, who only took statements from Army personnel who had not already given statements to the Military Board of Inquiry because their whereabouts were not known at the time the Military board conducted its proceedings. He apparently accepted what the Commanding Officer of the Simba Battalion told him and recorded statements from that information. It seemed he had a member of the Military Police attached to him at all times. His investigation was cursory, to say the least. He admitted that apart from interviewing the few people he had mentioned, he made no further inquiries. The other two policemen were equally as unhelpful, and it was no surprise when one of them admitted that the police had made no inquiries. *There seemed to have been a sinister pall of fear enveloping most of these civilian and police witnesses.*

I now turn to the military witnesses. The Commission ran into some serious difficulties when dealing with these. Some were administrative troubles, some were due to the personalities of the witnesses.

The Military Government of General Idi Amin stated in its first legal Proclamation following the coup that it was a government operating *within the existing Constitution.* That meant, and it has been reiterated on more than one occasion since by His Excellency the President, *that no one,* that includes the Army, *was above the law.* It was never claimed, nor considered, that the Military forces could do no wrong!!

Summonses to appear before the Commission as witnesses were not served through the usual channels, i.e., the police. The summonses with respect to military witnesses were sent through military representatives, Captain Musaka or Major Ozi. At some stage Major Ozi was assigned to a Court Martial. The burden of serving summonses then fell almost entirely on Capt. Musaka. Delays occurred as he, often times, due to the exigencies of the services, could not be contacted. When Capt. Musaka was found, the witnesses we wanted could not be easily traced as they were dispersed and deployed on various military duties. These I have referred to as administrative troubles.

The frustration became almost intolerable, and the impatience and annoyance with the Commission by the Army became a sore point with the military personnel. At one state it reached a deadlock and a confrontation. Lt. Col. Ali Fadhul, the Commanding Officer of Simba Battalion, refused to produce some documents, on what I considered no valid legal ground. As a result, the Commission was adjourned indefinitely. That was on the 5th of April, 1972. It was becoming apparent that the Army considered themselves to be above the law.

On the night of the 6th of April, I received a call from His Excellency, who expressed his displeasure that I had not informed him of the intended adjournment of the Inquiry. I replied that I was sending a letter to the Minister of Justice setting out my position. I sent that letter, dated the 7th of April, to the Minister giving a detailed account of everything that had happened, and in particular what my views and stance were on the attitude adopted by Lt. Col. Ali Fadhul. The contents of the letter were given to the President.

Shortly after the adjournment, it came to our ears that a journalist in another territory intended to write an article in a well-known London Sunday newspaper, *The Observer*, in which our Inquiry would be mentioned. We didn't know what the content of it was going to be. In case it would, or could, prejudice our Inquiry, we endeavored to have it stopped, but without success.

We arranged, therefore, to meet in my chambers on April 10th to read and discuss the article that had come out the day before in *The Observer* entitled, "*Americans Murdered in Uganda*" by David Martin. The article stated that a Ugandan Army lieutenant who had escaped to Tanzania had revealed that the two Americans were murdered by General Idi Amin's soldiers. Certain details regarding how the two men met their deaths were provided, as well as what was done with Stroh's car. As the article had a very definite bearing on the Inquiry, in particular where Mr. Stroh's car could be found, Mr. Grimley of Police Headquarters who is an expert on identifying engines of cars was asked to join us. It was obvious that speed was of the essence for the mission if we were to investigate and get anywhere with regard to the information contained in the article. We decided, therefore, to go to Fort Portal, where Stroh's car was supposedly burned, at once. The Police Air Wing was contacted and a plane was made available for the 11th of April to take the party to Fort Portal. I spoke to Mr. Hutchings of the Police Air Wing myself.

After we had decided to go to Fort Portal, I immediately spoke with the Minister of Justice to inform him of what was happening and what we proposed to do. I then told the Chief Justice of the High Court of Uganda of my plans.

As I am unable to fly, I went up by car on the 10th to Fort Portal which is situated at an elevation of about 5,000 feet and overlooks the mountains of the Rwenzori Range (often referred to as the "Mountains of the Moon") and the Mufumbiro volcanoes. Fort Portal provides a base for mountaineering in the Rwenzori Range. I stayed at the New Rwenzori Hotel.

On the morning of the 11th, I received a call from the Minister of Justice asking me to return to Kampala as His Excellency the President wanted me to resume the hearing of the Inquiry immediately. I said I would do so on the following day, *if* we had completed our mission, i.e., of looking for Stroh's car.

After breakfast, I visited the Commanding Officer of the Police who provided us with a handful of police and a Landrover. In a similar inquiry into the disappearance of a Mr. Lea a few years ago, 1,000 men were provided and a police helicopter to scour the suspected area for a missing diplomat. Be that as it may, at about 11 a.m. we proceeded onward to the area where we believed the Stroh car might be found. When we got near the Kichwamba Technical School, I suggested we speak to a few people there to see whether anyone had heard or seen anything of a burnt-out car being hurled over the side of the ravine, or had come across it in the valley. The school overlooks the deep valley we proposed to search. Our enquiries proved abortive.

I called on the Headmaster, who was comparatively new to the area to pay my respects to him and to seek information. He was of no assistance to us. After asking him, however, whether he had anyone on the staff who taught Natural History and who took parties to do practical work in the field, particularly in the valley, he said he had not but there was a mountain climbing team led by one of the masters attached to the school. He was sent for and before we could turn around, we had a party of the school mountain club team to assist us. This was our first stroke of luck. It was the end of term so they were able to accompany us without any interruption in their work.

We "crawled" in our cars along the road running through the Rwenzori Mountain Range, looking for probable or possible places where the car could have been dumped. We made the odd sortie in search of the car. We eventually reached the first barrier on that road. Meanwhile we had been joined by the Regional Commissioner of Police, and the Head of the Central Intelligence Division. We had drawn a blank and decided to call it a day, suggesting to the mountain climbing team that they could possibly assist us by searching the district during their vacation.

Both the Regional Police Commander and the leader of the team suggested that we ought not to exclude the possibility of the car being hidden in the other half of the valley beyond the barrier. As they seemed pretty insistent, we decided that as we had come this far, we would try the other half beyond the barrier on the following morning.

We decided to meet at 7 a.m. By this time the mountain climbing team had been augmented to about twenty, so had the police party. We started out without much hope. The second half of the valley—beyond the barrier—was wilder and the terrain more difficult, to say the least. Dropping sheer from the road was a deep ravine with thick forest.

We stopped at a place about 28 miles from Fort Portal, at what we thought was a likely spot, where a deep wooded valley ran from the road into the valley at the bottom of the ravine. The police were loathe to descend, as the place was allegedly infested with black snakes and populated by lion, leopard, baboons and elephants. The police were unarmed.

The schoolboys had no inhibitions. They went down at once. Mr. Grimley—the police expert on identifying engines of cars—who, like the boys, was unarmed, took off his coat and descended with them. It was an act of great courage. The young policemen were silenced and shamed by Mr. Grimley's example. They then joined the party. I stood in the eerie silence listening to the stones tumbling in the ravine as the party searched. Due to the thick forest, I could see nothing.

The suspense was such that Alfred Hitchcock could not have produced anything better. The searchers found the relics of a green Volkswagen and the skeleton of a truck but nothing else. It was obvious they had drawn a blank.

I and my party decided to walk back towards Fort Portal to do a recognizance. It was obvious that a car could be hidden in a thousand and one places, without being discovered, on this stretch of road. We picked out about three or four likely spots over a distance of about a mile and a half, and decided to return to the place where we had left our transport. We had walked about half a mile when we saw coming toward us the leader of the Mountain Club and an old man. The leader of the Club said the old man could tell us where the car was. We were a little skeptical. We asked him where it was and how he knew about it. He informed us that it was about a half a mile further along the road and he had seen it some distance down the side of the ravine in July, 1971.

He told us that he was a road foreman employed by the Ministry of Works and was working on this particular stretch of the road at that time. He explained that when they left work one day, about the 16th or 17th of July, 1971, there was nothing on the side of the valley. The following morning, they saw the car. He assumed it had gone over the brink during the night. Two days later he saw some men trying to push it further down the side, which he thought, at the time, was strange.

We had nothing to lose by turning back, so we went with him. Without hesitation he walked to a spot on the road which looked like a miniature road-side rest area and said, "It is there," pointing down a steep hill. The roadside rest area looked a probable place where a 3-ton lorry could have been parked across the road. (*The Observer* article had indicated that a 3-ton lorry had been used to transport the burnt car and dump it over the cliff.)

The leader of the Mountain Club went down like a flash and in no time shouted, "Got it." It was a thrilling moment. He came back and said, "It is a blue V.W." I said, "How do you know it's a V.W.?" He replied that he had one himself. Timorously, I asked him whether it was a left-hand drive or not. Mr. Stroh's care was a left-hand drive. He had not taken particular notice of that fact, so he went down again and reported back that it was a left-hand drive.

On his return he blew a whistle, which brought the other searchers back up, out of the valley. When they arrived at the scene, they all went down. In all, some 40 people saw the shell of a burnt-out VW car with its engine adrift, embedded against a tree.

We decided to go back to the hotel for lunch and it was arranged that Mr. Grimley and another man, who was the police photographer and scene of crimes expert, should return in the afternoon and photograph the car, and make an inspection of the remains of the car.

Wreckage of Nicholas Stroh Car

At 2:10 p.m., I was preparing to sit down for lunch when I was informed that the Minister of Justice wanted me to ring him up. Tired and famished as I was, I did. He appeared to be a bit testy and wanted to know when I was returning, as His Excellency, the President was anxious that I should resume the Commission hearing. In passing, he deprecated the fact that I had the "temerity" to keep Col. Ali Fadhul, the Commanding Officer at Simba Battalion, waiting. In the first place I did not know Col. Ali was waiting. I knew from my conversation with the President that he had sent for him, but no arrangements had been made for the resumption of the Inquiry. A bit disappointed with the tenor of the conversation and tired after our efforts, I was a bit sharp in my reply, saying that I was tired of the name Col. Ali, who had kept *me* waiting time after time, and asked the Minister *whether he really wanted an answer to the questions posed in the Inquiry.*

The Minister made no reply, so I informed him that *he was going to get one*, as we had made a discovery of the greatest importance. He didn't say anything. I don't know whether he appreciated the seriousness of what was being said, as he seemed so concerned about the resumption date of the adjourned Inquiry. Since I had no transport, I couldn't have travelled back to Kampala there and then on that day. I said I'd return on Thursday and could resume on Friday morning. He said, "Can I tell the President you will start on Friday?" I said, "Yes, yes, yes." The conversation ended.

I have gone into detail about this trip to Fort Portal because I was accused of holding my Inquiry "in secret." The accusation was given wide coverage in the world press. The President had said that "he had no intention of interfering in the Commission's work but he did not want it to operate secretly." As a matter of fact, no mission could have been less secret, and from the word "Go" the Minister of Justice and the President's own office knew about the journey, if not the reason for it. The above facts speak for themselves. As a further proof that the Minister of Justice knew I was in Fort Portal, I append to this report a telegram he sent to me at *Fort Portal*, which I received on the morning of the 13th of April.

I returned to Kampala on Thursday the 13th and found a letter from the Minister of Justice which was an answer to my letter of the 7th of April in which I explained to him the circumstances under which I had adjourned the Inquiry. The letter indicted that His Excellency the President had instructed Col. Ali Fadhul to produce the documents I had requested and, now that my concerns had been addressed, it was His Excellency's urgent wish that I resume the work of the Commission as soon as possible.

At this time, two articles appeared in the press carrying the captions, *"Amin Accuses Judge"* and *"Amin Chides Probe Judge."* The criticism, with respect, was unfair and unwarranted *in fact,* and *wrong in law.* Traditionally, the judiciary does not descend into the arena to defend itself. In accordance with such traditions, I did not do so at the time.

The newspaper report was understood by the outside world as an attack on my probity. I am therefore taking this opportunity of putting the record straight, if only in defense. In *fact,* I did not hold any secret sessions, far from it, as the above facts show. In *law,* I could have without asking anybody. I will cite a paragraph from Legal Notice No. 10 which established the Commission of Inquiry.

"… and I do hereby direct that the said inquiry may be held at such times and in such places as the *Commissioner* may, from time to time, determine and may be held in public *or in private,* or partly in public and partly in private as the *Commissioner* may, from time to time, determine."

The discretion given to me was absolute. Nowhere, with respect, can I find that I should previously have *informed* or obtained the previous consent of anyone in the world to hold a meeting in private if I wanted to. If I may be permitted to ask, if I had asked for consent, or informed His Excellency the President, would permission or consent have been given or withheld? If it were withheld it would have been in derogation of the terms of the Legal Notice establishing the Commission, and it could only be done by means of a decree or an amended legal notice.

I might also be forgiven for asking whether I would have been subjected to the same attack, if the missing car had *not* been found.

As to "secrecy," I would like to make one final observation. The Commissioners in "The Gold Inquiry, 1966" held some of their hearings in camera, and the Okoya Inquiry heard some of the evidence in Luzira Prison. Even if precedent were necessary, these two cases were at hand, well within the knowledge of everybody. No recriminations or denunciations, public or private, were made on those occasions.

That was not however, the most objectionable part of the attack. I had a complete legal and factual answer to it. The President's criticism went on to say, if he were reported correctly:

"If the Government was not kept informed of the doings of the Commissions of Inquiry, we the Government may feel that the judges are not with us."

Governments are always informed of the doings of an inquiry, in its report, as I am doing now. One is obliged to do so. If the warning meant that "judges must be *with* the Government" that would be a serious inroad into the independence of the Judiciary, which independence is enshrined in the Constitution, still extant. Judges are not *for* or *against* anyone. They, by their very judicial oath, are enjoined "to do *right* unto all manner of people, without fear or favor, affection or ill will." *Right* is the operative word. Traditionally, judges have stood as a bulwark between the executive and the people, within the terms of their oaths. Long may that be so. Any weakening of such a resolve could only lead to tyranny. If this phrase meant that I should, in the interest of Government or indeed anyone else, betray my trust to my oath, and did so, I would be a willfully perjured individual, void of moral worth.

In addition to my oath as a judge, in my oath under the Commissions of Inquiry Act, I swore:

"that I will faithfully, fully, impartially, and to the best of my ability discharge the trust, and perform the duties devolving upon me by virtue of the said."

My oath ended, "So help me God," meaning "so help me God to be a true and trustworthy man." That I have and shall always try to be and I serve notice on all and sundry that my integrity is unpurchasable. I am pleased to say that they are the feelings of my brother judges, who have been nurtured in the same traditions as well.

I think the Fort Portal part of this saga could very well be called "Mission Impossible." As a God-fearing person, I cannot but consider, especially in retrospect, the fortuitous presence—at least it appeared to be fortuitous at that time—of the road foreman *at that lonely spot, at that very moment of time* "*as the hand of God*" *intervening on the side of justice.*

Let me now move on to the next stage in the Inquiry, which could be only described as "stop-and-go." Mr. Grimley produced the commissioning plate found on the burnt car. On it was a number which the Licensing Officer verified from his records as the chassis number of a blue V.W. registered in the name of Mr. Stroh. There could be no shadow of doubt therefore that the car found on the 12th of April, 1972 on a heavily wooded slope of a ravine at Mile 26 on the Fort Portal Road was the missing car.

The finding of the car was a major discovery, changing the whole complexion of the Inquiry. It was obvious that, if possible, an affidavit should be obtained from Lt. Silver Tibihika of the Simba Battalion, who had given the information to the Tanzanian correspondent of the Sunday Observer about the location of the car. Such an affidavit was produced at the Inquiry.

The President responded immediately to the production of the affidavit, telling the press it was *false.* However, with the greatest respect, that was for *me* to decide, and no one else, as Commissioner of the Inquiry. These periodic excursions into the press could well have been taken as an interference with a matter which was under judicial review—almost directives.

From the facts contained in the affidavit it was obvious that Tibihika was at least an accessory after the fact for having participated in covering up the murders. Evidence was offered later to prove that he had been a member of the defunct government security force set up under the old regime of President Milton Obote. This was done to attack the credibility of Tibihika. He would also appear to be a deserter, although Lt. Col. Ali Fadhul charitably said he still considered him as an officer in the Uganda Army. There was also a further possibility that he wished the present Government to be discredited for another reason. There was a Commission running parallel with mine, concerning the activities of the National Trading Corporation. Lt. Tibihika's brother was deeply involved; indeed, he was the principal suspect and malefactor—the villain of the affair.

With all of these facts in mind, I approached Silver's affidavit with caution and reserve. I naturally looked for corroboration. Various arguments were put forth by counsel for the government for exclusion or expungement of the affidavit from the record—all of which seemed spurious to me. For example, it was argued that since the affidavit did not include the magic words "I swear these facts to be true to the best of my knowledge and belief," it was incurably defective. I note that no one had objected to Mrs. Stroh's affidavit which was in like form.

However, it was difficult at times to know what rules of procedure the government thought applicable to the Inquiry. If counsel had vouchsafed an answer, I think he would have said, "Only such procedure as is beneficial to my client."

As the affidavit was the first break-through, as far a positive information was concerned, on the subject matter of the Inquiry, we set about to test it by obtaining, if possible, further corroboration of what Tibihika had said in his affidavit. We had one fundamental piece of corroboration when we found Mr. Stroh's car where Tibihika had said it was. We asked Capt. Musaka to produce the mileage claims of *all* the officers of the Simba Battalion for the months of July and August, 1971. We got them. We returned them all *except* Tibihika's.

In order to appreciate the significance of that mileage claim form I propose to set out Tibihika's affidavit, long as it is, in full, in the body of this Report, drawing attention especially to the final paragraph of the affidavit concerning his mileage claims."

CHAPTER 14

AFFIDAVIT OF LIEUTENANT OF SILVER TIBIHIKA

I, Silver Tibihika, make oath and say:

In July 1971, I was a lieutenant in the Simba Battalion of the Uganda Army stationed at Mbarara. The Commanding officer was Lt. Col. Ali Fadhul and the Second in Command was Major Juma.

On the 8th of July 1971, I was outside the Battalion Orderly Room with Lieutenant Taban, the then Intelligence Officer at the barracks and saw a fairly heavily built white man with a slight beard come to the office block. He enquired for the Adjutant. The Adjutant later told me and others present that the man was a journalist who wanted to interview the Commanding Officer. The Commanding Officer was not in the barracks. I saw the journalist drive away. It was then about 10 a.m.

On the same day I had lunch at the Agip Motel in Mbarara. I sat with Captain Musaka. At another table sat some ministers and at another sat the journalist. I noticed a priest there whose name I did not know. Mr. and Mrs. Hoyle who manage the Motel know me well. The journalist left before I finished my lunch.

On the next day, that is the 9th July, the journalist came again to the barracks, I think at about 9 in the morning. I saw him drive in and stop at the Quarter Guard. I was at the Quartermaster's building nearby. About 15 minutes later I saw the car still there but did not see the journalist. About lunch time I saw him with his clothes covered in mud being forced by two Military Policemen to run with his hands above his head towards the Orderly Room. He went into Major Juma's office.

I never saw him again but later heard officers in the mess say that the European was "kalasi" which is a term used by Nubians to indicate that a person is dead. I do not know whether this statement is true or not. I remember that among the officers present in the mess was Lieutenant Taban, the Intelligence Officer.

Shortly before this I had heard Major Juma say "the Wazungu (whites) think that we Africans are shenzi (rotten)." He said that the European, by whom I understood him to refer to the journalist, had threatened to hit him, but the Major did not say what they had quarreled about.

On the afternoon of 9th July, Major Juma drove the journalist's car. Lt. Col. Ali Fadhul was annoyed and told him not to do so.

About four days later I was instructed by Fadhul to go with Taban to burn the car. Sergeant Major Stephen drove the car accompanied by Major Bindwa whilst Taban and I travelled in my personal car. We went to Rugaga Military training Area 50 miles away and there burned the journalist's car using 8 gallons of oil and 20 gallons of petrol. Fadhul had told us that to soak the upholstery first with oil and then pour the petrol would be more destructive. We waited until it was burned but still smoldering and then left it.

Fadhul told us about two days later, after he had been to Kampala that the matter of the two missing Americans had become serious. He told Taban and me to collect the remains of the two men and burn them to ashes. He told us to do our best to see that everything was destroyed. I had not myself seen any European other than the one journalist in the barracks at any time. Fadhul did not tell us where to find the remains but Taban directed me where to go. I drove with Taban and two recruits to a place pointed out by Taban approximately 10.5 miles from Mbarara on

Fort Portal Road. We then turned down a track on the left and stopped. Taban walked about 20 yards further and called me. I saw the rib bones of a person on the surface on a sand pit. The recruits used shovels and dug up the remains of two persons. There was some flesh on some of the bones which appeared to have been burned.

We collected the remains in two sacks and drove to the barracks. It was about ten at night and no one was in the Mess. We burned the remains behind the Mess using oil and petrol. The remains were almost entirely reduced to ashes except that next morning I saw a piece of arm bone and other small pieces of bone when we again put the ashes into the sacks. We put the sacks in a room in the Mess. That night Taban and I took the sacks to the river which flows under the bridge just before the Kikagati turn-off to the Kabale Road on the outskirts of Mbarara. After passing over the bridge we turned down a track to the right which runs down to the river. There is a place where the river is shallow and vehicles are washed, including military vehicles. Just above the shallow towards the bridge we stood on a mound and emptied the sacks into the river.

The following evening, we collected the burned car on a three-ton military lorry, breaking off the engine and gear box. I drove with Taban and Stephen in my car. There were twenty recruits in the lorry. We took parts of the car to the barracks and it was kept under guard at the Motor Transportation yard for the night. The lorry canopy was closed. Fadhul came and looked at the car.

At 8 o'clock next night, the same twenty recruits with the lorry and myself in my car leading the way, drove through Fort Portal to a place about 26 miles along the road to Bundibugyo. I know this road well from the time when I was an intelligence officer. The lorry stopped and the parts of the car were pushed over the bank of a steep valley with dense forest. The recruits had to go a short distance down the slope because the body of the car became stopped by a tree and had to be pushed again further down the valley.

When I returned to Mbarara accompanied by the lorry and recruits, I reported to Lt. Col. Fadhul who gave the recruits four days off duty.

With respect of the use of my car I made claims for mileage allowance from the Command Pay Office.

Silver Tibihika,
Sworn at Dar-es-Salaam, Tanzania, this 18th day of April, 1972.

CHAPTER 15

THE COMMISSIONER CONCLUDES "THEY ARE DEAD"

After the reading of Tibihika's affidavit, his mileage claim form was produced at the Commission of Inquiry hearing. Various military and civilian witnesses gave evidence to try to explain away items in the claim form and dispute the facts stated in his affidavit.

Justice Jones, nevertheless, concluded there was no doubt that the amount mentioned on the mileage claim form was paid by the military *as correct* and the veracity of all the various witnesses disputing the items on the mileage claim form and the facts mentioned in the affidavit was, at a minimum, "highly suspect."

"Taban was obviously a stranger to the truth. If he had not proved himself to be a liar, Lt. Col. Ali Fadhul in one fell swoop made out his witnesses Taban and Safi as liars when he said in his evidence that he had called *all* his officers together to lecture them on the missing Americans. To a man, the lieutenants had said at the enquiry that apart from what they had heard on the radio in their tongue, they had *not heard* anything about them from *anyone* or *discussed* it with *anyone, or heard anyone discuss it.* One of them slipped up by saying he had read something about it in the *Argus* newspaper. I watched and listened carefully to Stephen, Taban and Safi. I was satisfied that they had conspired to suppress or pervert the truth."

Further, the affidavit itself had "*the ring* of truth," in the words of Jones.

The Justice stated the fact that Stroh's burnt car was found where Tibihika said it was coupled with the mileage claim form was proof positive. The wealth of detail Tibihika provided regarding the method of burning the car, and gallons of oil and petrol used also "smacked of truth."

The judge next addressed Tibihika's account of collecting the two bodies which showed signs of serious burning that had been "ignominiously and indecently interred," said Jones, "in a shallow grave and exhumed at Fadhul's request." The bodies were subjected to a second burning behind the Officer's Mess and only an arm bone and small particles of bone left behind. These pieces were again put into two sacks and thrown into a river, a short distance out of Mbarara. The story of the final "ceremony" was "ghoulish and macabre in the extreme," Jones commented.

To ascertain the veracity of this portion of Tibihika's testimony, a mission was being prepared to scour the river after a pumping and damning operation. When the Attorney General told Jones that the President had asked the Commission of Inquiry complete its work within ten days or else it would be necessary to revoke the Legal Notice which established the Commission, the mission to find the remains of the two bodies had to be officially abandoned.

"So, we will never know whether that part of the story was true or not," lamented the judge. Jones concluded:

"When the affidavit is examined and tested, there is such a great body of corroborative material available that the only possible conclusion one can draw from it is that it is a true account of what happened, and I accept it as such."

Concerned that Tibihika, like most potential eyewitnesses to the murders—including the guards on duty at Mbarara when the two men were killed—might be in danger, as well as eager to question him further, Jones sought permission to travel to Tanzania to hear evidence on behalf of the Commission. Again, he was stonewalled by Amin. In response to his request, a "blocked-in announcement" in bold print appeared in The Uganda Argus newspaper. The announcement read:

> **"High Court Judges- A government spokesman issued a statement last night in connection with the jurisdiction of the Court judges appointed by the President. The statement reads: "All High Court judges appointed by the President have the power according to the law to preside and hear cases within Uganda and judges of the High Court have no jurisdiction to hear cases outside of Uganda. This statement is issued for the information of all judges in Uganda and this must be adhered to."**

This turn of events was something Jones said he had never experienced before and hoped to never again. It was a further example of "a disturbing feature of the Government's attitude to the Inquiry, i.e., sending notices and orders to the judiciary via the press."

Jones further noted: "To say it made my task extremely difficult, if not impossible, would be an understatement."

As a result of the bizarre public announcement in the newspaper, he sent a letter to the Minister of Justice setting out his position. The next communication from the Minister was a peremptory note directing Jones to complete the Inquiry within 10 days. Said Jones:

> "I was set a difficult task and had very little or no cooperation. In spite of His Excellency the President's directions about the production of all books asked for, I got none except a guard roll. The whole thing is unbelievable."

Finally, Justice Jones concluded the Inquiry stating with respect to both my father and Stroh "*that they are dead.*" Further, he said, it was obvious that the two Americans died an unnatural death. "They were in fact murdered by personnel of the Simba Battalion of the Uganda Armed Forces."

The two men were healthy people, with everything to live for, Jones reasoned.

> "One had a family in Kampala and the other was about to leave to join his family. They had not been involved in an accident, otherwise the police would have been informed. They had not been incarcerated, otherwise we would have been told. They had not crossed into another country, as suggested in an anonymous letter. They had little money and no change of clothing as they had only intended to stay one night. The Army went to a lot of unnecessary trouble dismembering, burning and dumping Stroh's car about 177 miles from Mbarara in a desolate spot, if they had nothing to do with their deaths, or if their deaths could be explained away—legally."

Still, from the evidence, there was no indication *where* the killings and first burning took place, or how they were killed. Jones wrote that from the evidence before him:

> "it was impossible to point an unerring finger at any particular person or persons who actively committed the offence. The material fell short of that. Lt. Tibihika himself may have had more to do with it than he cared to divulge. I have no doubt that had the whole matter been properly investigated, an answer could well have been found. Major Juma may well have had something more to do with the actual killing."

As to the reasons the two men visited Mbarara, Jones stated:

"Stroh visited Mbarara in his capacity as a journalist to enquire into conditions generally in Ankole on the Tanzania-Uganda border, and in particular to the alleged massacre in the Simba Barracks. He sought an interview with Col. Ali Fadhul to that end. The word massacre was used by Capt. Mukasa as the word used by Stroh to him. Mr. Burton Hoffman, in his affidavit, said that Stroh cabled him on July 5th, to say that he was going to investigate problems of discipline among Ugandan troops stationed in the area of Mbarara. Capt. Mukasa admitted that there had been fighting in the barracks amongst the troops in June. Father Seit, who visited Christian homes near the barracks on June 22, 1971, found children who were normally being taught in a school inside the barracks at home, because of "the trouble" in the barracks.

Siedle accompanied Stroh to put the finishing touches to, and to obtain photographs for, a book he was writing on aging missionaries. That he was writing such a book, was confirmed by a friend of his, a Mr. Essex, a lecturer at Makerere University, and by Fr. Seit, the White Father, and Mrs. Stroh."

As to the possible motives for the murders, Jones wrote:

"Mr. Stroh may have been too inquisitive, or insistent, or perhaps had "stumbled" onto something which the Army personnel wanted to hide. We will never know. That secret will be the burden of someone in that barracks, but let him or them rest assured that Nemesis will one day claim her pound of flesh. As for Siedle, the reason for his killing is inexplicable except for perhaps because he accompanied Mr. Stroh."

Jones also noted:

"the Bill of Human Rights and the Third Chapter of our own Constitution have not been repealed. There the fundamental rights and freedoms of the individual are enshrined. Murder is still an offense under the law of this land, wheresoever and by whomsoever committed. His Excellency the President has publicly stated that anyone responsible, whether highly place or not, would be brought before the bar of justice. I am sure he will honor his promise."

Jones concluded his Report stating:

"I lay down this burden with relief. Never has any inquiry been beset with such obstructions and confrontations as this. Let me end up with two quotations:

It is fundamental to any country which calls itself a democracy that there is a supreme court vested with power not only to settle disputes between the citizens but also to restrain the occasional unlawful activities of any of the various instruments of government (of which the Army is one) and even, if necessary, the Government itself. It is indeed correct to say that the degree of civilization reached by a country can be gauged by the standard set by, and respect paid to, its judiciary.

And finally in the words of Sir James Rose-Innes:

"The work of a judge does not catch the public eye like the work of a statesman but it is of supreme importance to the community. For the character, the integrity and the efficiency of its judiciary are a priceless asset to any country especially a young nation like ours. The confidence of all races and all sections of the people in the bench is the sheet anchor, equipped with which the ship of state may safely ride out storms which may overwhelm it."

His Excellency never loses an opportunity of exhorting people to fear God. The verse in Holy Writ goes a step further, "Fear God and set aside evil." (Proverbs, Chapter 3, Verse 7). Anyone who fails to do so is sowing dragon's teeth."

CHAPTER 16

BACKDOOR TESTIMONY

While the Ugandan Commission of Inquiry was publicly conducting its official investigation of the murders, Justice Jeffrey Jones was secretly sharing information with American officials—primarily Ambassador Ferguson. Had Amin discovered Jones was communicating with Ferguson, it would have meant certain death for the Justice and expulsion of the Ambassador. Both Ferguson and Jones knew at the outset of the Inquiry Amin himself had been present in Mbarara when the two men were captured and had personally ordered the murders. However, neither could openly accuse the sitting President of the country of committing the crimes within its borders.

Thus, Justice Jones had to awkwardly steer the Inquiry toward a finding that the Ugandan Army was responsible for the killings based entirely upon circumstantial evidence. That is, the judge had to pursue justice without naming the party he knew to be guilty and without stating the obvious motives for the killings, to avoid invoking the wrath of the President and inviting certain death to his doorstep.

As Ferguson said at the time in a State Department telegram later declassified:

> "Justice Jones has been doing a masterful job at getting at the truth in rather difficult circumstances (which involve, let it be said, the

credibility and accountability of a sovereign government.) While the final outcome cannot be assured, I believe we should be grateful that such an able and dedicated person is dealing with what is fundamentally a most difficult case."

Declassified telegrams reveal Ferguson and American officials were always at least one step ahead of Jones and the Commission of Inquiry for three reasons. First, the Americans began investigating the murders months earlier—within days of the disappearances when evidence was more readily available, i.e., before the cover-up effort was completed. Second, since everyone in Uganda expected the Commission to be a "whitewash," there was no point in coming forward with information. And third, eyewitnesses and other potential witnesses were concerned Amin and his henchmen, particularly Lt. Col. Ali Fadhul, might retaliate against them if they testified in Commission hearings. Since providing information anonymously to the Commission was not permitted, informants concerned for their own safety chose instead to give whatever information they had to American officials who could and would protect their confidentiality.

As Ferguson put it:

"The fact that Fadhul commanded at Mbarara with a well-known and well-deserved reputation for brutality and hair-trigger temper is the problem. As long as he has power by virtue of his Army position, to take reprisals against witnesses there will be no testimony at all."

Informants who had spoken to American intelligence, under a promise of absolute protection of identity, included a Catholic Father who had heard the confession of a senior officer of Simba Battalion, in which the officer confirmed the whole story of the murders in detail.

Then there was a letter from another lieutenant at Simba Battalion (not Tibihika) who stated his willingness to testify before the Commission only if his protection was guaranteed. According to declassified State Department telegrams:

> "This lieutenant's importance lies in the fact that he claims to have been an eyewitness to the murders of Stroh and Siedle at the barracks. His account in his letter differs from Tibihika's in that he says the Americans were strapped to oil drums and then shot and burned, whereas Tibihika says they were stabbed to death. Also, he says the orders for the executions came from Ugandan Army headquarters in Kampala, i.e., Amin himself, whereas Tibihika merely says orders for destroying evidence following the executions came from Army headquarters."

An expatriate doctor who hosted my father and Stroh for dinner their first night in Mbarara volunteered information about being questioned the following morning by the Army as to the nature of his conversation with Stroh.

Father You, a French Catholic White Father priest whom my father had befriended confided to American officials that my father and Stroh were dinner guests at his house their second evening in Mbarara. An Acholi officer named Okech met with the two men after dinner for three hours and provided details regarding the barracks massacre. Stroh took extensive notes, including writing down the officer's name and address in the same notebook, as well as Father You's. (Early articles regarding the killings stated soldiers found notes in Stroh's car indicating he had knowledge of the massacre of soldiers and "the notes in his car also indicated he had interviewed an Acholi officer about internecine strife within the Ugandan Army."[15])

The following evening, the Acholi officer went to the priest's house and told him the two Americans had appeared at the barracks at about ten that morning. The officer himself had been placed under arrest and

---

15.   U.S. Seeks Justice in Two Deaths in Uganda, Evening Star, August 27, 1970.

interrogated from 11 a.m. to 3 p.m. He had strenuously denied knowing the two Americans and had finally been released. He said the two men had also been placed under arrest at the barracks. The officer feared for his life and the information he provided could not be shared with the Commission.

About a week later, an Indian tailor from Goa who was a friend of Father You's casually mentioned to the Father that he had been at the barracks on business and had seen two Europeans out in the open rather than in the barracks, both of whom had beards and one of them had been severely beaten and was bleeding. Father You had asked for further details but the tailor knew nothing more. The Father said the tailor was very fearful and would not talk again about the incident if asked. Father You speculated my father and Stroh were probably killed Friday July 9th.

Said the American official, "I thanked the Father for his information and promised we would keep it confidential. Unfortunately, we cannot use it vis-a-vis the Government of Uganda as evidence the Mbarara army unit was responsible for the killings."

Recall Justice Jones was angered by Father You's apparent reluctance to provide information in his testimony before the Commission of Inquiry, as the following testy exchange between Justice Jones and the lawyer defending the Ugandan Army illustrates:

Lawyer: "Father You is a Catholic priest…"

Jones: "A role which I think he might have sheltered himself behind. I certainly did not get the impression that he told the whole truth."

Lawyer: "Mr. Commissioner, I suggest that a priest in the Holy Order is less prone to telling lies than most of the people who are not in the Holy Order."

Jones: "He told half the truth."

Lawyer: "But if it was half the truth, Mr. Commissioner, it could be a lie."

Jones was annoyed that Father You had been unwilling to testify that he had discussed the massacre at the barracks with Stroh and my father, information Father You had readily given to the Americans in confidence, unbeknownst to Jones.

Declassified documents reveal the Americans heard from a number of reporters who would not testify under any circumstances.

A father whose son was an Army officer and participated in the killings also contacted American officials. The father feared his son would be called before the Commission and charged. Would the son be willing to sign a confession? Since the son said authorities were threatening all soldiers who served at Mbarara at the time of the killings, American officials said, "We should be thinking about ways to get this soldier out of the country immediately after he testifies (if he agrees to do so) and to get him a job in Kenya."

There were two separate reports from people who had seen one or two bodies of white men floating in the River Nile near Chobe Lodge in Murchison Falls National Park:

"The informant states that while acting as an escort to a party of Americans in Uganda he saw the body of a white man floating in the water. He is convinced the corpse was a white man and gained the impression he had been dead some time. The man was wearing a red short-sleeved shirt with gray slacks and his hands had been tied behind his back with strong cord. He was either wearing a cap of gray or fawn color, or his hair was of that color. Corpse appeared to be that of a heavily built man probably six feet tall and possibly in early middle age. Informant is prepared to swear to the truth of his statement before witnesses but because of his connections in Uganda is anxious to appear as a witness if this can be avoided.

Please recall a report of an employee of the Ministry of Works who had seen bodies of two Europeans at approximately the same period of time in the same area not far from Chobe Lodge."

The Embassy had also received a letter from Mbarara which provided a lengthy, dramatic account of routine killings at the barracks:

"Sirs, you should know there are always incessant killings at the Mbarara Army barracks. The method of killing is very horrible and immoral. The ill-fated people being killed are members of the Langi and Acholi tribes. If you are arrested you are taken to room 3 or 4, assuming there are numerous people awaiting death but room 1 is where the killings take place. It is there where one's head is cut off from the body and fried. At the entrance of room 4 there's a fried head of a Lango tribesman. The time for killing daily is 5 a.m. The two Americans were held at the barracks guard room and slaughtered like goats innocently, like the Acholi and Langi tribesmen! They were arrested with the pretext that they were spies from Tanzania. It is probable that their heads were kept as they are whites. Gentlemen, it's a pity that Mr. Stroh and Mr. Siedle are now dead men!"

Mrs. Hoyle, the manager of the Agip Hotel in Mbarara told American officials that from July 10th through July 16th, Mrs. Stroh had called her almost nightly asking for information about her husband. Mrs. Hoyle made numerous fruitless inquiries. On July 16, Mrs. Stroh told Hoyle she had received information her husband's car was outside the Mbarara police station. Just after Holye said she would look to see if the car was there, her telephone line was cut. When she asked the telephone operator to reconnect her, the man refused and said, "You're finished." She stopped her investigation and contacted U.S. officials.

Finally, when Justice Jones's attempt to find the bodies of the missing men by scouring the river after a pumping and damning operation was thwarted by Amin toward the end of the Inquiry, American intelligence undertook a "quiet search" for the remains at a location pin-pointed by a testifying witness—unbeknownst to Ugandan officials or the Commission of Inquiry.

In short, Jones and American officials regularly exchanged information, working together toward a common goal. However, a great deal of the most sensitive intelligence they shared never appeared in the final Report of the Commission of Inquiry.

CHAPTER 17

JUSTICE FLEES UGANDA

J ustice Jeffrey Jones finished his Report and gave a confidential copy to the Americans well in advance but he did not submit it to the Government of Uganda until he fled Uganda—permanently—to the safe refuge of neighboring Kenya. The British High Commission secretly drove him over the border and after spending a few days in Nairobi, Jones went on to the port city of Mombasa where he boarded a ship, the M.V. Victoria for Britain and then retirement in Wales—the country of his origin. Not only was he fearful of premature leaks of his Report before he had sailed from Mombasa, declassified State Department documents indicate he told the Americans he did not trust the British High Commission "since they seemed more intent upon maintaining good relations with General Amin than in protecting their citizens."

Jones did not trust his own government to protect him.

According to declassified documents, Jones told the Americans that his completed and soon-to-be-released Report was "hard hitting" and would no doubt greatly anger Amin.

"The Report will flatly state that Stroh and Siedle were "murdered" by elements of the Simba battalion, Mbarara. Another point will be that Stroh went to Mbarara to investigate reports of a massacre involving Simba Battalion. Jones says his report also calls on the

President to punish those responsible for the murders as he publicly stated he would."

Jones was certain the Report "will never see the light of day as a consequence." Nevertheless, he said he felt obliged to write the unvarnished truth.

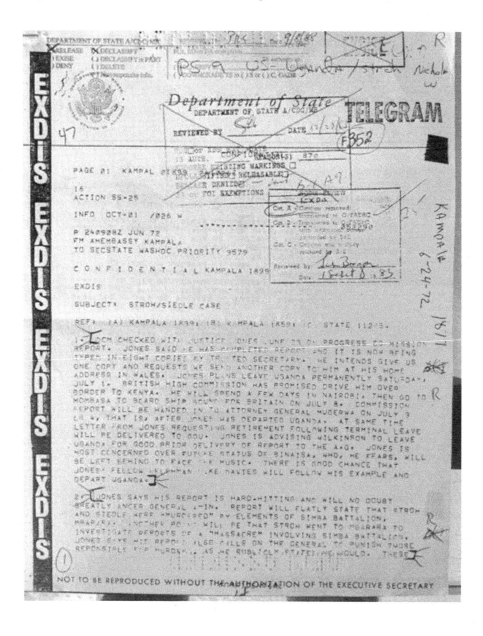

While he wanted to get out of Uganda as soon as possible, he found himself in a bit of a personal dilemma. Before leaving he wanted to collect three thousand pounds owed on his current contract with the Uganda Government plus twenty-three thousand pounds owed him as a pension. He said he would have preferred to be expelled, "as on the way out I would have asked for the money due me and would go willingly—knowing my Report was safely out of the country. I knew elements of the Ugandan Army would simply kill me if they found an opportunity."

Declassified U.S. State Department documents reveal at least three recent developments had caused Jones' renewed apprehension regarding his personal safety:

1. A warning to British citizens issued by Amin.

2. Chief Justice Kiwanuka told Jones he had met with Amin recently to ask for additional judges and Amin agreed but added, "Don't hire any British like that man Jones who gives me trouble and has a swelled head."

3. Reports of continuing instant executions of prominent citizens, the latest one being a report he had received from a Ugandan attorney that a former Uganda diplomat was shot dead while attending a dinner at the Kampala International Hotel.

By the end of the Inquiry, it was clear to Jones the independence of the judiciary in Uganda had ended and judges who opposed the President would be silenced. His worst fears regarding the safety of the judiciary were well-founded.

Former Chief Justice Benedicto Kiwanuka

On September 21, 1972, six months after Jones' departure from Uganda, Chief Justice Kiwanuka was abducted in his chambers at the High Court by members of the Ugandan Army. According to one report Kiwanuka had approached one of his friends the night before he was taken away to whom he revealed, "I am expecting them to come and take me soon. There is nothing to do but wait."

Like many other Amin victims, he was forced to remove his shoes and then bundled into the trunk of a car. Under Amin, a pair of shoes by the roadside came to mark the taking of a human life by state terrorism.

Kiwanuka had been incarcerated at Luzira Maximum Security Prison for his alleged role in the failed 1969 attempt to assassinate Obote, where he remained until Amin released him following the 1971 coup. Kiwanuka had then been appointed Chief Justice by Amin and served the country as an outspoken and courageous jurist. He had made several rulings against the

Government and military, protecting individual human rights in the weeks before he was abducted.

Approximately a week after he was abducted, he was viciously killed by a hammer wielded by a military officer at Makindye military prison, as other officers looked on. A Study by the International Commission of Jurists in May, 1974 concluded:

> "The independence of the judiciary has been undermined by direct attacks on individual judges, by the repeated interference of the armed forces, and above all by the arrest and subsequent murder of the country's Chief Justice, Benedicto Kiwanuka, in September 1972. The authority of the civilian court has been further undermined by the transfer of important parts of their jurisdiction to try civilians to a Military Tribunal."

Declassified U.S. State Department documents indicate officials recognized if the Government of Uganda did not make the Commission of Inquiry Report public—with its conclusion that the two men were, in fact, dead—it would be difficult to have their estates probated. Said U.S. officials:

> "The Department of State wishes to be of maximum assistance to the families in this matter. At the same time, we would hope to find a satisfactory solution without seriously impairing our relations with the Government of Uganda. We have no desire to embarrass President Amin or the Ugandan Government by insisting they make the Report public or by unnecessarily making use of our secret copy of the report without its being officially released. The U.S. Government would understand if the Ugandan Government should decide it is not in its best interest to publish the Jones Report. However, for purposes of probate the courts here must have adequate assurance that the two men are legally dead. In this respect, certificates may be more useful than the Jones report. If

the Government of Uganda is willing to issue death certificates for Stroh and Siedle, pressure by the families for release of the Report would almost certainly terminate.

We do not think it would be desirable for the Embassy to indicate to the Government of Uganda that we have a copy of the Commission of Inquiry Report. Conceivably, knowing that we would not press for release of the Report and in the interest of clearing up what could be a continuing irritant in U.S.-Uganda relations, Amin might feel the death certificate/ex gratia settlement arrangement is the best way out of an embarrassing situation."

But Amin was full of surprises.

Contrary to the dire predictions of Justice Jones and the Americans, the Commission of Inquiry Report was published by the Government, in full, but was accompanied by a Government White Paper. The very brief (four-page) Government rebuttal began by stating:

"Justice Jones was appointed as the sole Commissioner, not necessarily as a Judge of the Uganda High Court, but because he was considered to be a person capable of carrying out the inquiry."

It was an indication of his misunderstanding of this role, said the Government, that from the beginning he appeared to conceive of the proceedings as if they were court proceedings.

"He expected the Inquiry to be conducted in much the same way as a criminal trial which it was not. The Commissioner overlooked the fact that commissions of inquiry are often resorted to as the only means of ascertaining facts which a normal Police investigation and court trial would be unable to unearth. It was for these very reasons that the present Commission was set up."

Also:

"Commissions of Inquiry generally arising as they do from difficult or unusual circumstances require quite special efforts of coordination and special administrative arrangements on the part of everybody concerned and do not have the advantage of the day-to-day smooth running of, for instance, a court of law."

Further, in the Government's view, the words Jones had chosen in his Report revealed he had not started the investigation with an open mind.

"To quote his own words: "The Army is on trial," "I saw rocks ahead.""

It was, therefore, not surprising, said the Government, that the Commissioner would see in every recalcitrant witness (a not uncommon feature in inquiries), an agent of a general plot to frustrate the Inquiry. The Government considered it unfair that the Commissioner did not acknowledge the overall ready cooperation of Government Departments, the Army and the Police.

The Commissioner's prejudiced mind hampered his work. "Even before he started the enquiry, the Commissioner placed more reliance on newspaper articles written by biased foreign correspondents." Jones' lack of faith in the Government was exemplified by the manner in which he left the country, secretly and without taking leave of anybody, and by the way his report was delivered to the Government, i.e., by post.

Finally, the Government accepted the findings of the Commissioner that the two men went to Mbarara and did not leave alive, having met their deaths somewhere in Mbarara at the hands of unidentified persons. The Government also accepted Tibihika may have had more to do with the deaths than he cared to divulge.

Declassified U.S. State Department documents indicate that a group of Ugandan Army colonels had met with Amin prior to his receipt and release of the Report, insisting they see it before anyone else other than the President saw it.

Amin released the Report to the public at a press conference which included U.S. and Ugandan Government officials, plus about ten members of the press, television and radio. In his accompanying remarks, Amin recalled his personal friendship with Nick Stroh and the fact they had been at the Kampala International swimming pool together only a week prior to Stroh's disappearance. He recounted his decision to appoint a military Board of Inquiry and then a judicial Commission to ascertain all the facts. He said the Government had now decided to publish the Report so that the facts would be available to all. He observed that the case had caused some misunderstanding between American and Ugandan governments and he hoped release of the Report would eliminate any misunderstanding for Uganda wanted good relations with all friendly nations. He then stated the Government was working on an arrangement to compensate the families and that he planned to write a letter to President Nixon on the subject.

When the President asked press representatives if they had any questions, a reporter from the BBC said, "We'd like to see the report," whereupon the General handed one copy to each reporter present.

Amin later would shock his own advisers and American officials by insisting upon making an offer of settlement in connection with my father and Stroh's murders directly to President Nixon in a letter, only to then send the letter omitting the settlement offer:

August 1, 1972

Dear President Nixon,

I am sending this letter by the hand of my Minister of Foreign Affairs, Mr. Wanume Kibedi, with whom I have entrusted a dual task: first handing you a copy of the Commission of Inquiry Report in the case of two of your citizens who disappeared in Uganda; secondly putting to you my thoughts on this matter and my proposals for settling this problem finally.

You will be aware, Mr. President, that this incident has without doubt given rise to some awkwardness in the relations between our two countries, but our hope here is that with the publication of the Commissioner's Report, the way will now be laid open for removing all misunderstandings between our two countries.

Allow me, Mr. President, to renew to you the assurances of my highest consideration and esteem.

General Idi Amin Dada

President of the Republic of Uganda

The end result was far better than anyone had hoped for—the Report was made public, death certificates were issued, estates probated and an ex-gratia settlement paid.

A year later, from the safety of his retirement residence in Swansea, Wales, Justice Jones responded to a letter of appreciation from a representative of the Stroh family.

"It gave me ineffable pleasure to know that my efforts in the matter of the Inquiry into the disappearance of two American citizens were appreciated. This was more so in light of the vilification and character assassination by Amin in the accompanying Government White Paper.

There has also been a conspiracy of silence in some quarters where I had expected some comfort."

Jones had started to write an account of his secretive departure from Uganda but abandoned the idea. "Suffice it to say that there was a story but not the lurid one bruited about by the press. My movements to Britain were monitored by the British Government. I have since dubbed my departure as "Operation Scarlett Pimpernel."

Since his return to England, he had had very little news from Uganda. His letters were interrupted and letters to him were all edited by the President. Three of his friends were expelled, or deported at short notice. One of them had assisted the Inquiry, when he went to search for Stroh's car.

Jones wrote:

"From the very start, I realized that the Commission was to be a delicate thing to handle. Shortly after the public hearing had started I realized it was to be my last assignment. I had resolved from the word "go" that this was not going to be a whitewashing exercise which the Government had fondly hoped and thought it would be."

Jones ended his letter saying:

"I was greatly concerned for the two families, and not a little distressed, that I could find no way of cushioning them from the stark and horrifying facts that emerged during the hearing. It was necessary, from every point of view, that I made incisive findings. My heart went out to them. I would be grateful if you would convey to them the sentiments I have expressed above.

May God walk with them."

CHAPTER 18

BACK AT LAST TO OUR LAST HOME

The morning after my meeting with General Muntu I was awaken by a call from Major Kabijamu.

"Good morning, Mr. Siedle, Kabijamu here. General Muntu has arranged for you to travel to Mbarara with Major Albert Kareba. He will be calling you soon to go over the itinerary. I am still working on getting in touch with Lt. Silver Tibihika and some other soldiers who were at the barracks when your father was captured. We will have contacted them all before you get to Mbarara."

Major Kareba soon called and told me he would stop by the hotel that evening around 6:30 to introduce himself. He would be attending a farewell reception hosted by Ugandan Army senior officers for a visiting foreign military adviser which was being held on the top floor and rooftop patio of the Sheraton. If I would like to attend with him, I was welcome to come along. We would leave Kampala at 9 the following morning, the Major said.

Since I had the day free, after breakfast I took a taxi back to the Makerere University campus where I used to live.

In the light of day, the campus did not seem as forbidding. The neglect and destruction were more visible but did not seem as sinister as the other night. The outside walls of the faculty apartment buildings were stained and window glass was missing from all buildings, including the University library. Laundry was hanging from the balconies of the faculty apartments, as well as spread out to dry on the un-mowed grass. When I had lived here, every faculty apartment had a corresponding servant's quarters in a separate building nearby where our laundry would be handwashed by servants and hung to dry. These days, faculty evidently did their own laundry. The faculty apartments had fallen into such disrepair they were indistinguishable from the servants' quarters.

The University Guest House my father and I had stayed our first few days in Uganda—where I, in protest had refused to get out of my bed—was in the best condition of any of the college buildings. It too had deteriorated to the point of looking more like a college dormitory than the colonialist club-house it had once been. As I walked into what used to be the formal dining room, I recalled our first night's dinner when my father had whispered to me, "You can eat this same traditional English meal, including the hot vanilla custard for dessert, served by a waiter in a starched white uniform, in East Africa, India or any other former British colony. That's pretty remarkable given that tasteless British favorites, such as hot custard, and formalities, such as starched white uniforms, are particularly ill-suited for the heat and humidity of the tropics."

These days, the Guest House formal dining room was divided into two offices by a sheet hanging from a rope stretched across the middle of the ceiling. The grass and clay tennis courts near the Guest House which had always been meticulously maintained for faculty and visiting dignitaries, were no longer in use.

I then asked my driver to take me across the campus to Livingston Flats, the three-story faculty apartment building where I once lived. This time I was determined to see the interior of our old apartment.

As I entered the building, the hallway walls were dirty, and the hall windows were boarded. Four young children initially ran up the stairs away from me as I approached, then, with encouragement, they slowly crept back down. By the time I took their pictures, they were all smiles. Encouraged by their friendliness, I knocked on the door of our old apartment, No. 4 on the second-floor landing.

When a young boy answered, I asked for his mother. A curious, friendly slender petite young woman came to the door. While she didn't seem to fully understand what I was saying when I asked if I might see my old home, she was still willing to let me walk through and take a look. The apartment was the same, only older, dirtier and sparsely furnished. It was a simple apartment with polished concrete floors, a small living room-dining room combination, a small kitchen, two small bedrooms with a dark interior hallway between them and a sink, shower and tub bathroom with a separate toilet. The bedroom doors were locked by the professor whose apartment it was when he left in the morning for work, the young woman told me. Apparently, she was hired help—not a wife or family member trusted with full access to each and every room.

When I had dreamed of returning to Uganda I envisioned—assuming I was able to talk my way into the apartment—sitting for hours meditating in this space which once meant so much to me.

But today there was no time to even say a final prayer as I stood in our last home, or to commune with my murdered father's spirit. Other people lived here now and the energetic young children needed to be fed. The pressing daily demands of the living left little room for honoring the memories of the long departed. Still, I had done my duty and come back to this place to which I had imagined returning so many times. And, for reasons I will never know, a young housekeeper had kindly allowed me—a stranger—to enter and inspect what was now another family's home.

I remembered one of the last evenings my father and I spent together here, in this apartment. Before I left Uganda for Norway, on my seventeenth birthday, my father had taken me to dinner at a Maoist Chinese restaurant in Kampala. He had given me my first high quality 17-jewel Swiss watch—now that I was old enough to care of it. Later that evening in this small apartment we listened to the Voice of America on the shortwave radio as we quietly packed our few family belongings—mainly books and clothing—for the long journey back to America. The battery-powered shortwave radio was our only source for timely news from the outside world.

There was an air of nostalgia in the living room as we each silently reflected on our time in Africa. From his journal that evening:

> "Soon our flat will be empty. Most of our books are now packed and it's beginning to look bare. Soon voices will echo from the hard surfaces of the walls and cement floor. Here I have lived for two years, loved and been lonely—worked and rested. A womb-like place, quiet and private. To lose a home, to be uprooted, to begin a round of living in hotel rooms, catching flights, long waits at airports—I dread it. Still, there will be an emptiness in this little flat and I will feel tears at finally delivering the keys and shutting the door. This leaving, this heart-wrenching. I am a creature of territory with a need for familiarity. How lost I feel without my turf."

He thanked God for his blessings. Among them he listed that his rebellious son was so changed. He could now talk to me. I was even reasonable and polite to him, he wrote:

> "He is a fine son and now my job is to raise him and help him to be better than I am—to let him learn from my history and not repeat it, to stand on my shoulders as it were."

What happened next as I stood in our former living room was as startling as anything I have ever experienced in my lifetime.

Peering out the picture window at the trees growing up on the hillside behind the building, I suddenly realized that all these years, in the deepest magical-thinking recesses of my child's mind or soul, I still believed—decades after the murders—if I came back to this very spot in the universe, I would find my father just as I had left him. He would still be here living as we had, perhaps slightly older, but pretty much the same—frozen in time.

When I was very little, my father would read poetry to me at bedtime. His favorite poem to read was The Tiger by William Blake:

> Tiger, tiger, burning bright
> In the forests of the night,
> What immortal hand or eye
> Could frame thy fearful symmetry?

He delighted in the fiery imagery used throughout the poem which conjures the tiger's aura of danger. As a single father, he did not understand the poem scared the hell out of his little boy. I would ask him instead to read again and again my favorite, *Little Boy Blue* by Eugene Field, a sentimental poem about a little boy who dies one night but his toys remain forever loyal to him, awaiting his return.

> The little toy dog is covered with dust,
> But sturdy and stanch he stands;
> And the little toy soldier is red with rust,
> And his musket molds in his hands.
> Time was when the little toy dog was new,
> And the soldier was passing fair;
> And that was the time when our Little Boy Blue
> Kissed them and put them there.

> "Now, don't you go till I come," he said,
> "And don't you make any noise!"
> So, toddling off to his trundle-bed,
> He dreamt of the pretty toys;
> And, as he was dreaming, an angel song
> Awakened our Little Boy Blue

Oh! the years are many, the years are long,
But the little toy friends are true!

Ay, faithful to Little Boy Blue they stand,
Each in the same old place
Awaiting the touch of a little hand,
The smile of a little face;
And they wonder, as waiting the long years through
In the dust of that little chair,
What has become of our Little Boy Blue,
Since he kissed them and put them there.

Like the little toy dog and the little toy soldier in the poem, over the years, I had subconsciously believed my father would be there awaiting the touch of my hand, the smile of my face. He might have collected some rust and dust but he would be otherwise unchanged over the many, the long years.

But the poem is about parents who lose a child suddenly in the night and remain true to him, even after his death. Since the boy cannot come back to play with his toys, they will remain standing in the same old place forever, awaiting his touch, his smile—symbolizing the parents' endless love for their son.

Instead, he, my only parent, had unexpectedly been taken from me and all things familiar in my world had been snatched away. I needed for him to still be here, still loving me, and for decades I had clung to that belief.

Now I could finally see… he was gone.

It was as if two realities, inner and outer worlds, had collided and I had to choose which to believe and live in—whether to finally let go of a past reality which had been too painful to give up for so long.

I thanked the young woman and slowly walked down the stairs of the apartment building I had, in a prior life, run carefree so many times before.

My taxi driver was patiently waiting in the parking lot and as I entered the car, I asked him to take me to the University's outdoor swimming pool, squash courts and basketball complex where I spent nearly every afternoon as a teenager. It was a small pool for a school with a student population of 40,000 but most of the African students and faculty did not know how to swim and were afraid of water, I learned. African mothers, I was told, taught their children to fear water to keep them from wandering in and drowning, as opposed to teaching swimming for safety.

On the other hand, the university pool was a popular meeting spot for the foreign faculty and their children. Coming here to the pool area had been an important part of my daily routine—a time for exercise and to see friends—which was a lifeline to me since I did not attend school and had no peers to interact with during the day. The pool area was empty now and the water had an unhealthy yellowish tint.

I paid the driver and walked up the hill to the Student Canteen where I would go in the evenings to socialize with university students who were largely in their early 20s. Here I would drink sodas and buy cigarettes to share. Cigarettes, a luxury in Uganda, were sold individually and in five, ten and twenty packs which made smoking more affordable to the masses. It was considered a gracious gesture to offer cigarettes and no one would refuse—even if they did not regularly smoke.

Where I had gotten the courage, first arriving in Uganda—at 15—to walk across the campus alone in darkness to sit and talk with African university students I had nothing in common with, I don't know. But my rapid socialization strategy worked back then—within weeks of reaching out to others, I had made so many friends that I was never alone.

From the Canteen, I walked further uphill toward the Main Administration Building with its unique 20th century British architecture—including the imposing bell tower. This was where my father and I collected our daily mail. I then passed by the Faculty of Social Sciences building where his office had been. Behind Main Administration, I found an open chapel and went inside. A broken stained-glass window in the chapel read, "Blessed are those who believe without seeing."

Surely this pilgrimage of mine was all about believing without seeing—flying blindly. Decades after the murder, I had made a herculean effort to risk returning, alone, to the scene of the crime… and for what? What did I expect to gain? Greater knowledge of the facts surrounding his murder, or something more? Where did my belief that anything good would come of this journey, itself come from?

For whatever reasons, God had allowed me to return. That alone was a miracle. Many survivors of traumatic events never have the chance to retrace their steps—to go back in search of answers to questions that haunt them from the past. In a sense, I had been fortunate. My childhood traumas, although severe, had not crippled me. Twice in my lifetime, I had been able to revisit these tragedies.

My first deeply personal journey was at age 32, when I felt compelled to return to the Caribbean island of Trinidad and meet the Muslim Indian mother I had been taken from as a toddler. My friends and work colleagues in Boston, upon hearing the purpose of my journey—reuniting with the mother I had never known—were eager to help. An older salesman at the company where I worked was so deeply moved that he insisted I take his pricy Leica camera with me to photograph the reunion. He confided he had never known his mother and knew how important this trip would be to me. A partner in the Boston office of the accountancy Price Waterhouse, with whom I did business, contacted a partner in the firm's Trinidad office asking the latter to greet me upon my arrival and assist in any way he could—which he graciously did my first visit and on many other occasions in the years to follow.

When my flight landed in Trinidad, a uniformed immigration officer upon reviewing my U.S. passport sternly asked:

"Where are you staying on the island?"

"The Trinidad Hilton," I responded.

"What is the purpose of your travel, business or leisure?"

"Leisure," I said.

"When and where were you born?"

"I was born on June 22, 1954, here in Trinidad but I have never been back since then," I curtly responded but then added, "I've come back to finally meet my mother."

His eyes shifted from me to my passport which indicated I was born on the island. He then smiled and said nonchalantly, yet sincerely, "Welcome home."

In that moment, I tearfully realized for the first time it was, indeed, a homecoming.

Even as adults, it was difficult for my mother and me to put the past behind us and rekindle our relationship, without prejudice.

When I finally sat at a kitchen table face-to-face with her in Trinidad, she asked provocatively, "Did you bring me a present?"

"No," I responded bitterly, taken aback by her expectation of a reward from the child she had abandoned—which felt outrageous to me. "Why should I have? What did you ever do for me?"

"I am your mother—I gave birth to you!" she said angrily.

"Yeah, and that's the last thing you *ever* did for me," I snarled.

The family relation she was living with—who was a pastor, slightly younger than my mother—joined us at the table and gripped our hands. "Look, you two are going to have to work this thing out. It's not going to be easy, but it can be done. I will help you in any way I can," she said.

From that dismal starting point—with the lowest of expectations, and plenty of assistance from others—our relationship slowly blossomed over the following days and years.

I discovered she was a mother who still had love to give, not the train wreck I had been led to believe. I discovered, as a grown man, a fundamental belief I had held about myself since earliest memory—that I was the son of a mother who did not love me—was a lie. She *did* love me and had not meant to abandon me forever (in a moment of hysteria) following her divorce from my father. I learned the beliefs you hold about yourself are so incredibly determinative, you'd better make damn sure they're true. The truth about my mother—which I learned as an adult—changed my life. I would never again think of myself as a motherless child and my mother went to her grave knowing she had not been forgotten by her son. I came back for her.

As I sat in the University chapel, the same questions I had asked myself time and again over the decades flooded my brain: Could I have prevented my father's death? Could I have saved him? Did my teenage anger and fighting with him contribute to his death in any way—make him less eager to live, or more willing to take unnecessary risks? Did I care enough? Was I careful enough? How could I not have seen what was coming?

I walked out of the chapel into the courtyard where students were casually reading and talking, as they sat or lay on the lawn under tall trees shading them from the afternoon sun. A familiar feeling of dread came over me as I wondered about these students' dreams and aspirations. What standard of living could they reasonably expect, what level of professional accomplishment? Why even bother to pursue an education? What difference would it make when the next ruthless dictator, deadly disease or natural disaster came along to destroy everything? Why did they even try? Couldn't they see how pointless it was for them to try to get ahead, to try to build something on the shifting sands of this chaotic land? Compare these students, this educational environment with the impatient, competitive, hyper-aggressive American business and law students I knew—each convinced he deserved a Ferrari, a salary of a million bucks a year and to be on the cover of Forbes magazine. My American peers knew exactly what they were entitled to and demanded it all.

That had never been me. I had returned to life in America but my internal reality remained deeply rooted in Uganda—worse still, stuck in a traumatized memory of the country at its worst moment in time.

Even with my return to the relative stability of America, in the years following my father's death, I had remained fearful of impending devastation, unsure of my ability to handle the next catastrophe that might come my way—grateful for my mere survival and afraid to tempt fate by asking for too much. I understood only too well the words of Abraham Lincoln, "If I am killed, I can die but once; but to live in constant dread of it is to die over and over again."

A college guidance counselor had once warned me, "You have a tendency to give up too easily. Watch out for that—catch yourself whenever you're about to quit and instead, double-down on your effort." She was right and awareness of this tendency would be my best defense against it.

Despite my pessimism, I pushed myself to finish college at the top of my class and went on to a competitive law school, segueing into finance and investments once I discovered how incredibly boring law could be.

I had no sense of entitlement, just a vague desire to see if I acted "as if" I could succeed—if I half-heartedly went through the motions—I might break free of the doomed trajectory of my life. Each small step along the way required a huge leap of faith. Yet there was hardly a moment when I truly believed I would prevail, or that an unforeseen disaster would not prevent it.

The lesson I learned early in life was: In the end, all is lost.

CHAPTER 19

ROOFTOP COCKTAILS
WITH SENIOR ARMY OFFICERS

Major Albert Kareba was friendly and lighthearted when I met him for the first time that surreal evening on the Kampala Sheraton's rooftop patio. He was looking forward to a festive night at the city's trendiest (and costliest) nightclub, complete with an open bar—a rare treat for even senior officers in this impoverished army.

As we shook hands in the waiting area outside the club, I told him I'd been here before—decades earlier when it was called the Leopard's Lair disco. Given that Albert was in his early 30s, this was news to him—ancient history. The Ugandan Army senior officer's farewell reception for a foreign military adviser was polite and subdued at the outset but, thanks to the free booze, grew more raucous as the evening wore on.

It was a cool night and while the patio was brightly lit, looking out over the city was near pitch-black darkness in every direction. The officers were all lean, appearing to be in their 40s, dressed in suits and ties. There was not a single military uniform in the crowd. Most of the officers wore cheap but smart, double-breasted suits. This was Uganda's military elite and I had no idea what to expect from them. Given the nation's bloody past, these men had to be more ruthless than their cruelest adversaries to have survived. The officers looked at me as curiously as I looked at them. Who was I to be invited to attend this function they seemed to be asking? Major Kareba gave them an answer they were satisfied with.

"His father was killed by Amin's soldiers in 1971 and he has come back to find his body." The officers nodded affirmatively. It seemed I had paid the price of admission to this club of waning warriors.

Author at Ugandan Army Reception,
Kampala Sheraton Rooftop Patio

As Major Kareba introduced me around, the soldiers spoke of the years they had survived living out in the open fighting during the Ugandan Bush War (also known as the Luwero War, the Ugandan civil war, or the Resistance War). This guerilla war waged between 1981 and 1986 was fought by the official Ugandan government and its armed wing, the Uganda National Liberation Army against several rebel groups. Most notable of the rebel groups was the National Resistance Army (NRA) headed by now-President

Yoweri Museveni. It has been estimated that approximately 100,000 to 500,000 people, including combatants and civilians, died across Uganda during the Bush War. The officers spoke of the hardship they endured living year-after-year in the bush, moving camp frequently—living away from parents, wives and children.

The NRA had little equipment back then—only a small arsenal of captured weapons. The officers laughed as they recalled that new recruits had to practice shooting with wooden rifles. They had no uniforms. Many soldiers wore rags since the clothing of new recruits was torn after only a few months in the bush and could not be replaced. Hardly any of them had shoes. They talked about the ever-present hunger and disease. They ate whatever they could find, kill and cook. Soldiers scrounged for food on abandoned fields or planted cassava or matooke (plantain bananas). Some found nourishment in cooked cow-skins, cassava peels, grass, or tree bark. Many fellow soldiers had died of starvation during the war, yet tonight these officers could joke about having been forced to eat every animal, rodent, bird, and insect imaginable to survive. Others suffered or died from malaria and intestinal illnesses as a result of contaminated food and drinking water. Medicine was in short supply and bandages were so scarce that soldiers were forced to look for mattresses in abandoned houses to rip apart and use for dressing wounds.

There was one unspoken rule this night—no one spoke of killing or fighting. For good reason.

While Museveni's troops generally had a reputation for being a well-disciplined army, in certain parts of the country killings, rape and other forms of physical abuse aimed at noncombatants were common. Thousands of suspected rebels were taken into detention, followed by torture and maltreatment. The NRA also reportedly used land mines against civilians. Child soldiers were common in the NRA's ranks, even after it had become the regular Ugandan Army. Homes and belongings were destroyed, and herds of cattle looted. A group of more than 1,700 former cattle owners joined together long after the Bush War had ended and sued the government at the

High Court in Kampala, frustrated that most of their complaints had been in vain—even met with hostility by the Army—and the little compensation provided, inadequate.

These well-groomed fighters sipping cocktails were the chosen few who had not merely survived but for whom those years in the bush had paid off with promotions and relative riches. Good thing, because they were not paid as soldiers fighting in the bush before Museveni took control of the country.

They told the story of a new recruit in Amin's Army who had foolishly asked his superior officer for his "pay." The response had been:

"What do you need to be paid for? You have been given a gun. Go out and use it."

In other words, take what you need from those unarmed or otherwise too weak to defend themselves. Your gun is a license to steal.

One senior officer who was very dark-skinned and lean had a half-closed badly scarred eye. What had happened to him, I wondered? He was the only obviously wounded figure in the crowd.

The departing foreign military adviser who was white, gray haired and distinguished, was well-liked by the officers. What country or armaments manufacturer was he affiliated with? He seemed as suspicious of me as I was of him. But this night, it didn't matter.

He was ending his tour of duty and mine had just begun.

CHAPTER 20

A PANAMANIAN JUNGLE NIGHTMARE

When the officers began to order shots of Waragi—the highly-popular locally brewed industrial triple distilled gin (which, when adulterated with high amounts of methanol, has been known to kill)—I wasn't surprised. Uganda has been ranked as *the world's* leading consumer of alcohol per capita by the World Health Organization and Waragi, is dirt cheap. It derives its name from "war gin" because it was produced locally from cassava, bananas or cane sugar in protest to the high cost of British gins. A large glass of this badass liquor goes for approximately 25 cents, making it easily accessible for Ugandans. But I had learned as a teenager, nasty tasting Waragi was not for me.

Instead, I said goodnight to my new drinking buddies and careened back to my room early, leaving plenty of time for a good night's sleep. After thrashing around in bed for a few hours, I finally fell into a deep slumber.

It began with an itch. In my dream, a half-dozen winded U.S. Army soldiers straggled into a clearing in the Panamanian jungle. It was humid yet cool in the heavy shade of the trees beneath the jungle canopy. The earthen floor smelled moist and rich, so fertile that it was teeming with insect and plant life. A yellowy, white-furred albino sloth hung from a branch high above. The ugly animal seemed lifeless.

This jungle on Ancon Hill in the Panama Canal Zone was familiar to me. It had once been pristine rainforest, long before incursions by the French and American canal companies. Time and again its dense growth had been hacked back by gangs of workmen swinging machetes to create paths, its stone cliffs exposed from excavations for gravel to build the Canal's massive concrete system of locks.

Despite all the human intervention, the jungle here was still congested—every hard-fought man-made opening quickly reclaimed by Mother Nature. Lower branches of trees and palm fronds drooped onto the flourishing bushes below. The weakest in the struggle for nutritious sunlight—lichen and ferns—carpeted the jungle floor. Vines inched toward the heavens, wrapping around and strangling host trees, then fell toward the ground, crisscrossing one another haphazardly. In the midst of this tangle, a slender Royal Palm tree stood straight in an irregular world.

As a boy, from ages 8 through 12, I had lived with my father in housing for civilian residents of the Canal Zone—employees of the Panama Canal Company—in the Gorgas Apartments in a clearing below. I had flown on rope swings from these trees out over its glens, howling into open air. My childhood friends and I built villages of 2 to 3-foot low stone wall "houses" up here on the hill in the afternoons following the school day at Ancon Elementary.

Boys and girls paired off as homesteading couples, clearing the land of rock as they fortified their dwelling walls. It was easy, being warmly accepted in this playground society. No girl ever shirked from innocently playing my mate for an afternoon.

Between the jungle on the hill and the civilization below was a border of avocado and mango trees, at which we young boys threw stones aiming for fruit. A few bites from the green mangos tasted good and tart before we threw the rest away. The sweetest were the ripe yellow and orange. We would rip the skin off with our teeth and chew down to their stringy pits. The only wildlife we could see from our homes below were countless "neques" that ran harmlessly about like little brown rabbits across mowed fields. Formally named the Central American agouti, they had rounded backs, slim little legs, naked ears, and a dark, reddish-brown color with long straw-colored black-tipped hairs on their rumps. When small boa constrictors occasionally lost their way and slithered down the hill, they quickly became some boy's pet. We knew jaguarondi, puma, jaguar, ocelot cats and other large animals lived in this jungle. We heard stories of their sightings from soldiers on patrol. And when a large animal met its death, we learned of it from the vultures circling above. The more vultures, the larger the animal, we figured.

At the very top of Ancon Hill stood an Army radio transmission tower erected upon an underground concrete communications bunker built during World War II, surrounded by chain-link fencing and barbed wire. The fence, once reached, our hiking was over—the adventures of the Zone's youth were officially restricted to non-strategic land areas. However, our inability as children to restrain our curiosity and comply with adult military rules was never dealt with harshly. A mild reprimand from a young soldier was enough. We were not hostiles—just American kids fooling around. Exposed iron pipes, whether for ventilation of the bunker or drainage, popped out of the ground about the hill. There were other curious remains, such as crumbling concrete steps and foundations, and abandoned rusting generators to fuel our imaginations. We could picture elaborate secret chambers beneath the ground and used the accessible remnants as props for our games. In the Atlantic and Pacific ocean waters there were fences too, only these were to protect us from the ravages of the sea, rather than to protect military secrets. At all the Zone's beaches, shark netting had been stretched underwater to protect swimmers—so ever-present was the danger of attack.

The Panama Canal Zone was a remarkable place for a young boy to grow up. This was the narrow strip of land where the pirate Henry Morgan had once transported gold and other stolen treasure from one ocean to another with his would-be captors in hot pursuit. The "forty-niners" bound for California from the Eastern United States had crossed here in their rush for gold. For centuries the Isthmus of Panama had been considered one of the most pestilential spots in the world. Malaria, yellow fever and a cornucopia of intestinal diseases were endemic to the area. The sanitation of the Isthmus and the provision of a clean water supply were grave obstacles that had to be overcome for the Canal to be built. Eventually conquered, they required ever-constant vigilance in the rainforest environment.

For the workers who built the canal, it had been a grand and noble effort. "The adventure of a lifetime," the survivors would say. But for those of us who followed in their footsteps and were a part of maintaining its operations decades later, it still remained an extraordinary experience. We, too, felt part of an immense, daring enterprise. We were content with the lifestyle provided by our government and grateful for the opportunity to be a part of something so much larger than ourselves.

The strategic military importance of the Canal was readily acceptable to the American civilian and military inhabitants of the Canal Zone in the mid-sixties. We civilians agreed to confine ourselves to those areas that did not house soldiers, armaments or communications equipment. We did not question what transpired at so-called "research" facilities and beyond barbed wire. We honored the intermittent guard posts where we were obliged to identify ourselves. In exchange for these limitations to our freedom of movement and access to information, we received a comfortable, secure way of life—far better materially than the quality of life we would have enjoyed at our middle-income level in the U.S. None of us were wealthy; none of us were poor. We were all well cared for.

Like most Americans post-World War II, we trusted our government and military. We took pride in our nation's achievements. None was more tangible and impressive than the Panama Canal itself. Yet our beliefs about the American way of life would soon be challenged here by the oppressed Panamanians, and later by the civil rights movement and opposition to the Vietnam War in the United States.

The Gorgas Apartments, where we lived, sat adjacent to the sprawling Gorgas Hospital and related buildings, such as the Walter Reed Research laboratory and morgue. The French were the first to build a hospital on Ancon Hill. Their poorly designed facility, lacking screens to keep out mosquitoes and surrounded by stagnant water for their breeding, unfortunately had been more effective spreading malaria and yellow fever than treating the diseases. Having inherited the property, the Americans made improvements over the years. Its buildings now fanned out along both sides of the road up Ancon Hill, which was lined by majestic Royal Palm trees. The buildings were connected by walkways that provided shelter during the long rainy season from mid-April to mid-December. The architecture was uniform and government-issue, built to last forever like American post offices and courthouses, but adapted to the tropical environment. After work—once most of the staff had gone home—we children could sneak into any of the buildings that did not house overnight staff and patients. The lab technicians at Walter Reed Research facility were kid-friendly and gave us white mice for pets when we asked. When a laboratory was shuttered, we rummaged through the trash and collected dozens of beakers, test-tube racks and other equipment to supplement the store-bought home chemistry kits which were so popular with American kids those days. We salvaged reddish-brown rubberized sheets that had been tossed into the hospital-waste dumpster, unaware and unconcerned about their prior clinical use, and made wizard dunce caps and capes out of them—outfits that, had they been white, would have looked strikingly similar to Ku Klux Klan robes. For a few days our gang of boys could be seen stealing through the jungle on Ancon Hill oddly dressed in these homemade outfits. But we soon discovered that non-breathing rubberized sheets were far too uncomfortable and hot for the tropics.

The Gorgas Apartments were built for families of Americans who worked for the Panama Canal Company. Some of the neighborhood Dads worked as pilots navigating the commercial ships along the 50-mile passage through the Canal. The commercial ship captains, unfamiliar with the workings of the Canal, were required to place their vessels in the hands of the Panama Canal Company's experienced pilots for the slow passage. Each vessel's safety was guarded by well trained personnel and a multitude of navigational aids and mechanical safety devices.

On weekends my father would shepherd me onto ships from around the world docked in the Canal to meet the crews and collect coins for my swelling international collection. The crews were friendly and willingly gave me pocket change from their distant homelands. The H.M.S. Intrepid was an icebreaker, my father explained, built to withstand plowing through frozen seas and grazing icebergs, like the one that had sunk the Titanic. She was returning from a journey to the South Pole when her crew gave us photographs of penguins they had taken.

We lived at the crossroads of the world, a numismatic paradise. Not only was it easy to gather foreign coins, but because this was the only place in the world where United States and local (Panamanian) currency was interchangeable, finding rare U.S. coins long out of circulation in the U.S. still in use in Panama, was simple enough for curious boys like me and my friends. We convinced the tellers at the Panama City bus station to allow us to sift through their battered wooden change drawers where we found rare Indian head pennies, Buffalo nickels, Mercury dimes, Liberty walking half dollars, zinc coated steel pennies minted during World War II and other U.S. coins, many fifty or more years old, still used in poor, remote regions of the country.

Our family, consisting of a divorced man and his son, was unique at the Gorgas Apartments. Here there were no divorcees; every child had a mother who was expected to be involved in the school and after-school lives of her children. Every mother also belonged to the society of American housewives. There were no working mothers. Living in the Zone was not the adventurous lifestyle my father had yearned for since, as a young man, he had left his wealthy suburban hometown to work on a ship bound for South Africa. He left seeking racial and cultural diversity, none of which was to be found here.

Since my skin was brown, inherited from my Moslem Indian mother, the other children sometimes insulted me by calling me "Panamanian." Yet, unlike my white father, I found comfort in the structure and conformity of the Zone. My father had a good job; we lived in a stable family-oriented community and could afford a housekeeper to cook and clean up after me. I wanted to be white, middle class and very American—like everyone around me. So as a half-white and half-Indian, half American and half Trinidadian, son of a divorced American father and an absent East Indian mother, there were a few uncomfortable moments finding my place in Zone society. But in a short time, I did. I was even one of the more popular boys—and the girls liked me too!

In 1964, soon after our arrival in Panama, Americans and Panamanians alike celebrated the fiftieth Silver Anniversary of the completion of the Panama Canal, which was called one of the "Seven Wonders of the Modern World." My father told me stories of the massive difficulties encountered by the men who worked to build the canal. The black and white photographic history of its construction put faces to the stories. It was an engineering masterpiece, he declared. What for centuries had been considered impossible—to tame the forces of nature and link the two oceans—was accomplished by Americans within a ten-year period! "Think of the magnitude of the task," he whispered as he tried to capture my imagination and swelled with a nationalistic pride that was rare for him.

"Imagine trying to build a trench and locks wide and deep enough to accommodate the largest ocean-faring ships, in a swampy jungle where yellow fever, malaria and dysentery were rampant. You would have to build homes, roads, hospitals, schools and assemble a workforce from thousands of miles away. Equipment to excavate and move tons of earth and rock would have to be transported to the area or even invented specifically for scope of the project. Since the time of Charles V of Spain, the first monarch to grasp the significance of a canal joining the two oceans, the nations of the world had failed to fulfill the dream."

At age 8, I was too young to marvel at the Canal's mechanical workings or appreciate the engineering challenges. But the tales of human sacrifice and suffering the men who had built the canal endured, I understood. The health obstacles they encountered were as formidable as the weather, terrain or engineering. In Panama, my father began teaching me about common Third World diseases such as malaria, yellow fever, elephantiasis, syphilis, gonorrhea and leprosy and his teachings continued with kwashiorkor and cholera through to my 17th birthday in Africa. The lessons began with my asking him what was "wrong" with the sickly, scarred or deformed people we encountered in our travels—the emaciated malnourished child with the belly swollen with fluid, the beggar with the grotesque enlarged leg covered in open sores, or the elderly woman with a milky film over her eyes. But he was not merely answering his son's questions, he too was learning as we went along. After all, the worlds he exposed me to in childhood were also new to him and far different from his privileged suburban American upbringing.

While unrelated to his profession, my father had tremendous curiosity about developing world health problems. He visited the Palo Seco Leprosarium or leper colony established on an ocean-side 500-acre fruit farm in the Canal Zone which had about 100 patients. In Uganda, years later he visited another colony. Leprosy, a potentially horribly disfiguring disease, terrified me, but my father assured me with the detachment of a research scientist, that leprosy was now treatable with sulfa drugs. It seemed cruel to him that these unfortunate souls were still forced to live in isolation due largely to ignorance and superstition.

Despite my fears, I usually wanted to go with him on his journeys to strange places, including mental hospitals and juvenile treatment facilities.

"Children were not permitted to visit leper colonies," he said, "because while not contagious among adults, the risk of contracting the disease is much greater for children." But when he went into the shanty villages in the hills above Panama City, to visit the "casas de brujas," or homes of witch "healers," I was with him. Only then I chose to wait in our car while he met the witches in the wooden shacks with corrugated steel roofs they called home.

In Panama, my father had been a social worker in a psychiatric hospital treating both military and civilian patients. In the early sixties, psychiatry was still considered a highly questionable field, hardly a science, and was associated with frightening, uncomfortable human frailties or deviancies. In the Zone, any deviation from suburban American norms of the period was as unacceptable as weeds in its lawns manicured with military precision. Mental illness—like prostitution and drug usage—did not belong inside its policed borders. Maladies such as these had their place—in the noisy, dirty streets of Panama City. When life in the Zone proved too boring or confining, the men—including my father—stole into Panama City to satisfy their appetites and thirsts.

My father would observe with great annoyance that the Canal Zone was "more American than America." He was not alone in his criticism of the Zone's segregated, rigid society. Decades earlier it had been said:

> "The Canal Zone is a narrow ribbon of standardized buildings and standardized men working at standardized jobs."

> "A drearily efficient state where every American looks and behaves exactly like every other."

The Canal Zone's legal status, society and government were as peculiar as the geographical alignment of the Canal. It was not a state, territory or possession of the United States. The area of land was granted in perpetuity to the U.S. by the Republic of Panama for the specific purpose of building, operation and protecting the Canal. Subject to this limiting condition, the Zone was, in effect, a government reservation where private enterprise was not permitted except those directly related to the waterway and its operation.

The Zone was created in a bold stroke of American imperialism. Under the terms of the treaty between Panama and the U.S., the U.S. exercised complete and exclusive sovereignty. The U.S. Government was responsible for providing civil government. In the 1960s, the Zone's population, including uniformed personnel of the Armed Forces, was slightly over 42,000—mainly composed of civilian employees of the Panama Canal Company and the Canal Zone Government, the uniformed and civilian employees of the Army, Navy, and Air Force and their dependents. The Canal Zone Government was under the authority of the Secretary of the Army.

In short, the Zone's quasi-military, civil servant society hardly mirrored life in America. And while America was changing rapidly in the turbulent 1960's, Zone society stood still.

For thousands of Panamanians and blacks who labored on the canal, it was more like South Africa than America. Neighborhoods were labeled 'silver' and 'gold' to distinguish between white and non-white areas. Blacks lived in separate more modest communities with deceptively attractive, cheery names like Rainbow Village. Panamanians were not allowed in the Zone—except as workers or servants. There was hardly a trace of Panamanian culture.

While the United States and Panamanian flags were supposed to be flown side by side at civilian locations in the Zone under an agreement (reached in 1963 under President Kennedy), Kennedy was assassinated before his orders were carried out. Residents of the Zone were reluctant to abide by this agreement which barely acknowledged Panama's existence. One month after the President's death, the Panama Canal Zone's Governor issued a decree limiting Kennedy's order. The U.S. flag would no longer be flown outside Canal Zone schools, police stations, post offices or other civilian locations where it had been flown, but Panama's flag would not be flown either. The governor's order infuriated many Canal Zone residents who interpreted it as a U.S. renunciation of sovereignty over the Canal Zone.

In response, outraged residents began flying the U.S. flag anywhere they could. In January 1964, students at Balboa High School, with adult encouragement, on two consecutive days hoisted the American flag alone in front of their school—just to piss off the Panamanians.

So, it was no surprise to my father when nearly 200 Panamanian students, in response, marched in protest into the Canal Zone carrying the Panamanian flag. In a struggle that ensued, the flag was torn and the angry Panamanian students began running through the streets past our apartment building down the hill to the security gate between the Zone and Panama City. Thousands of Panamanians stormed the border fence from outside. The rioting lasted 3 days and resulted in the deaths of 22 Panamanians and four U.S. soldiers, serious injuries to several hundred persons, and millions of dollars in property damage. Cars with Canal Zone license plates caught in Panama City were rocked by the crowds and once their American occupants were permitted to flee, the cars were overturned and set on fire. American-owned businesses in the city were set afire. The recently dedicated Pan Am building which (despite housing an American corporation, was Panamanian-owned) was torched by Molotov cocktails sent flying through its windows. The next morning the bodies of six Panamanians were found in the debris. "Yankee Go Home" was scrawled on walls throughout the city.

The Panamanians didn't stand a chance though. Our military presence was massive in this place of great global strategic importance. In the days that followed, American armored tanks noisily rumbled through the streets, down the Hill to protect the Zone's entrance gates. We smelled the tear gas fired into the crowds in Panama City and heard gunshots in the distance. Order was restored within days. My father had been visiting friends—the family of an American ship pilot who lived in Panama City—when the rioting began. He called to reassure our housekeeper and me he was safe and would be home soon. I didn't worry about him—he was fluent in Spanish and unlike other Americans of the time, he preferred Hispanic culture to his own. He safely made his way back into the Zone at night after having been trapped in the midst of the chaos for two days. He told me he and the ship pilot had worn metal U.S. Army helmets to protect themselves from stones thrown by the crowds at their station wagon as they approached the Zone's gates. He showed me pictures he had somehow taken of the rioting and people throwing gasoline-filled bottles at the Pan Am building as it burned.

Torched Pan Am Building, Photo by My Father

Although my father first disappeared in Panama during the riots of 1964, he returned home safely that time. In 1971, when he disappeared, he did not return.

At age 17, I could not have conceived his death would haunt me for the next fifty years. Friedrich Nietzsche, the German philosopher, once famously said: "That which does not kill us makes us stronger."

Bullshit. The truth is that which doesn't kill us... leaves us deeply wounded.

Today, I know that no one walks away from tragedy without being profoundly touched. And murder leaves its special scars. We are forever haunted by the spirits of those we love when they are violently taken from us without the chance to say goodbye.

I have learned that when life seems brightest, you may be shaken to your very core. Your roots charred in a single blinding moment, by the strike of a massive bolt of lightning. This I promise you: You will never again walk so fully erect, without bending to clutch your stomach in nervous spasm, flinching in the face of perceived danger (real or imagined) or gasping for breath when struck with fear. You will be tested by this raw, savage blow. In the end, life or death you may choose. Yet your walk through the fire is preordained.

The soldiers in my dream wore clean, starched olive-green uniforms with their names printed in black on white tape sewn above their pockets. They were new to the jungle. They had not slept in hammocks under trees with mosquito netting tied into the branches forming a netted cocoon, as I had. They had no bites on their backs from mosquitoes that found their way through the hammock canvas. Yet they were not falsely confident or ignorant of the dangers of the unfamiliar environment. They proceeded intelligently with caution and were well intentioned. Their commander instructed them to stop in the clearing and review their progress. As they gathered around their leader to study a map, he began to scratch the back of his neck and down his starched collar. He continued talking, quietly, because there might be hostiles within earshot. Another soldier began to scratch his neck too. Now the commander scratched his arm. One by one all the soldiers began scratching. As the final members of the detail straggled into the clearing, they too, within moments, were scratching. Since the scratching was controlled and subtle, no one in the group noticed that everyone was engaged in it.

I was the only person not scratching. I observed carefully what was happening. A deep sadness came over me as the men scratched more and more feverishly.

Then they were no longer scratching. Their skin was burning from a caustic chemical that had leaked onto them, first invisible, now black and bubbling. Now they were fighting for their lives. Some threw off their shirts, screamed out and rolled on the ground. No one understood why, in this spot, at this time, they were suddenly experiencing great pain. Only I knew the history that would explain this seemingly mad turn of events. This was the very spot where my father had been murdered. I couldn't explain the connection between their itching, then burning skin and my father's unsolved, unmourned murder. Yet intuitively I understood.

The horror of the murder still resided in this remote location, inflicting pain upon those who ventured into it.

CHAPTER 21

ON THE ROAD TO MBARARA

I wasn't sure how to dress for my journey—complete with military escort—to Mbarara. On the one hand, I wanted to be comfortable and casual, as well as for others to be comfortable with me. On the other, I wanted to impress the military personnel with my presence. I wanted them to respect me as they would a senior officer or important civilian. Above all, I didn't want them to think I was a crazy kid who had come to Uganda on a lark to pursue some poorly thought-out mixture of personal emotional baggage and muddled "investigation." Of course, that's exactly the way I thought about what I was doing. I was a kid when my father was murdered and that kid—upset, confused and overwhelmed by the task which had been thrust upon him—was still inside me. What did he know about conducting an investigation of any kind?

While I did not want to ignore my feelings, my trip to Mbarara would involve intense fact-finding, not just grieving. There was so much I needed to learn, see, and do in the seven days I had in the country. I had to make use of my forensic training and relentlessly pursue answers. However, having returned to the country, city, if not actual spot where my father was brutally murdered, some of the people I interviewed might have actually participated in his murder. While the military was assisting me at the moment, at any time military helpfulness could easily turn to anger if I pushed too hard or asked the wrong questions. That's exactly what happened to Stroh and led to my father's death.

I chose to wear blue jeans, sneakers, and a starched white long sleeve shirt. The shirt would convey my official, lawyer-like, senior officer status. The jeans and sneakers would be comfortable.

Major Albert Kareba met me at the Sheraton promptly at 9 a.m. dressed in a starched white, long-sleeve Ralph Lauren button-down shirt, khaki slacks and brown tassel loafers. He brought with him his Olympus camera, Sharp electric organizer, cell phone and beeper. In short, Albert was better dressed and better equipped than I was.

We would be driven to Mbarara by Albert's regular chauffeur, a friendly chap named Meddie, in a new air-conditioned Pearl African Safaris Toyota touring van with expanded sunroof, permitting passengers to stand to view and take pictures of wildlife. Times had changed. In my day, we safaried in rugged Land Rovers with thinly cushioned seats, worthless shock absorbers, and windows which were difficult to slide open in lieu of air conditioning.

Albert had the demeanor—good manners and self-assurance—fitting for the Army Protocol Officer. He seemed to be worry-free and pleased with his lot in life. He knew he was fortunate to have landed a plum job that involved catering to dignitaries.

He had recently taken on tour a visiting American four-star general who had come to assess the security in the region in light of the problems Uganda was experiencing along its borders. Albert proudly told me he also had been involved with security for a visit by Nelson Mandela, who was enormously popular in Uganda as the leader in the fight for freedom in South Africa. The Ugandan soldiers I met with, who had fought against Amin and Obote, also considered themselves freedom fighters. Only they had freed Ugandans from brutal black leaders, not apartheid.

It would be a four-hour drive to Mbarara and we were both *really* tired. Albert had stayed late toasting Uganda Waragi with the other senior officers and slept only three hours. But since he had finally eaten—albeit at 3 a.m.—he said he was only slightly hung over. Not sure what to expect in Mbarara but knowing this would be the most demanding leg of my journey, I had spent much of the night worrying in bed, before my nightmarish dream about the Panamanian jungle.

Author and Major Albert Kareba Riding To Mbarara

Albert explained that as an officer, the Army paid for his housing and living supplies but only gave him a small salary. He and the other officers supplemented their incomes as best they could. He had a brother in Kansas who worked as a software designer who sent him electronics which Albert would sell for two or three times his cost. As he explained the mechanics and economics of this business, it was clear he knew what he was doing and had a keen interest in making money. Since I was a successful entrepreneur, as well as closer to his age than most visitors he escorted, we talked easily about everything from business opportunities in Uganda, such as health clubs and exporting African artifacts, to Army pension benefits. After years of devastation, Uganda was rapidly rebuilding and growing, Albert said. The question in my mind was who would want to do business in Uganda given the limited wealth of the people and very real risks.

The last time I had traveled the road to Mbarara, I told Albert, I was hitchhiking to Rwanda with my twenty-something friend Jack Peden. Jack was a good-natured Californian hippie who, immediately following graduation from college was comfortable traveling alone around the world, living out of his backpack on a shoestring budget. My father invited him to sleep on our living room sofa for a while, after which Jack migrated to the nearby campus dormitory rooms of Makerere University student friends he made.

I have no idea where or how I met Jack, but in Uganda in the late 1960s it didn't take long to meet every member of the small European and American community, including visitors. He was every bit as unlikely a friend as all my friends back then but, in Uganda, there was time—lots of time—to get to know people of all different ages and backgrounds.

Nearly ten years apart in age, Jack and I almost certainly would never have been friends back in America. I would have hung with kids my own age who shared the same interests and were moving forward toward the same goals in lockstep with me. But in Africa I discovered that almost anyone is worth spending the time to get to know.

While a relaxed sense of time and broadening of awareness helped me and other Americans adapt to, as well as appreciate life in Africa, when we eventually returned to the U.S. years later, our lack of focus made us strangers in our homeland. We spoke too slowly, asked too many questions and paused too long before responding to everyday demands. We acted like bewildered tourists even though we appeared to be indistinguishable from other Americans. It would take us a year to adjust back to the rapidly changing, fast-paced American lifestyle.

Jack persuaded me, somewhat reluctantly, to accompany him hitchhiking along the Mbarara road to the Rwandan border and then possibly onto Lake Kivu, one of the deepest lakes in the world sitting on the border between Rwanda and Congo. Rwanda was unsafe even then and I didn't share Jack's unbridled curiosity about the country. After a few uncomfortable days on the road with Jack—who, unlike my other older friends at Makerere, had no knowledge of Uganda—I cut the trip short by hitching a ride from the town of Kabale, a mere 10 miles from the Rwandan border, in a development agency's Land Rover back to Kampala. Jack, who dismissed my safety concerns, went on alone. He was surprised and a little annoyed by my last-minute change of plans but we parted on good terms. I would see him again in a week when he returned to our flat in Kampala exhausted and in need of a hot shower.

About halfway to Mbarara, after two hours of driving, Albert and I stopped in the southern town of Masaka. During the Amin years and Obote's second regime, Masaka had been the scene of intense fighting and bombing, Albert told me. In the 1979 Battle of Masaka during the Uganda-Tanzania War, the Tanzanians captured the town following an artillery bombardment to thwart a threatened invasion of Tanzania by Amin. The Siege of Masaka, a battle of the Ugandan Bush War in 1985, left the already pummeled town further damaged. We stopped to view the remains of two buildings which had been destroyed. In Kampala I had seen widespread damage caused by neglect and civil disorder, but this was the first evidence of massive destruction caused by war.

A couple of hours later as we were comfortably reclining in the back of the touring van driving down the road, Albert nonchalantly said, "That's the Simba Battalion barracks on the left." He pointed to a cluster of low buildings too far from the main road to clearly see. Without any advance warning to me, we had reached the place where my father was last seen alive and reportedly tortured and killed. But we weren't headed to the barracks just yet. Albert said we had an hour to check into our hotel and have lunch before our 2:00 appointment at the barracks.

Town of Masaka Bombardment Remains

"Before we go to our hotel, can we stop at the Rest House where my father and Stroh reportedly stayed the last two nights before they were killed?" I asked. "The Commission of Inquiry Exhibit of the Guest Register showed that my father had stayed in Room No. 3 for two nights, the 7th and 8th of July."

Albert, who was from Mbarara, didn't know for certain the Rest House to which I was referring but he instructed our driver to take us to a hotel he thought might be it. The hotel was too big, not at all similar to the architecture of the many modest Rest Houses the colonial government had built throughout the country pre-independence. I dimly recalled the appearance of the building from when I had stayed there a year before my father and Stroh, whilst hitching to the Rwanda border with Jack Peden. I remembered a long, single story flat building with rooms spanning out to the right and left of a central entrance hall. This hotel was two stories and not long in shape.

Albert wasn't sure where else to take me. Then he remembered there was another building that, while now abandoned, could have been a Rest

House in the distant past. As we approached, I could see the building was boarded shut and showed signs of years of neglect. The corrugated steel roof was rusted and caving, all windows were broken, paint was peeling and the concrete foundation was crumbling. As we walked to the front of the building, our driver, Meddie, asked a passer-by what it had been used for. We were told it was an abandoned government building which squatters had been permitted to inhabit. It looked like the Rest House I remembered but I couldn't be sure. I had only stayed there a single night decades ago. It would have been difficult to recognize the building under the best of circumstances.

And nothing about this journey was "under the best of circumstances."

Now, we couldn't even be certain we had found the Rest House where my father had spent his last two nights of freedom. We couldn't go inside to see if there even was a Room No. 3. As I milled about the front of the building, I came upon an old sign that had fallen years ago and was enmeshed in tall grass. As Albert helped me untangle and stand it up, the sign clearly read "Rest House."

Mbarara Rest House

Remarkably, this old wooden sign still lay where it had fallen decades earlier— well-preserved and legible, although its wooden legs were broken— and had never been carted away for firewood by squatters. I silently thanked God for giving me enough reference points to keep going, knowing I was on the right path. God, it seemed, had not only given me a sense of obligation but was leading me to fulfill my duty.

CHAPTER 22

SIMBA BATTALION
ARMY BARRACKS

Albert and I sat on the patio of our hotel at a restaurant table under an umbrella advertising Nile Special beer, "produced in the town of Jinja, the source of the Nile at Lake Victoria," which shielded us from the blazing sun as we ate our lunch of crispy, well-done steak and chips. My father and I had eaten steak almost daily in Uganda—beef was plentiful, cheap, and as long as the meat was cooked well enough, any parasites would be killed, he had told me.

My hotel room was clean and simple, and while I knew I wouldn't be getting my best night's sleep here, I was comfortable with the accommodations.

After lunch, Meddie drove us to the Army barracks. As we approached, I saw on the left side of the road beyond the rusty gate to the barracks and sentries, a mural of an enormous ghostly grey lion painted on the wall of a building. The painted lion sat resting in the upper right corner of the wall of a split-level structure built into the side of a small slope. To the left and below the floating lion were double barred jailhouse doors leading from the side into the lower floor of the building. The haunting lion was the symbol for Simba Battalion—Simba being the word for lion in Swahili—the unit of the Ugandan Army that was stationed at the barracks.

As we drove closer and my eyes fixed upon the lion mural, I sensed this building—in its lower, most forbidding level beyond its jailhouse doors—was where my father and Stroh had been killed or suffered intensely. I had a vision of the two men, their weakened, half-dead bodies being carried by soldiers, feet dragging through the lower-level doors. Perhaps it was just the dramatic impact of the sight of the iron bars and ghostly lion, but I felt strongly I was finally at the place where my father had been murdered.

To the right of the road as we entered the Simba Battalion barracks sat two crumbling concrete lions perched on the grass on either side of a walkway.

To the left was the upper level of the jail or lock-up facility which the military guards referred to as the "Quarter Guard." It was a long concrete building with small, barred window openings every few feet—windows set so high that neither prisoners locked inside nor outsiders could see through to one another. Like the lions, the road and all the buildings near the entrance gate were crumbling. Only a few concrete walls remained of what had once been the Administrative Offices. The roof and all window frames were long gone and tall grass sprouted with abandon along the base of the walls. Poured concrete foundation floors remained revealing the dimensions of the old offices. Plainly visible on a lone still-standing wall were the words, "Officers Car Park Only" hand painted in white. Some of the barracks had been completely destroyed, all were substantially deteriorated, yet the buildings remarkably still housed soldiers. This Third World Army could still domicile soldiers here; after all, these conditions were hardly different from the impoverished homes the soldiers had come from. The barracks were every bit as appropriate for these soldiers at this point in time in Uganda as Fort Dix or any American military base is for American soldiers.

We turned to the right and drove down a straight mile-long stretch of road that ran the length of the barracks. On both sides of the road tall grass grew in fields surrounding abandoned rusting military vehicles—tanks and personnel carriers. These vehicles which had sat here for decades since the days of Amin and Obote, were reminders that Uganda had at one time spent heavily on defense and received substantial military assistance from many foreign countries, including the U.S., Britain and Israel. The country reportedly spent $100 million on defense in 1971 alone—proportionately more than any other country in Africa until it began having difficulty buying arms because it could not pay.

What had come from all this military spending and assistance? The monies, personnel, armament and other resources had been squandered by leaders seeking to settle longstanding inter-tribal grievances. The outcome from purchasing all the toys of war—planes, tanks, and artillery—was over a million Ugandans killed. So much of the constructive work of the people—supported by well-intentioned foreign government aid—schools, roads, and housing had been destroyed by weapons of destruction bought by vengeful leaders.

As we drove past the long rows of doorless, windowless cement block rooms where the soldiers lived, I was surprised to see women among the men. Married soldiers were allowed to bring their wives and children to live with them in the barracks, Albert told me. Entire families were camped out, cooking over open fires. Across the road from the barracks were open-air latrines and water facilities. Surprisingly, these areas were not kept clean even though the Army clearly had resources to ensure basic sanitation. Perhaps still reeling from corrupt leadership and massive losses, the Army lacked the discipline or esprit de corps to manage even its own living conditions.

Albert introduced me to Lt. Col. Rutambika, Commanding Officer of Simba Battalion, who was a very dark-skinned African with refined Arab facial features. He wore a black beret and camouflage fatigues. His face conveyed sincere concern and sympathy—he wanted to help me, I believed.

Rutambika was responsible for this remotely situated, impoverished, uneducated and largely unskilled military force. He had virtually no resources to work with. His large, dark, sparsely furnished office with a single bare light bulb dangling several yards from the tall ceiling and surrounded by ruins, was the very best the barracks had to offer. He had the ultimate perk—his own bathroom with what appeared to be a flushing toilet.

It was dark in his office when we met with him mid-afternoon, but the hanging light was not switched on. Albert and I sat across from each other at a table with seating for five which extended in front of Rutambika's desk. Albert introduced me first, explaining who I was, why I was here, and that this was a personal inquiry, not an official investigation. He then asked me to speak. I emphasized that I had come to learn how my father had spent his last days and how he died. I did not need to know who killed them—I already had a good idea of who participated in the killings.

Rutambika said we would be meeting with two people: Lt. Silver Tibihika, who was now retired living on his small farm in Mbarara, and another soldier, still active in the Army, who was a new recruit at the barracks at the time of the killings. Albert and Rutambika knew both of these men well. I was eager to hear from Tibihika since he was the key witness to come forward and give testimony to the Commission of Inquiry—without him there would not have been sufficient circumstantial evidence for the judge to conclude the two men were murdered by the Ugandan Armed Forces—but also because it was clear to me, as well as the presiding judge, he had not told all he knew.

Tibihika did not go so far as to indicate in his affidavit how either of the two men met their deaths. In fact, he claimed he never saw my father at all—at least not while alive. He did testify he had been ordered to, and did, supervise recruits to dig up the remains of two persons and burn them. That was as close as he came to saying he knew my father to be dead.

Tibihika was described to U.S. Embassy officials, in a declassified State Department telegram, "as one of the better educated men in the Ugandan Army, trained as an officer rather than commissioned from the ranks and having completed an officer's training course in Israel." He was also the brother of a prominent former political figure.

Lt. Silver Tibihika and Author

Tibihika shuffled into the room in a guarded, lackadaisical manner. He was a short, poorly shaven, portly man who appeared to be nearly too frail to care for himself. His hair was closely cropped, and he had a thick mustache. He wore probably his best dress shirt—white with a frayed inside collar. The whites of his eyes were cloudy yellow and bloodshot. His jaw moved in a continuous sideways grinding motion as if he was chewing tobacco, but he wasn't. He looked to be a heavy drinker and smoked his cigarettes down to the very filter so as not to waste a single precious puff. He carried a slim zippered portfolio under his arm as he was directed to sit down next to me.

I stood to greet him and shake his hand. If I approached him with the right combination of emotional appeal and financial incentives, would he now—decades after the murders—be willing to tell me more?

CHAPTER 23

THE REMARKABLE STORY OF THE MASSACRE AT MBARARA

T ibihika began by telling us the remarkable story of the brutal massacre at Simba Battalion barracks on June 22, 1971. I had never heard the complete story before and, to the best of my knowledge, it has never been told elsewhere.

At times, Rutambika and Albert interjected confirming Tibihika's statements, as well as adding their own comments about what they had heard over the years regarding the bloody incident.

After Amin took control of the country in January 1971, he set about consolidating his base in the army by relying heavily on his Nubian supporters and eliminating suspected opponents, including 75% of the thousands of Langi and Acholi soldiers. Two weeks before my father and Stroh arrived at the barracks in early July 1971, there had been a massacre of about 500 soldiers, which Tibihika personally witnessed. In the morning, all Simba battalion soldiers were hurriedly awakened then summoned, to the parade grounds. As they stood in the bright sunlight, an order was given to the crowd to kill those fellow soldiers whose names were called out—Langi and Acholi soldiers.

"How were they killed?" asked Rutambika.

"They were all beaten to death, pounded with fists and pieces of firewood by the soldiers standing around them."

Rutambika and Albert were incredulous. "All 500 were beaten to death? Were some of them shot?"

"No, not a single shot was fired."

"Were some soldiers stabbed?"

"No, no one had thought to bring their knives with them to the parade grounds," he said.

We were all struggling to picture what Tibihika was telling us. It was inconceivable hundreds of soldiers would, without discussion or dissent, rush to obey an order to beat to death 500 fellow soldiers standing alongside them—soldiers with whom they may have just shared a morning cup of tea or coffee—using nothing but their fists and firewood. It was logical to assume that if a decision had been made to murder 500 soldiers at one time in one place, an efficient means to accomplish the objective would have been employed by those in command—not bloody bludgeoning.

Here we were somberly sitting, with our heads bowed as if in prayer, in a dark room in the ruins of the barracks 26 years after the abhorrent event, struggling to break free from our presumptions of rationality. As we descended into this horrendous underworld, we desperately wanted to bring our notions of order, sanity and reason with us.

Mass murders should make sense, we demanded.

But, of course, there was no command given to suddenly, simultaneously murder 500 soldiers—an order which might have given rise to an immediate mutiny. Rather, a list of names of soldiers to be killed was read aloud and the list just kept growing... and growing... and growing. The soldiers had no idea when the killing started, it would continue for so long. No one imagined the unimaginable.

Tibihika went on to explain that following the beatings, the hundreds of dead bodies had to be disposed of. This was a monumental task. Again, no plan had been made in advance for getting rid of the hundreds of corpses. The bodies were piled onto trucks and then tossed into neighboring farmlands on a 17-mile stretch of road between Masaka and Mbarara.

No one had forewarned, or notified the farmers.

The shocked farmers didn't know what to do with the bodies dumped onto their land. There were too many bodies for the farmers to bury but leaving the bodies exposed to the hot sun caused them to decompose nastily. The farmers pled with the Army to clean up the mess. Rutambika and Albert confirmed that over the years they had heard accounts from neighboring farmers about soldiers' bodies that had been dumped on their land in 1971. Rutambika told the story of three soldiers presumed dead and carted off with the other bodies who actually crawled back to the barracks severely injured—only to be killed immediately.

"It's hard to feel sorry for soldiers who are so stupid as to crawl back to the very people who had just tried to kill them, only to be killed again," Albert quipped and we all laughed nervously.

Killed again. How funny was that?

"Why would any soldiers have crawled back?" I asked.

"Because they had nowhere else to go," was the somber answer.

Poor, uneducated, badly beaten, psychologically devastated after having been savagely attacked by their colleagues and far from their homes—what else could they do? Instinctively, they crawled back to their former refuge nearby hoping all had been forgiven, or forgotten, or it had just been some terrible misunderstanding.

Rutambika told of another wounded soldier who crawled out of a pile of bodies to a farmer's house nearby. The distraught farmer contacted the Army for assistance. The Army quickly responded—shooting the soldier on the spot and leaving the bloody corpse in the farmer's home.

The murderous madness began at dawn and continued all day through to dusk. The disposal of bodies went on until late in the evening. Even the officers who ordered the bloodbath had no idea it would go on for so long and so many would die. Once inflamed to kill, it was hard for the commanding officers and soldiers to stop themselves.

This was the massacre at Simba Battalion Nicholas Stroh had heard rumors of and, with the assistance of my father, had travelled to Mbarara to confirm with the Commanding Officer, Lt. Col. Ali Fadhul. When Stroh arrived at the barracks approximately two weeks after the massacre, on July 8, he was told Fadhul was not there. The following day, Stroh returned and Tibihika saw him taken into the office of the second in command, Major Juma. Juma ordered the killing of my father and Stroh, and Lt. Samwala actually killed the men, according to Tibihika. This information was not included in his Commission of Inquiry affidavit. He did not place any of the blame on Fadhul, even though he was in command at the time. Juma was to blame, said Tibihika. Fadhul was not at the barracks when the murders occurred.

I accepted Tibihika's account of events in the moment because I had not yet combed through the Commission documents carefully enough to understand that, while Juma was at the very center of the Inquiry, and, in the words of the judge, "was a consummate liar… and… made an appalling impression on everyone," Ali Fadhul *was* at the barracks by the time of the killings.

Tibihika emphasized he himself wasn't there and had nothing to do with the killings. Sensing he was scared of being implicated, I decided to shift my questioning to what he could tell me about my father and Stroh's bodies.

"What could you tell about how the men were killed from the condition of their bodies?"

"Nothing really—they were decomposed. The bodies fell apart like chicken meat falls off the bone. When you picked up a limb, the meat and flesh just fell off," he said using his hands to illustrate. He grimaced as he described the smell of the rotting bodies and the motion of the flesh and underlying musculature falling from the bones of the two dead men.

We all found his statements regarding his inability to divine from the bodies how the two had met their deaths hard to believe.

"Had they been beaten?" I asked.

"Were their throats cut?" asked Albert.

"Were their heads severed?" asked Rutambika.

"Had they been strangled?

"Had they been shot?

To each question, Tibihika shook his head and responded he did not know. It was nighttime, hard to see, he said, and the recruits actually handled the bodies, not him. He did not get close enough to the bodies. The recruits stood between him and the bodies.

I then showed him a picture of my father taken a few weeks before he was killed. He did not recognize my father as one of the two bodies.

Sensing I was getting nowhere asking about his direct knowledge, I shifted my questioning to what he thought happened to the men, based upon any rumors he may have overheard or his knowledge of other killings undertaken by the Army at the time. He said he had heard no rumors whatsoever.

"I guess I find it hard to believe that two white men were killed—an event that attracted worldwide attention—and there was absolutely no discussion of it among the soldiers. That defies human nature," I said.

Rutambika and Albert came to Tibihika's defense initially. At that time in Uganda, they said, people who were caught even discussing something they had heard or seen were often killed. People would have been afraid to discuss anything so dangerous. But the soldiers did not let him entirely off the hook. They kept pressing Tibihika and he began to give a little.

He referred to Stroh's large physical form on several occasions, in order to make different points. This seemed odd to me because my father and Stroh were both approximately 6 feet tall, although Stroh was 12 years younger and 50 pounds heavier.

"Mr. Stroh was such a big man the soldiers who were small boys could not have beaten him or fought him head-on. Most likely the small soldiers would have shot him from behind, in the back of the head."

"What date and time were they killed?" I asked.

"They were killed the same day they were taken prisoner—probably between 6 and 9 in the evening," said Tibihika. As I mentioned earlier, since first viewing the Quarter Guard lock-up with its ghostly lion mural, I had a vision—which was growing stronger as we sat questioning Tibihika—that my father and Stroh had not been killed quickly. I had a sense they suffered intense, lingering pain. But perhaps it was my own intense, lingering grief I was feeling.

"If they were shot in the back of the head, would they have been shot at the barracks? Did you hear any shots?" I asked.

"No, they would not have been shot at the barracks because then the small soldiers would have had to struggle to lift and remove the bodies. Stroh was much too big to have been killed at the barracks and then removed. He must have been killed where the bodies were left—out in the bush away from the barracks. I heard no shots," he responded.

"Were they beaten before they died?"

Quietly and without emotion Tibihika answered, "Yes, they would have been beaten—everyone would have wanted a chance to hit a muzungu."

Albert and Rutambika looked at me and nodded in agreement. We all knew the seething anger toward whites many Ugandans harbored that, if given the opportunity, could explode into rage. In 1971, while Ugandans beating and killing their fellow countrymen was commonplace, it was nearly unheard of to attack whites—except in connection with a theft or burglary gone wrong. Tibihika was speaking candidly.

In the midst of questioning Tibihika, I mentally withdrew for a moment to marvel at how remarkable it was to be back in Mbarara talking to a man who very likely played a role in my father's murder decades earlier. I thought of all the people—including those in the room—who had helped me on this journey to find peace with my father's death. I had come a long way from a shaken, orphaned, penniless teenage victim of an international tragedy completely beyond my control to the adult who sat in this room judiciously investigating the matter. Yet, even now, I was helpless to get Tibihika to tell me all he knew.

As he was getting up to leave the room, Tibihika added, "The person I saw out in the hall when I came in who is, I believe, waiting to talk to you was a new recruit at the time. He is more likely to have been in situations where rumors were openly discussed—among the new recruits. The new recruits did not talk to me since I was an officer and since I was not one of the senior officers at Mbarara close to Amin, the other officers did not speak freely with me either after the incident."

We all acknowledged some truth in what he was saying. He had fled Uganda after the killings because he was viewed as an outsider and his knowledge of what happened was a threat to Amin and his loyal officers. On the other hand, he had stated in his affidavit that the sole basis for his belief that the two men were dead was that he overheard officers in the Mess saying so—a rumor. If rumors weren't circulating at the time of the killings, then the only way he could have known about the killings was if he participated.

As pitiful, disheveled, and battered as he appeared before us, Tibihika was a survivor. He had been an outsider at the very center of an international incident which destroyed Amin's credibility and reputation worldwide. He deserted Amin's Army, fleeing into Tanzania when his life was threatened. He knew he was considered untrustworthy by Amin's close associates. He struck back at Amin and his henchmen from a neighboring country which opposed Amin—where Amin could not harm him.

Declassified U.S. Department of State telegrams reveal Tibihika's escape to Tanzania was neither reckless nor solitary; rather, it had been carefully planned with help from numerous well-positioned parties.

After Tibihikia sent an anonymous letter to the Commission of Inquiry offering to testify if his confidentiality and safety could be assured—which Justice Jones shared with American officials (because the Commission could not offer confidentiality)—the United States government had assisted in his flight over the border to where he could safely and openly testify. London Observer reporter David Martin, with whom he met initially in Tanzania, sent a message to Uganda and seventy-two hours later, Tibihika's wife, children and two brothers were brought safely into Tanzania.

Tibihika retained counsel of his own choosing to advise him. Early in the morning having completing his affidavit for the Commission of Inquiry, Tibihika had balked at signing it after discussing his position with a local lawyer. His lawyer advised signing the deposition was equivalent to signing a confession he was an accessory to murder after the fact. After an entire morning of arguing, Tibihika had finally agreed to sign.

Later Tibihika, whose family had joined him in Tanzania and was destitute, pressed for financial assistance from the American Embassy, as well as the Stroh family. Declassified U.S. State Department documents indicate that Tibihika walked into the U.S. Embassy in Dar es Salaam saying he had been told they would be able to assist him financially and could also contact the Embassy in Kampala for him about a reward offered by Mrs. Stroh.

Long before the Commission of Inquiry commenced, Mrs. Stroh had sought the State Department's advice on whether she should offer a reward for information regarding her husband's fate. American officials advised against it—no one was likely to come forward owing to fear for their own lives. Witnesses who testify for money were not worth much in an Inquiry of this sort, she was told; credible witnesses were asking for confidentiality and safety, not money.

Department officials harshly concluded at one point:

"Like everyone else around here Tibihika seems to think the Stroh family is a gold mine available for the asking. If he calls again about the matter, tell him the Embassy has no funds for him and the Stroh family has not offered a reward for information. Perhaps he should apply to the Tanzanian Government for assistance as a destitute Ugandan refugee."

Later, however, State Department officials softened as to Tibhika's plight indicating, that while a reward might look like a payoff before the case could be considered closed, no one would particularly care about a payment to Tibihika afterwards. There was "no doubt Tibihika was in difficult straits in Tanzania."

Tibihika's Commission of Inquiry testimony implicating Amin and his loyal senior officers also served another purpose for him. As Justice Jones commented in his Report, Tibihika's brother was the principal suspect in the activities of the National Trading Corporation which was the subject of another Commission of Inquiry running parallel with the Commission investigating my father's murder. He had struck a blow in his brother's defense by pointing the finger at Amin in my father and Stroh's case.

Once Amin was out of power, Tibihika returned to Uganda and managed to survive the second Obote regime which was even more brutal than the Amin years. He settled in his home region of Mbarara to enjoy a peaceful retirement on his own small farm and now, in his twilight years, he was on good terms with the current government and the military.

Tibihika had survived with all of the grace, character and charm of a rat.

He was nervous, wily, conniving, singularly unappealing and devoid of credibility. Later, as Albert and I reflected on the day's events over dinner at our hotel, I realized the moment Tibihika walked into the room carrying a skinny (empty) zippered portfolio, I should have known he was going to answer every question as if he were the lawyer and I wasn't.

Tibihika was an intelligence officer, by his own admission, entrusted to handle the cover-up operation following the murders. However, he was no leader of men and I do not believe torturing or killing the two men was his idea. He was neither easy to respect nor hate. I felt sorry for him. His life, so harsh, had netted so pitifully little. There was another reason not to hate him. Whatever his role, the testimony he gave in his affidavit ended ten months of silence following my father's disappearance. Coming forward as he did—telling only some of what he knew and did—was still enough to establish culpability on the part of the Army that was crucial to the ex-gratia settlement I eventually received from the Ugandan government.

Tibihika, in saving his own and his brother's necks, had also come to the aid of the survivors.

CHAPTER 24

BLOODY CELL WALLS

With Tibihika dismissed and now waiting in the hallway, we interviewed a second soldier who was congenial, well-known, and obviously well-liked by all men in the room. He wore a black beret and fatigues as he was still an active officer in the Army. He quickly got to the point: He knew nothing. He was just a young, new recruit at the time and had heard no rumors. Only the officers would have known what happened to the two men, he said.

If he truly knew nothing, why would General Muntu have brought him to me to be interviewed? It didn't make sense.

I was certain he and Tibihika were both lying, or at least not telling me everything they knew. The murders, international media attention, as well as military and civil investigations would have likely dominated discussion at the barracks for months. The officers would have known more details and talked about what they knew amongst themselves; the new recruits would have known less but probably talked more freely, as they tried to figure out what their leaders were doing.

I told Albert and Rutambika I would like to walk the barracks grounds with Tibihika and have him guide me through what happened 26 years ago. We all drove back toward the entrance gate in the Commanding Officer's truck, Albert and I sitting in the back seat with Tibihika between us. As we were getting out of the truck, my pant leg got caught on the driver's rifle barrel. Thankfully, the rifle did not discharge.

Tibihika led us to where the administrative offices had once been and pointed to the ruins of Major Juma's office. He testified he had last seen Stroh being "frog-marched," i.e., seized from behind roughly and forcefully propelled forward, toward Juma's office by two military police from the Quarter Guard. In a strange, distant voice, Tibihika observed Stroh must have told the soldiers who were pushing and beating him that my father was waiting for him at the Rest House and would tell American officials if Stroh came to harm. Otherwise, how would the soldiers have known to go after my father?

A few years after my father disappeared—after reading the Commission of Inquiry Report—I had come to the same conclusion as Tibihika: Stroh had unintentionally played a central role in bringing about my father's death.

The record was clear that my father hadn't gone to the barracks and pissed anyone off—Stroh had. My father knew better. The only way the soldiers even knew of my father's existence and whereabouts was because Stroh, new to Uganda and unfamiliar with its people, had told them—in hopes of saving himself.

Major Rutambika indicated where the Officer's Mess had been, and Tibihika pointed to the spot on the ground where he claimed he had, following orders, burned the bodies.

Of all the buildings at the barracks, the Quarter Guard lock-up facility near the entrance gate was most intact. I asked Tibihika to lead me to the cell or cells where my father and Stroh would have been held captive. While making it clear he had no firsthand knowledge, he led me to the upper-level cells. Declassified U.S. State Department documents reveal that while touring the barracks in March 1972, Commission of Inquiry members had visited these cells in the Quarter Guard and saw "very bloody walls."

The Commission, as well as Mrs. Stroh, sought—unsuccessfully—to have analysis of the blood by a chemist, as well as photographs entered into evidence. A simple blood test would have quickly established the men were dead and had been killed by the Army at this location. Little wonder Amin had opposed testing.

As I examined the crude cells, there was no blood on the walls. But around the time of the murders, evidently someone had bled badly here.

"Would they have been held in one or two cells?" I asked.

Quarter Guard Prison Cell

"They would not have been put in the same cell," he said, but, he may have misunderstood my question and meant they would not have been kept in the same cell with other prisoners. There were occupants in the lock-up this day, but security seemed lax, and I did not witness any signs of brutality. No one objected to my taking pictures.

It was strange Tibihika had nothing to say about my father. He never saw or met him, he said. He did not recognize my father's picture.

Tibihika could not even identify my father as being the second body he unearthed and burned.

Why not—was my father beheaded? Were the two men killed at separate times, in difference places?

The most obvious explanation for why Tibihika had never seen my father was that once taken from the Rest House my father was never brought to the barracks. Instead, he was killed somewhere else soon after he was seen being taken away in a black Zephyr car.

The Commission of Inquiry Report had been confusing and included conflicting statements regarding who had last seen my father alive, when, and where. In one paragraph of the Report, the judge wrote that my father was last seen on July 9th by the Rest House cook being taken away by three Africans dressed in Special Forces shirts.

"Where he was taken to, no one knows. That was the last that was seen of him," wrote Justice Jones.

Tibihika testified in his affidavit that he had not seen "any other European other than the one journalist in the barracks at the time." He also testified he had seen Stroh having lunch with a priest at the Agip Motel the day before. My father was also at the lunch according to the testimony of the priest—indeed my father arranged the lunch with the priest whom he knew—but Tibihika did not mention seeing my father at the table. The judge, several paragraphs later in the Report, wrote that Major Juma, the second in command at the barracks admitted to "seeing both Stroh and Siedle, but no more." Where or when Juma saw my father is not indicated anywhere in the Report. I assume it was at the barracks, even though Tibihika claimed he never saw my father there.

The lack of thoroughness regarding my father's fate—the willingness to accept he simply vanished from the barracks into thin air, or was an invisible man at the lunch table with the priest and Stroh—reflects the obvious bias of the Inquiry. From the very beginning, as the title of the Inquiry and first *Newsweek* article clearly indicate, the foremost concern was what had happened to Stroh.

Stroh's name preceded my father's in the title of the Inquiry—even though alphabetically, Siedle should have come first. The Report focused upon Stroh but the same vigilance was not shown regarding my father's movements or motivations. There is no mention that my father was guiding Stroh in gathering intelligence about the massacre, including introducing Stroh to his missionary contacts in Mbarara. Rather, the explanation offered by the press for why my father had accompanied Stroh to Mbarara was that he was "putting the finishing touches on a book he had written about the elderly in Uganda." In fact, he had completed the book and left the manuscript at the printer's before departing for Mbarara. Eventually—after his estate was settled and the publisher's bill paid—I received a few copies of his book, *The Last of Life: Old Age, Missions and Missionaries in Uganda.*

THE LAST OF LIFE:
Old Age, Missions
and Missionaries
In Uganda

BY ROBERT L. SIEDLE
SOCIAL WORK DEPARTMENT,
MAKERERE UNIVERSITY,
KAMPALA

It is possible to surmise from a careful reading of the Report: (a) At least one person (Major Juma) saw my father at the barracks imprisoned with Stroh; (b) My father was mistreated similarly to Stroh; and (c) He was finally killed along with Stroh. However, only the brief mention of Juma having seen both men alive provides a basis for the conclusion that my father arrived at the barracks alive. Still unanswered were the questions of why Tibihika insisted he had never seen my father alive and could not identify the second body he and the recruits unearthed and burned as my father's.

I walked down the hill on the side of the lock-up facility to the lower level where I earlier sensed my father had endured prolonged suffering. Peering through the peeling grey painted iron bars of the lower gates I could see grey painted bolted wooden doors to cells and an orange oil barrel in the hallway. I decided not to push my luck by asking my hosts for permission to go into the lower-level cells where abused prisoners might have been hidden. I wasn't eager to find out whether my hosts were being entirely truthful when they assured me torture in Uganda was long over.

Albert took a picture of Tibihika, Major Rutambika and me standing together in front of the lower-level wall, the ghostly lion hovering above in the background. Throughout our walking tour of the barracks, Tibihika's demeanor was hesitant and suspicious, but when he surprisingly asked if we wanted to drive to where he found the bodies he had been ordered to burn, his mood lifted. He *wanted* to show us the spot, it seemed… or maybe he just wanted to take us far away from the barracks.

Pulling Albert and Rutambika aside, I explained that I wanted to drive to the spot alone with Tibihika, in hopes that he would speak to me more candidly without the others present. I didn't tell them I also wanted a chance to offer him money to tell the truth and for him to be able to accept it without having to confess in the presence of the others that he had been lying all along, or be concerned he would have to share the reward with others. Albert told me to be careful since Tibihika would be taking me far out into the bush and, once there, might make a desperate move.

"Do not be led too far away from Meddie and our car," he said.

It began to drizzle as Tibihika, Meddie and I left in the touring van. As we rode, I thanked Tibihika for testifying before the Commission of Inquiry. Absent his affidavit, the Commission would not have been able to conclude the Ugandan Army was responsible for the murders. I wanted him to believe that whatever involvement he may have had in the murders, I was grateful to him—he did not have to fear me.

We were driving slowly through the African savanna along a straight stretch of road about 10 miles from the barracks when Tibihika suddenly told the driver to turn off the road. While he had told us repeatedly over the course of the afternoon that he had not been back to the spot where he found the bodies since the day he collected and burned them, he very quickly and without hesitation directed the driver toward a lone tree in the grassy plain. Tibihika and I got out of the car and walked further into the bush, leaving Meddie far behind—exactly what Albert had told me not to do. I was somewhat concerned for my safety, but I was so occupied with the immediate task before me—moving forward to learn all I could—that I didn't have time for fear. It was still drizzling and getting darker as I kept pumping Tibihika for more information.

"Mr. Siedle, I don't want to lie to you," he said, "I could tell you I know more, but I don't. I would tell you if I did." Then he pointed to the exact spot under the tree where he had found the bodies and said, "If you dig here, you will find remains of the men. I was given two gunny sacks to put the bodies in but they were too big for the sacks, so we left some parts behind here."

"You're certain? I really don't want to make the effort to dig here if you're not sure we'll find something," I said.

"If you dig here, you will find remains—body parts," he assured me. Now was not the time to begin excavating.

It had been a long, exhausting day and it was almost dark. We were wet, itchy and dirty from trekking through the shoulder-high, rough and hairy elephant grass with razor-sharp pointed tips as we made our way back to the waiting van and our driver. Meddie had to shift the van into 4-wheel drive to pull us out of the gray, clayish mud and onto the asphalt road.

As we rode back to Mbarara, it seemed the right time to explore whether money might motivate Tibihika, or refresh his memory.

"There's something I wanted to mention to you privately—without the others hearing. You know, I am willing to pay you some money if you can be of greater assistance," I said.

He quickly turned to look at me and asked, "How much money?"

"A thousand dollars," I carelessly responded.

After a brief contemplative pause, he once again stated, "I really don't know anything more… Mr. Siedle, I could lie and take your money, but I really don't know any more."

Maybe if I had offered more—in that instant—he would have told me all he knew. Later, when I did increase my offer, it was too late. He was resolute, claiming he had already told me all he knew.

Albert was waiting for us back at the hotel and, with Tibihika present, I told him about our trek to the tree on the savannah. Tibihika declined my offer to buy him a drink which I thought was very odd because he certainly appeared to be a heavy drinker. He was probably still uncomfortable with me and had spent enough time responding to my questions for a day. He agreed to meet us at 9 the following morning and left for home. Albert and I agreed to go to the sauna first and then have dinner.

An attendant gave Albert and me each a towel and colorful East African Kitange fabric sarong to wrap around our waists in the sauna. The last time I had wrapped myself in Kitange cloth I was a teenager on safari swimming and camping overnight at Lake Victoria.

We were joined in the sauna by three stout African men and one woman. The sky was dark now and there was only the dim bulb in the sauna for illumination. We all had had at least one beer and were joking and laughing. I was surrounded by a sea of sweating, flabby flesh which rippled with each new joke. A man laughingly told me that when African children misbehave, their parents tell them if they don't stop, the parents will feed them to the muzungu.

The children are told white people eat little African children.

Everyone laughed. They were all speaking in English—which I really appreciated—out of courtesy to me. If they had wanted to exclude me, they could have spoken and joked in Swahili. It felt good to be included in the banter. Albert and I looked at each other after the joke and he said to me,

"That's why Tibihika said everyone would have welcomed the chance to beat a white man." The reality of simmering racism was hardly news to me but as I descended ever deeper into the dark world of imprisonment, murder, massacres, beatings, torture, dumping and burning bodies, even uglier truths were emerging:

Beating or killing a white man may be more appealing to Africans than beating or killing a black man.

To incite a group to kill a large number of people, start off slowly and add victims as the bloodlust grows.

Disposing of one or two bodies is manageable by burning or burying the remains.

Disposing of hundreds of bodies is a real problem which can tax local resources.

Shooting a person in the back of the head without warning prevents the victim from putting up a fight.

Killing someone where you can leave him relieves you of the burden of moving the body.

Since I, as the survivor of the murder of a loved one, felt compelled to investigate my father's killing on my own, I had no choice but to follow the evidence, ask one unholy question after another and live with the answers. Both the questions I asked, such as "was my father decapitated," and the answers I received were deeply disturbing.

Survivors of murder victims are almost always left with unanswered questions—even if the crime has been supposedly "solved." In recognition of this fact, an American organization I have been in contact with—Parents of Murdered Children—even offers an Ask the Experts service which allows survivors to ask experts in bereavement, crime scene investigation and forensics their questions, as well as seek a second opinion.[16] Based upon readings on the POMC website, I had once explored the feasibility of transporting

---

16.   https://www.pomc.com/sos.html

ground penetrating radar—which has been used to find ancient ruins and locate massacre sites—to Uganda to search for my father's remains.

There is a lot to learn about murder—knowledge which most people thankfully go through life never needing.

At dinner, I told Albert that Tibihika had encouraged me to dig for the remains. I thought it odd Tibihika claimed to know so little about my father's death but was so certain if I dug, I would find his remains.

"Africans believe until you find and bury the bones of your loved one, you will not find peace," Albert explained. "Tibihika may be offering you a way to be more at peace with your father's death."

I told Albert that I, too, believed finding the remains of my father and burying them properly—with an appropriate ritual—would bring me some peace.

"But is it even possible the remains would still exist? How much does the human skeleton decompose over 25 years if not in a coffin and not buried deep in the ground?" I asked.

With great confidence that suggested actual experience in such matters, Albert said, "If animals do not destroy or move the bones, skeletons normally take around 20 years to dissolve in fertile soil. However, in sand or neutral soil, skeletons can remain intact for hundreds of years. Given the sandy loams—a type of soil made up of sand and varying amounts of silt and clay—in the area, the bones could still be there even after 25 years."

"Then what should we do?" I wondered aloud.

"We should dig. It's the only way you will know you have done everything you could to find out what happened to your father. We will hire two porters in the morning to do the digging."

I knew he was right but had never envisioned getting this far—to be actually digging up my father's body.

"What do we do if we find the bodies? What will we do with the remains?" I asked.

Albert, the Army Protocol Officer, knew exactly what had to be done in this surreal circumstance. Extensive protocols existed under both Ugandan and U.S. law which had to be carefully followed.

"If we find the bodies, we will have to contact the American Embassy in Kampala, the Ugandan government, the Stroh family, local health authorities, and then probably have autopsies completed here—before dealing with the issues and documentation related to return of the remains to the U.S.," he said very matter-of-factly.

Albert then added, "U.S. law requires that when—as in your father's case—the remains are not embalmed, the U.S. consular officer will alert U.S. Customs and the U.S. Public Health Service in advance, faxing copies of the consular mortuary certificate, local death certificate, affidavit of foreign funeral director, and a formal statement from competent foreign authorities stating that the individual did not die from a communicable disease. This statement generally is required even if the exact cause of death is unknown in order for the remains to enter the United States."

There were lots of steps that would have to be taken before my father's remains could be returned to the U.S. and laid in a final resting place. The only way to proceed with this monumental task was to take one step at a time.

CHAPTER 25

DIGGING FOR THE BODILY REMAINS

A nother night of fitful sleep.

I was at a hotel in the middle of nowhere and if Tibihika wanted to stop me from unearthing the remains of the two dead men, he would make his move tonight.

He could easily kill me—just shoot my hotel room full of holes. Under Amin, such an attack on a lone individual would have gone unreported. Amin was known to fill a room with people he wanted dead and then blow the entire room to smithereens. It was also hard to calm my mind because my investigation was moving forward so quickly. For years it had been impossible to learn anything. The circumstances surrounding my father's murder had remained a mystery. Now it appeared I was about to solve the mystery. After hours of tossing and turning, I finally fell asleep.

I awoke exhausted but my extreme fatigue seemed fitting. How are you supposed to feel when you go digging for your father's body? This was hard, painful mental-emotional work. At breakfast, Albert told me he too had had nightmares about his combat experiences, which was unusual. He said he never dreamt about those days. For the first time, it occurred to me that helping dig up my painful past was having an effect on him as well. We both had painful memories which were being unearthed.

When Tibihika was an hour-plus overdue, I had doubts he'd show. Albert, who knew the routine of farmers in the area, was confident Tibihika had risen early to do his chores and would come after he had finished. When Tibihika finally arrived driving a light Japanese truck, he had a much younger woman in the car with him who he said was his wife. His wife needed him to take her to the doctor, he said. She did not look well.

Albert persuaded him to lead me to the site of the remains so the porters could begin digging while he went to the doctor with his wife. We only had a few hours to dig because, according to Albert, we had to be back in Kampala by 5 p.m., which meant we had to leave by 1 p.m.

That was news to me.

I didn't understand why it was important to get back to Kampala by that hour. I wanted to have enough time to be thorough in our digging because it seemed unlikely we'd find the bodies immediately. If we were off by even a foot in our digging, we might miss the remains.

"Take him to the site where he can dig and determine there are no remains to be found and be back in a few hours," said Albert to Tibihika.

"Let's not assume there are no remains to be found," I said, concerned about Albert's instructions.

Had Albert spoken to his superiors and, after telling them our plans to excavate, been instructed not to go too far? Did the Army and Ugandan Government really want me to unearth evidence of past atrocities? Uganda's economy was on the upswing; Uganda was rapidly becoming a favored American trading partner and a force for stability in the region. A story about finding the bodies of Americans who had been murdered in Uganda's bloody past was in no one's best interest—except my own.

Albert stayed at the hotel while Tibihika, Meddie, and I drove in the van to the site, picking up two young men along the way to do the digging. It was a bright sunny day but, for some reason, it was harder for Tibihika to find the ancient tree today than yesterday in the rain. Leaving the main road, we inched along a narrow grey clay pathway. Having reached the end of the pathway, we parked the van and made our way on foot through knee-high elephant grass past a few bushes. The further we walked, the thicker and taller the grass grew until it reached a height of about six feet.

The tree under which we would dig was by far the tallest visible on the savanna but since it was growing in a small depression surrounded by high grass it did not appear to be towering from the road. The porters, who were barefoot, led the way, hacking back the stocky grass with their pangas (machetes). "This is the spot," Tibihika declared and as the men began to dig, he left to take his wife to the doctor. I stood in the tall elephant grass to the side of the diggers, away from the tree with Albert's camera strapped around my neck ready to snap pictures the very moment we found something. A trench about eight feet long, three feet wide was dug and the men said they would go down four feet. Digging was easy as there was hardly a stone in the soil. The air was still.

The tree was Y-shaped, forking into two major branches about 10 feet above the base. The leafy smaller upper branches grew to the left and right as much as they grew upward so that the tree shaded a large patch of ground. Where the two major branches split out from the trunk, a dark, mossy mass grew on the bark. A hive of angry bees throbbed around the mass high above which made me nervous but, for the time being, the bees seemed to be keeping to themselves. Every now and then, a bird warbled in the distance, reminding me of the haunting song of mourning doves— birds that filled me with unbearable sadness when I first heard their cries lying in bed at dawn following a sleepless night in New England, after my father's death.

In the distance, mist shrouded the snow-capped peaks of the astounding Mountains of the Moon which my father and I had crossed a year earlier while on safari at Queen Elizabeth National Park photographing lions, elephants, gazelle and giraffes.

Author at Uganda Equator

We were on our way to Kilembe—on the banks of River Nyamwamba, at the foothills of the Rwenzori Mountains—where Uganda's largest copper mine was located. Along with workers, we travelled up the mountain from the base camp to the mine entrance by chairlift, swaying in the breeze high above tall, dry grasses. Smoking was absolutely prohibited, we were sternly warned. Once, when a lit cigarette accidentally fell from the mouth of a miner sitting in his chair into the dry grass below, it had immediately caught fire horrifically roasting the workers dangling helplessly above. My father convinced the shift supervisors to give us a tour of the deep veins of the mine, which they were proud to do after providing us with white overalls, black rubber boots and white lighted hardhat helmets.

Author on Chairlift to Kilembe Copper Mines

Author and Robert Siedle, Kilembe Copper Mines

Robert Siedle and Workmen, Kilembe Copper Mines

More recently, not too far away, a group of Americans and six other foreign tourists were hacked to death by Hutu rebels while on a mountain gorilla watching tour. Insurgent groups have made it clear that Westerners will be targeted in Uganda.

Kidnapping for ransom is only a concept in Africa, said Robert Pelton in *The World's Most Dangerous Places*.

"If you're tagged, expect to be bagged."

Suddenly I felt pain on my temple and the men we hired to dig started yelling, "Run, run, run." I ran as fast as I could from the swarming bees which was difficult because I had Albert's camera dangling around my neck. The bees kept chasing me no matter how far or fast I ran. The men then yelled, "Get down on the ground!" I fell to the ground landing in the hairy deep grass. The bees were soon gone and I suffered only a single sting. Since the men hadn't unearthed anything yet and the bees were ever-present, I didn't know what to do next—dig deeper, wider, elsewhere or give up?

While the porters had also been stung running from the digging site, a few minutes after gathering their breath they were eager to return and continue. Their enthusiasm to resume digging seemed odd to me.

I pulled Meddie aside and asked, "What did you tell the men we were digging for?"

"I didn't dare say," he said. "But I think they believe we are looking to recover some of the treasure wealthy Indian businessmen were rumored to have buried around the country when Amin expelled the 90,000-minority Asian population in 1972, giving them only 90 days to leave."

By way of background, many Asians, i.e., Indians, Pakistanis and Bengalis were brought to East Africa by the British during their colonial rule. Originally, they were sent to help build the East African Rail system. Their descendants, and other immigrants who followed them, found their way into various businesses and professional positions. Many others, perhaps a majority, came immediately after World War II, providing much needed technical and professional services in these countries. By the mid-1960's, the Asians in Uganda enjoyed great financial success, forming an important part of the merchant and business sector of the country, especially in the cities. They also occupied prominent positions as teachers, engineers, lawyers and doctors. Yet because their customs and culture were totally different from those of the Africans, they never fully integrated themselves into the society. Moreover, their economic success came to be greatly resented by the native population of Uganda, who felt that the Asians were exploiting them.

Ironically, when Amin seized power in January 1971, many Indian businessmen were relieved. There had been fear surrounding measures introduced by his predecessor, Obote, over entry permits and economic reforms aimed at redressing the balance of power between Africans and non-Africans—all of which served to hinder Indian business activity. Amin, on the other hand, initially offered residence permits, granted import licenses to businesses and generally relaxed the rules on trade to the benefit of Uganda's Asians. Asian businesspeople started to repatriate capital and investments back to Uganda.

Ugandan Airlift: Ugandan Asians arrive at London Stansted Airport on the first of several specially chartered flights to Britain, shortly after Amin expelled them from Uganda. (Photo by Evening Standard/Hulton Archive/Getty Images)

So, it came as a shock to them when, nineteen months later, Amin ordered the deportation of the country's Asian population, many of whom had lived in Uganda for more than 100 years. Most of the Asians expelled felt settled in Uganda. Their parents were born in Uganda, and it was regarded as their home country.

Many Ugandans were not in favor of the expulsion, especially those employed by Asian businesses. They saw Asians as job-providers who had skills essential to the proper functioning of the economy. The expulsion put many African Ugandans out of work. Yet there were others who welcomed the expulsion.

As reasons for his expulsion order, Amin cited that the Ugandan Indian community were "bloodsuckers" who had exploited the local economy and refused to integrate with black African people after a century in the country.

Amin's order created a diplomatic crisis involving Uganda, India and Great Britain. Most of the Asians eventually emigrated to Great Britain since prior to Uganda's independence, the colonial government had offered British nationality to people of Indian origin and a majority chose to become British nationals. Those who emigrated to the UK, as holders of valid British passports, had the legal right to settle there. However, most of them had never lived in the UK before and the British government neither anticipated, nor was prepared for their arrival.

As the first groups of British Asians reached London, they told stories of Ugandan officials cutting up their passports to harass them, and subjecting them to physical violence. The Ugandan army visited the houses of many Asians during night time, threatened and beat them. As each group of refugees arrived from Uganda, they reported increasing violence and vandalism by the army. Similar mistreatment was reported by Asians who migrated back to India, Pakistan and Bangladesh.

Despite government assurances that the Asians would be permitted to carry with them personal effects to the value of 10,000 Uganda Shillings and 1,000 shillings in cash, the Ugandan authorities stripped the Asians of all their wealth and assets prior to their forced departure from the country. There were army checkpoints on all major roads and any gold, jewelry or money Asians were carrying was forcibly taken. Since Asians were also unable to access their bank accounts, many landed in Britain without a penny to their name.

Similarly, despite government promises that no property would be confiscated, the departing Asians received no compensation for the stores and various businesses they were forced to leave behind. The house owners and shopkeepers could not find any ready buyers since Amin had issued a decree that the Asians should sell their properties only to Ugandans, and not to other Asians. There were also cases where houses, shops and business premises were occupied by Ugandans by force and the Indian owners were simply thrown out.

Amin made several subsequent statements promising to compensate these people, but no compensation was ever paid. When Museveni took power in 1986, he invited the expelled Indians back to Uganda, offering back some of their possessions and providing incentives to reboot the economy. Many returned in the 1980s and 1990s and went on to, once again, dominate the country's economy.

It seemed plausible the porters would believe we were looking for buried treasure given that I am half-Indian and may have looked like the son of a wealthy Indian businessman. Whatever the reason, the men went back to digging without my prompting and despite the fact I had said I was willing to give up. They certainly seemed to believe there was something of great value to be found in the ground and I saw no good reason to dissuade them from the notion. Meddie and I watched the porters from the distance through his binoculars initially and gradually drifted back toward them.

After another hour of digging another ten feet, I told the men to stop.

We had found nothing, and it seemed unlikely we would. I was tired and disappointed, but the likelihood that Tibihika 26 years later accurately identified, and directed us to the very spot where parts of the bodies lay was remote. If he had been there with us, reassuring me, I probably would have continued the digging, but he wasn't. The fact that he hadn't come back seemed telling, I thought. He had probably sent me on a pointless search to appease me. Regardless, I had gone as far as I could without some encouragement.

Having given up the search for bodies, I desperately needed to go for a run to clear my head. After my father died, I had embraced long distance running as a means of handling stress. It was comforting to know I could always run—whenever and wherever I was. Since I'd be spending the entire afternoon in the van on the road back to Kampala, I'd brought my running clothes and shoes with me to the dig hoping to sneak in some late morning exercise. I changed into my running clothes and told Meddie to go on ahead—I would meet him back at the hotel which was about 8 kilometers away. But Meddie drove slowly—marginally ahead of me—the entire way, never letting me out of view. He knew jogging alone on the side of the road in a killing field was not safe. I had run an average of forty miles a week for the past 20 years, including alongside the Panama Canal and the pyramids at Giza, from the beaches of Saipan to the Caribbean, but never before had I been followed by guards at my heels.

Author, Killing Field, Mbarara

We found Albert at the hotel sitting outside with Tibihika drinking beers. He said he was trying to get Tibihika to talk more but had no success.

"Isn't it time to start getting rough with him? He's wasted our time. We found nothing under the tree," I said.

"I don't think it would be wise to push him too hard and risk his refusing to talk to us at all. After all, we can't force him to speak," said Albert.

Albert may have been right, but I wasn't ruling out anything that might help me get to the truth.

I gave Tibihika my business card, told him I would be in Kampala at the Sheraton for the next few days and if he had more information, he should please call me. I would pay him. He said he might have been a little confused in where he directed us to dig. He would look again and, if he found the right spot, he would have the bones dug up and sent to me in Kampala before I left. That seemed more than a little unlikely, but still, I hoped he would call before I left or even write once I was back in the U.S. Maybe he would feel safer once I left the country.

While I was finishing with Tibihika, Albert was talking with the porters, negotiating payment for their efforts. They told Albert they should be paid $150 U.S.

"That's outrageous," said Albert, "What would you get paid if you had done the same job for my parents who live here in Mbarara?"

"We would charge them $5 U.S.," said one porter.

"Well, would it be fair to pay you the same as my parents would have for the work?" asked Albert.

"Yes, that would be fair," said the porter in response to Albert's reasoning. Albert gave him $5 plus $1 for a tip.

On the way back to Kampala in the van, Albert and I both slept a couple of hours. I told him I wanted to treat him to a really fine dinner to thank him for all he had done for me. He said his favorite restaurant was called Le Chateau Brasserie Belge which was Belgium-owned and pricey. He and Meddie dropped me at the Sheraton around 6 p.m. and Albert agreed to meet me there at 9.

Back in my room, I had a message from Megan, my Canadian doctor friend who, not having heard from me for a few days was checking in to hear how my "mission" was going. I invited her to join Albert and me for a late dinner.

Albert showed up late at the Sheraton lobby—around 10—and after brief introductions, the three of us jumped into a taxi to the restaurant. I wasn't sure it was a good idea to bring Megan along since I had a good relationship with Albert and whether introducing a white Canadian woman doctor might disturb the dynamic between us was unclear. Still, I wanted to tell Megan about our trip to Mbarara and get her reactions. Albert, the protocol officer, was easily gracious and Megan, the visiting international healthcare worker, responded like a trained diplomat.

"I visited your country ten years ago," Megan said, "and I have never forgotten its beauty." That sounded sickly sweet to me but she was genuine. Megan really did seem to have a deep sensitivity for Uganda's infirmed and God knows Uganda had enough pain and suffering to touch the heart of anyone who had the capacity to care about the health and well-being of others.

It was late when we finished our dinner of steaks, mussels and fries. The kitchen closed but somehow Albert convinced the chef to bring us ice cream. Afterwards, we drifted to a quiet bar which, for no apparent reason, was popular with whites and wealthier Africans. It reminded me of the Ugandan bars I had gone to as a boy of 15—not drinking alcohol (although I certainly would have been served booze if I had the cash), but fraternizing with grown-ups from all over the world.

Tonight, I was one of the adults in the bar and, as I looked around, I wondered: Who are these people and what brought them here?

Were they brave adventurers boldly travelling to distant exotic lands, or just hopelessly lost drunks?

CHAPTER 26

THE MANY FACES OF GRIEF

Grief is an intensely personal experience which has the potential to be massively transformative.

There are a million ways to die and a million ways to grieve. There is no right or wrong way to grieve the loss of a loved one. All that matters is that we find our way toward healing.

A woman at my church in Florida is suing the tobacco companies for the death of her husband from lung cancer. While church members seem to understand bringing the lawsuit is something she feels she must do to honor her husband's memory—a necessary part of the grieving process—there is also a hint of disapproval in their voices when they talk about what she's doing. They feel she hasn't fully accepted the loss of her husband and worry the protracted litigation may delay acceptance. Some might say she's stuck in her anger about the loss and, by now, should have moved onto acceptance.

But who is to say what is an appropriate, or healthy response to a loss?

While there are recognizable stages of grief many survivors pass through over time and norms regarding the length of each stage, to treat grief as an illness which should be cured quickly is to deny both our humanity and mortality. If someone who loses a loved one to cancer devotes the rest of his life to searching for a cure, or raising money for charities involved in cancer research, is that life-long commitment excessive or unhealthy? Isn't there a danger that if we do not spend enough time wrestling with the difficult questions and feelings the death of a loved one produces, we may lose our capacity to love deeply and our lives will lose the richness they once had? Today, I believe, people are more likely to be rushed through their grief than languish in it.

Death of a loved one often imposes an obligation on survivors. More accurately stated, survivors often recognize, or impose upon themselves, an obligation to the dead.

My father's initial disappearance, unsolved murder and missing body— a mystery that stretched on for years—gave rise to complicated and, at least in my case, delayed grief. I did not begin to feel the full weight of the devastating loss of my father until five years later—in 1976—years before "delayed grief reactions," "survivor's guilt," and "Post Traumatic Stress Disorder" were widely recognized. The therapists I initially saw didn't connect the panic and intense sorrow I was feeling with the murder years earlier. Instead of seeing justifiable grief, they saw intense emotional distress seemingly unrelated to any precipitating event, i.e., they saw psychological abnormality.

Fortunately, as I learned to better express my feelings and understanding of complicated grief in the therapeutic community improved (post-Vietnam war), my journey into psychotherapy eventually resulted in a positive outcome. But it was a bumpy road with lots of misconceptions.

One common symptom associated with post-traumatic stress disorder, survivor's guilt—i.e., guilt about staying alive and the things I failed to do—was the last reaction to my father's death to surface. It has, *to this day*, proved most difficult to overcome. I had left Uganda for a month-long scenic vacation in Norway *just days* before my father's disappearance, after having helped pack all our belongings, confident he would follow safely behind me. How could I have abandoned him to frolic in the fjords? Why hadn't I seen the looming danger? Did I deserve to live while my father deserved to die for taking unnecessary risks?

If only I had been with him, I could have prevented, or at least mediated, the confrontation between him and the Army, I thought early on. Only later did I come to understand I would have been helpless to save him had I been there, and, for sure my father would not have wanted me with him. He died with the comfort of knowing his son was safe with trusted friends in Norway—far out of Amin's reach. He had not risked his son's life on this final mission—only his own.

"It wasn't supposed to happen," "we almost made it out safely" and, most intense of all, "you don't leave behind those you love" were phrases I choked on during involuntary flashbacks to the murders, both in and out of therapy.

It was my personal responsibility, as his son, to protect him because there simply was *no one* in Uganda who loved him more.

Other survivors of the murdered loved ones struggled in their own ways.

My aunts—my father's two older sisters—disapproved of my father's adventurous lifestyle, recklessly traveling to dangerous parts of the underdeveloped world on unclear missions. It was no surprise to his sisters that their younger brother's life—lived "irresponsibly"—ended tragically surrounded by unanswered questions.

My aunts' conflicted feelings about my father and how he lived led them to have only limited interest in what had actually happened to him. Their obligation was to establish he was indeed dead and then clean up the practical mess his unanticipated demise created—to hold a funeral, bury the body if one could be found, carry out the terms of his will, sell the family car, collect life insurance and Social Security Survivor benefits, sort through the contents of the apartment once shipped back to the U.S., and get his son started in a life of his own. The findings of the Commission of Inquiry, though inconclusive, were sufficient to secure a settlement from the Ugandan Government and that was good enough.

My kindly aunts did not need to know more, and to the best of my knowledge, they were never haunted over the years by any sense of unfulfilled obligation to their murdered younger brother. But they were both second mothers to me.

For my mother who had been divorced from my father and living apart from us over ten years, my father's death meant the end of her dream that one day the family would be joyously reunited. She claimed to have never stopped loving him but now they would never again be together—at least not in this world.

My mother, Betty Zenobia Khan, was a petite Muslim Indian woman of Pakistani origin whose ancestors migrated to the Caribbean island nation of Trinidad and Tobago in the mid-nineteenth century as part of the great Indian Diaspora. Following the abolition of slavery in the British Empire in 1833, Indians, as indentured laborers, were brought by the British to work in sugar cane plantations in the Caribbean. The first Indians arrived in Trinidad on May 30, 1845 and the immigration of indentured Indians continued until 1917 when it was banned by the government of India.

My mother's grandfather was a Pathan, a fiercely independent mountain dwelling people who are renowned for their courage and the military prowess they demonstrated resisting the British in India for a generation, as well as fighting the Russians in Afghanistan. Her grandfather came to Trinidad of his own free will, unlike the thousands of destitute Indians who were imported to Trinidad as indentured laborers. In addition to his military experience, he was a very talented jeweler and a successful businessman. The family lived upstairs from his jewelry store on busy Frederick Street, the main shopping street in the capital city of Port of Spain.

My mother was one of four sisters, each approximately five years apart in age. She was a very beautiful woman, slender with light brown skin, long black hair and brown eyes. She was said to be the most beautiful woman in Trinidad but her sisters were beautiful too and they were all pursued by many men. She wrote that she was the third child of parents "who did nothing but spoil their children with pretty clothes, lots of toys and all that money can buy." Despite his success as a jeweler, her father had an active, restless mind which led him to send away for books on invention and work unsuccessfully on the development of devices such as a perpetual motion machine. (While it is widely accepted today that the laws of physics do not allow for a machine that can work indefinitely without an external energy source, at that time it was considered possible to create such a device and many tried!)

My mother wrote of her father, "After many months of hard work and the expense of materials, when his inventions did not stay alive, he would die a little. Each time he failed to make a perpetual motion machine he drank a little more. I guess he loved his whiskey most of all and this was to destroy not only his beautiful jewelry but his life as well."

My mother's only brother, Ismith Khan, left Trinidad to study sociology and creative writing in the U.S. and became a well-known Caribbean writer. His first and best-known novel, *The Jumbie Bird*, published in 1961—the year before Trinidad and Tobago's independence from the British Empire—is highly autobiographical and tells the tragic story of his proud grandfather's quest to restore the dignity of the Indian people in Trinidad through repatriation to India, as opposed to further assimilation into a Creole society still under British rule.

Like her mother before her, my mother was a devout Muslim. However, in her youth she was not unduly encumbered by somber religious beliefs, I am told. She enjoyed being a socialite, attending parties, dancing and receiving lots of attention from men. As she grew older and her life became harsh and lonely, her thoughts increasingly, desperately turned to Allah.

Despite her happy upbringing and beauty, my mother's luck in marriage was not good. Her first husband, who was East Indian, left Trinidad to study dentistry in Indiana and, once there, married another woman, committing bigamy. My mother learned of her husband's other marriage from a social welfare officer in Trinidad who had received an inquiry from the American wife regarding whether her husband's other marriage in Trinidad had been legally recognized. My mother was left with an infant child to raise on her own. She managed to do so by living in her parents' home and working for the Board of Tourism.

A cruise line poster she had posed for caught the lustful eye of an adventurous American (my father) who was able to get her phone number from an Indian airport officer who was like a brother to her. The romance began when she agreed to have dinner with him, she told me.

Two later colorful photos of my mother wearing a necklace made by her father, one smiling demurely in an orange sari in front of a white Hindu temple and another looking somewhat frightened with a giant red and blue feathered Macaw perched upon her arm were included in the January 1953 *National Geographic* story, Happy-Go-Lucky Trinidad and Tobago: Britain's Caribbean Colony. Said the magazine, "East Indians ... give parts of the island an Arabian Nights atmosphere complete with soft Hindustani accents, plaintive Oriental tunes, sloe-eyed beauties with bangles and nose ornaments, and snow-white mosques and temples."

My parents were married in Trinidad in 1952, shortly after my older brother was born.

My mother loved my father deeply, but their marriage lasted only seven years. She did not want the marriage to end; it was he who insisted on the divorce. The day before their divorce my father wrote in his diary, "Betty tried to persuade me not to get a divorce, but there doesn't seem to be much reason to go on… We got a very simple Muslim divorce… I really didn't want it and neither did she, but under the shadow of an unhappy life together in the past, it seemed best," he wrote.

My mother already knew how difficult it was to raise a son alone and believed that a son needed, most of all, the protection of a father. She knew she could not handle the responsibility for the care of her two infant sons, as well as her teenage son. My father, on the other hand, very much wanted his two sons with him so she agreed to let him take us. A rich (by Trinidadian standards) white American man could provide her children with support, protection and U.S. citizenship—a future far more promising than she could offer in Trinidad. But my mother told me, years later, she never believed she was giving up her children for good when she let us go with our father. She believed she and my father would eventually reunite and that she would be able to see us in the interim. That was not to happen. Soon after they parted, my father wrote in his diary, "Betty wrote and wants to see the boys. I told her she was welcome to if she paid her own way to come to see them." It would be five years before she, accompanied by her now third husband, could pay to come visit us in the Panama Canal Zone and by then it was too late. She was a stranger to me. (Her third and final husband, a struggling portrait painter, later disappeared—never to be heard from again—while they were travelling through the Miami International Airport terminal a few years later.)

My mother wrote three poems about the dissolution of her marriage to my father and the decision to let her children go. Each poem is written from a different perspective, in the voice of a different member of the family. The first poem, A Child's Love, is written in the voice of my brother and me. The second poem, A Man's Love, reflects what she hoped my father was feeling about the loss of his loving wife, as opposed to what he may have actually felt. The final poem, A Mother's Sacrifice, tells of her feelings about losing her husband and children.

THE STORY

A CHILD'S LOVE

Please tell mummy that I love her
Tell her that I forgot to tell her
Tell her that I miss her
It hurts to be without her
How I miss my mummy every night
Tell her that I miss her tucking me in bed
I miss her lullabies, her goodnight kiss
The songs my mummy sang to me
The stories my mummy read to me
Also, those special ones she made up just for me
Tell mummy that I am really missing her
So very much, I am crying now
I don't know why but I wish she was here now
I'd hug and kiss my sweet lovely mummy
I know she would kiss my tears away
She used to kiss all my hurts away
Please tell mummy I'll keep our secret
I promise from tomorrow I won't cry
I promise I'll learn how to smile
I promise I'll grow big and strong and brave
I'll eat my carrots, I'll take my tonics
Even if its bitter medicine

I'll go to school, I'll study much, I'll do my homework, exercises and exams

Until the day she returns, she'll be so proud of me

I know my mummy loves me because she told me so

I know my mummy prays for me also

She taught me how to bow and say my prayers, like this:

God bless mummy, God bless daddy, and God bless everybody

And now I lay me down to sleep, I pray the Lord my soul to keep

Please, God. Goodnight.

A MAN'S LOVE

Dear God, I don't know why I did it (divorce)
But she is gone and I miss her so much
The tender softness of her nearness
Her soothing hand upon my brow
The fragrance of her perfume everywhere
The little shining earrings she used to wear
Dangling like precious diamonds from her lovely ears
The lacy hanky she always left behind
I often found them on the floor or anywhere they dropped
I even loved her gentle scolding, her nagging words, her foolish temper
Her feminine touch after making up
Her comforting arms around my clumsy body
I miss her pressing me closely against her warm bosom
The little kisses from my cheek to my neck
The bigger kisses that make a man so weak
I long for her to gather me once more in her arms
Or lay my head upon her lap
I miss that warmth and softness that gave me so much strength
That bosom was my cradle and my heaven
I'll fall asleep breathing her body's special scent
Her wonderful hugs, her kisses of blessings on my cheek or forehead
For all the greatness of that woman's touch, I am humble
And a deep emotion comes within my soul
So, I can stand up and breathe freely and deeply; I am a man
I feel physically and spiritually refreshed and clean
Once I was loved by a woman of value and I am grateful
She is gone but not forgotten.

A MOTHER'S SACRIFICE

Time stood still

For me, my world had come to any end

I had to tear out my heart and send it away

I had to make this sacrifice that was too much for me

I think I went away from myself for a little while

Whatever happened to me I did not care

I knew my love, my dreams, my everything

Had come to an end and time stood still

The children must go with their father

I had no other choice

They say I was sick

A mother not capable of her duty

To take care of her own children

Of two small boys like twins

Could I bring up and protect them, alone, me

Some people say they don't know

How I had the heart to do it

But I knew what was best for them

To keep them meant a selfish love

Wanting their love, companionship and help

To make me feel wanted, a job maybe, a salary to mind them

To look after their bringing up, training, schooling and health

But I wanted something better than this for my little sons

I wanted them to become somebody

A better education and all the advantages of an American citizen

And most of all, a father's protection

Maybe I was wrong (about the father he died)

But I still think

They are much happier and better educated

Otherwise, they will always be my two little loves, children.

Gerta Stroh—Nicholas' wife—in her sworn statement to the Commission of Inquiry indicated that on Tuesday July 6th, her husband told her he would leave the next day for an overnight trip to Mbarara to investigate reports of a massacre at Mbarara barracks in late June. On the morning of Wednesday July 7th, her husband hastily threw a few toilet articles in an attaché case. There was no room for an extra set of clothing and he did not take his wallet or passport with him. His final words were, "See you tomorrow." In her statement she wrote:

> "As the wife of a journalist I was accustomed to his frequent delays on trips, and there were times he was unable to give me an exact date for his return, but once he committed himself he would always either telephone or send a telegram to inform me of any change. When my husband failed to return by Thursday evening I voiced my concern to a journalist friend and an American Embassy official. On Friday evening, July 9th, when my husband was not back to attend a reception in honor of the new American Charge d'affaires and a reception given by the Canadian High Commissioner, I was certain he was no longer free to move about as he wished.
>
> From Friday July 9th through Monday, July 12th, I contacted a number of people to aid me in the search for my husband. I contacted journalist friends of the Western Press both in Kampala and Nairobi; I spoke to the White Fathers Missionaries near Mbarara; I called the Agip Motel at Mbarara and Securicor in Masaka. On Monday morning, July 12th, I reported all I knew about my husband's movements to the American Embassy together with a photograph and a personal description. I made arrangements for a missing person's announcement on radio and television.
>
> On Friday evening, July 23rd, my husband's cousin, Peter W. Stroh arrived in Kampala to be of assistance to me and my children and

to help make inquiries into my husband's disappearance. All leads having proved futile, we decided nothing further was to be gained by our presence in Uganda. We left Kampala for home in Michigan on Thursday, July 29, 1971."

German-born, Mrs. Stroh who had a young son and infant daughter to care for, did all she could have—calling all the right people and taking aggressive, appropriate action. Declassified U.S. State Department documents indicate she was "understandably distraught" and often angry that American and Ugandan officials were not doing more to find her husband and those responsible. In particular, she:

"felt Embassy personnel could and should have done much more in the early stages to find out what happened to her husband. She claimed she obtained much more information on her own than from the Embassy and had given the Embassy many leads. She spoke of the outstanding support she received from the local press corps and indicated she might have to turn to the American press if she was not satisfied U.S. Government officials were doing all that was possible."

While the Department of State reacted immediately to the sudden disappearances by calling an emergency country team meeting and restricting movement of American personnel outside of Kampala, the Embassy did not share with her evidence it had uncovered in the first five days after the disappearances—that two whites were being held at the barracks and Lt. Col. Ali Fadhul had been seen driving Stroh's car—due to the necessity of protecting sources and to keep from arousing media attention which might have panicked Fadhul into killing the two men, if they were still alive.

Embassy officials did not investigate Mrs. Stroh's leads because they had already determined through their own investigation Stroh had been arrested at the barracks and hence their job "was not to determine where he was but to get him out alive"—again, "if he was still alive." Mrs. Stroh told agency officials she believed Amin, who was at Mbarara barracks when her husband and my father first appeared, must have known the two men were being held in custody. Remarkably, the Embassy disagreed with her, instead maintaining Amin was somehow unaware of the presence of the two white men at the barracks—one of whom (Stroh) the General openly admitted was "his friend."

Said the Embassy:

"For understandable reasons, Mrs. Stroh approached the problem as if the central concern of the Government of Uganda was her husband. In fact, the central concern was the rapidly deteriorating security situation revolving around the Acholi and Langi tribes. It is highly unlikely in this period that the Government of Uganda was mainly concerned with two American citizens. We realize this is obviously extremely difficult for Mrs. Stroh to accept.

She should be made to understand that in view of the nature of our sources the Embassy could not reveal to her in the first five days matters which we were actively pursuing. Moreover, as our investigation continues, we still face precisely the same problem with regard to sources. While Mrs. Stroh may be critical of the U.S. Government's handling of the matter, she should be reminded that despite accepted principles of international law which require a receiving state to allow consul of a sending state to see and communicate with its citizens detained by the receiving state without unreasonable delay—a principle clearly stated in Article 36, Vienna Convention of which the U.S. is a party, Uganda is not a party to the Convention. Thus, immediate consular access to her husband and Siedle is not assured."

Once she returned to the U.S., Mrs. Stroh claimed the whole affair preyed on her mind much more than when she was in Kampala where she kept occupied and was able to do something about the situation. Back in Michigan, she had to rely on others for information and action and nothing seemed to be happening soon enough, she said. She told agency officials unless she heard something more definite soon, her only hope would be to go to the news media.

Approximately ten years after the murders, when I was in law school, I wrote to and then spoke with her by telephone. Her voice was shaky as it was still very difficult for her to talk about the tragedy. Gerta left Uganda on July 29, 1971, never to return and died in California of cancer approximately 15 years later. Did she feel she and the government officials involved had done all they could have and should have? While I do not know for certain, I do not believe Gerta ever found peace about the death of her husband in her lifetime.

Peter Stroh told me Nicholas' daughter Kristina lived in Manhattan where she was working as an actress. While I had never thought of reaching out to her over the years, since she and I were both living in the same city at the time, I asked to meet her. We shared something in common—all our lives we had been known as "the kids whose fathers were murdered in Africa by Idi Amin." Peter asked Kristina whether she would like to meet with me and when she agreed, gave me her telephone number. So, when I called, she was not surprised. Our initial conversation was awkward, carefully slow, and sensitively deliberate. She already had plans for the evening I proposed to meet for dinner but said she could break them. She too seemed to feel it was important for us to meet. I chose a cozy neighborhood restaurant where I was friends with the chef and often took clients. I wanted to ensure we would not be interrupted or rushed through our meal. We needed time to ask every question we ever had over the decades—questions that the other might be able to answer.

What would happen when I connected with the daughter of the other man who was killed with my father 27 years later, I wondered. Would our meeting open old poorly healed wounds, or conjure up the anguished spirits of our fathers?

After World War I—one of the deadliest conflicts in the history of the human race in which over 16 million people died—a staggering percentage, perhaps 30 percent of the dead, were never found. Their families and loved ones had to accept these soldiers would never return, even though there were no bodies to confirm they were indeed dead. Following the War, spiritualism rose in popularity as many people sought to communicate with those who had died through séances. While communication with the dead through séances may seem far-fetched, few would dispute that when we get together with others who share our grief for a loved one and collectively remember the deceased, it is possible to experience, to some degree, their presence.

Kristina had a kind, honest face and although she said she struggled with weight, she was not heavy. After I introduced myself, as we sat down, she mentioned I had pronounced my last name differently than she had pronounced it over the years when she repeated the story about how her father and another man, Robert Siedle, were murdered in Africa. My last name had always been part of her life's story, from the day she could first tell it. She had learned to pronounce Siedle, which is German, properly from her mother. I, on the other hand, pronounced my last name in a manner that was easy for Americans to say. Kristina never knew her father, she confessed, since she was six months old when he disappeared and had no memories of Uganda.

"What was it like there?' she asked, "Was it a wild jungle?"

"Not at all," I laughed, "The university campus where our families lived was not remotely jungle-like. At that time, in the late 1960s and early 1970s, it was very much like any tropical university campus."

I described living conditions in Uganda and told her what my life there with my father had been like. She said her mother had struggled to raise her and her brother on her own, never re-marrying and had died a when Kristina was 16. She had taken a year off from school to care for her mother in the final year of her illness.

Her older brother had never shared any memories of her father; her mother and the extended Stroh family did not speak of Nicholas often, she said.

While it was terribly important to me to have all my questions about my father answered at this point in my life, Kristina was 15 years younger and did not seem to have the need to dive deeply into her father's death. Perhaps she would seek answers later in her life—perhaps she never would. People grieve differently.

Relations between two governments were involved—Uganda and the United States—and neither country investigated the disappearances of the two men as if they were searching for a loved one. Rather, a diplomatic accommodation had to be reached. Uganda's President had to be permitted to save face internationally for the murders he had ordered or committed. An attempt by the Army to hide the Mbarara massacre had failed—backfired—and Amin's brutality was exposed to the world. Still, America needed to maintain a positive relationship with Uganda for trade and security reasons. Amin needed to be persuaded to make a token payment of reparations—without admitting guilt—which would serve as proof the U.S. government was responsive to the families of its citizens abroad, including one very wealthy and influential family.

According to declassified State Department documents, the agency rightly assumed that my family was much more interested in cash compensation than the question of responsibility at the time. The wealthy Stroh family on the other hand, was at least initially focused on prosecuting those responsible. But the truth about what happened to the two men, exactly how they met their deaths, when, where and by whose hand, was largely irrelevant to the resolution. Everyone knew Amin was ultimately responsible and an admission of guilt by a despotic foreign sovereign for murders committed in his own country was never going to happen.

The single person who possibly fought for the victims as exhaustively as their families would have, was Justice Jones.

Jones was the man-in-the-middle of the international controversy—a Welshman whose homeland was not directly involved in the fight.

He was so pessimistic the Ugandan Commission would be able to arrive at a meaningful conclusion, due to the rampant destruction of evidence, killing and intimidation of potential witnesses and other Amin heavy-handedness that he pleaded with American officials for assistance. Upon instructions from Washington, the U.S. officials responded they could not participate in the investigation or hearings and could not provide evidence or witnesses.

As the American Ambassador to Uganda advised in a declassified State Department telegram:

"While occasional attendance by an Embassy officer at the sessions of the Jones Commission hearings in the capacity of an observer would be beneficial in demonstrating publicly the Embassy's interest in the proceedings, I believe there are other important considerations that suggest such attendance would be unwise. As the Department of State is aware from our regular reporting on the substance of these proceedings, the truth about what happened to Stroh and Siedle is beginning to be placed on the record through the efforts of Justice Jones. I believe we are now approaching the point where the Ugandan Government will become increasingly apprehensive that the final result of the Inquiry will place it in a very bad light. For us to now make a display of official interest in the proceedings themselves, as opposed to the final outcome, would add discomfort to the Government of Uganda and probably exacerbate bad feelings that seem likely to result from the Inquiry. Proceedings are being fully reported in the press and we, of course, have our own channel for receiving reports on everything that develops. The only purpose of attendance by an observer would thus be to make a public gesture with no substantive benefit.

I suggest we maintain our posture of aloofness from hearings, on the basis that we have requested the Ugandan Government to conduct an Inquiry into the disappearances and advise us of the result, and we await a reply from the Government when it has completed the necessary investigations."

While Justice Jones stopped short of naming those responsible for the murders in his Report, he risked his own life and ended his career pursuing justice on behalf of the families and upholding the rule of law in Uganda.

CHAPTER 27

SOMETIMES THE VERY BEST YOU CAN DO IS SURVIVE

I met Major Allichema—the next to last soldier General Muntu had arranged for me to interview—late Sunday afternoon downstairs in the lobby of the Sheraton. He apologized for not being able to meet earlier in the day but his wife, he said, had some "psychiatric problems." As I sat down on a chair facing him in the crowded room, he looked at me intently, then nervously peered around to the right and left behind him.

"Is it safe to talk here?" he asked.

"Yes, it's safe," I said, "but we can go anywhere you like to talk. If it's too crowded here, we can go someplace quieter."

It was cool and sunny, so I suggested we sit outside. He agreed outside would be better and chose a table at the patio restaurant where he could sit with his back to the wall and observe anyone who approached us.

It was understandable Allichema would ask about safety. I was reminded of a 1974 study I had read by the International Commission of Jurists in Geneva entitled, "*Violations of Human Rights and the Rule of Law in Uganda*" which stated in its preface that a factor obscuring the scale of the internal repression and loss of life among the African population in Uganda was "… the great reluctance of Ugandans, even though living abroad in exile, to make public statements about these events for fear of reprisal action against their families or friends in Uganda." According to the ICJ, without exception all eyewitnesses to violations it had spoken to had "demanded that their names and identities remain strictly confidential. We are satisfied that it is the universal fear of reprisals which is responsible for this reticence."

Also, Allichema knew that all of the eyewitnesses to the murder of my father and Stroh, except Tibihika (who was forced to flee the country) and Ali Fadhul (who was in prison on death row) had been killed.

Allichema began by saying General Muntu had asked him to speak with me because he had been at Mbarara barracks at the time my father and Stroh had been killed. He was not reluctant to speak with me because he, like me, was a victim of what happened in Mbarara—as he would more fully explain. The events at the barracks on June 22, 1971 were so horrible that ever since that fateful day he had been unable to work on the anniversary. He then paused for a moment and asked somewhat awkwardly, "Have we gotten started yet with the interview?"

"Yes," I said even though I wasn't sure what he was getting at or what I was doing for that matter. "Would you mind if I took notes?"

"No, not at all, I assumed you would," he said. As he later revealed, Allichema was used to being interviewed by foreign reporters and having them take notes as he spoke.

He was a tall, thin, healthy-looking man who appeared to be in his early 50s. He had a clean-shaven angular face and a full mouth with big, healthy white teeth. He said he was one year away from retirement. He had served in the Ugandan Army for decades through political upheavals, military coups, tribal massacres and endless bloodletting. He was a member of the old guard—career military trained by the British. He was proud of his knowledge of proper military procedure and was well-spoken. His eyes were lively as he talked, perhaps a bit nervous. The thick-lens oversized black frame prescription eyeglasses he wore reminded me of rock and roller Buddy Holly, or a nerdy engineer. He spoke like an engineer in a methodical, clear manner. It was apparent he took very seriously his obligation to provide me with a comprehensive account of what happened. If he subsequently remembered something he should have told me earlier, he would stop talking about the current matter and refer back. From Allichema I would receive the most complete explanation of what happened at the barracks I had ever heard.

"Over the years, the Mbarara incident has been referred to in articles alternatively as a massacre and an attempted mutiny. Which was it?" I asked.

"It was, in fact, both," stated Allichema much to my surprise.

The chain of command at the barracks at the time was as follows: Lt. Col. Ali Fadhul was the Commanding Officer; second in command, never referred to in any of the accounts, was Major Alai. Alai died driving back to Mbarara drunk from a wedding days before the killings. Major Juma, third in command, was the only one of the three senior officers not newly commissioned. He had been promoted by Amin for having assisted in the military coup.

Following the coup, Amin rewarded many men who had been helpful to him by making them officers in the Ugandan Army. Uneducated, unskilled and completely lacking relevant military experience, these men had to be trained. Career officers, like Allichema, naturally resented these men and had little respect for their capabilities. All the newly commissioned officers sent to Mbarara for training were Muslim, as was Amin.

Major Juma enlisted in the Army in 1967. Allichema pointed out with disgust Juma was a taxi driver before Amin promoted him to Major.

"Juma should never have been given any responsibilities beyond being a taxi driver," he said.

Lt. Col. Ali Fadhul, the Commanding Officer, was not present when Stroh first arrived, and also was not at the barracks when the killings occurred. Major Juma, according to Allichema, was the officer in command at the time of the killings and gave the order to incarcerate my father and Stroh.

While Allichema maintained Fadhul bore no responsibility for the killings, he had no fondness or respect for the man—indeed, he held Fadhul responsible for many other deaths, including his own beating.

On June 21st, Allichema, who was a musical band director in the Army, drove to Mbarara from an officer's wedding where he had been responsible for the musical arrangements. He stopped along the way to arrange the burial of Major Alai who had been second in command at Mbarara before he was killed driving drunk. Allichema arrived at the barracks on June 22nd at 7 a.m.

Early that morning, as many as 2,000 soldiers were awakened and summoned to appear on the parade ground by Amin's group of newly commissioned officers. While these officers had been sent to Mbarara for training, they had ideas of their own. Once the soldiers had assembled, some of the newly commissioned officers, including Ali Fadhul, began shouting out names of soldiers to be annihilated from a list. The soldiers whose names were called were kicked and beaten to death by fists and with pieces of firewood. Initially 300 soldiers belonging to the Acholi and Langi tribes were beaten to death but the bloodbath did not stop once all the Acholi and Langi tribesmen were dead. Ali Fadhul and the other officers called out the names of other soldiers to be murdered. After a while, the butchery moved from the parade ground to other areas in the garrison. Soldiers to be slain were now taken to the Orderly Room, the group of administrative offices where the most senior staff had their offices.

As the bloodshed continued, the remaining seasoned soldiers began to object to killing the new victims and resist the instructions shouted by Amin's henchmen. Around this time Allichema himself was singled out and attacked in Ali Fadhul's office.

Allichema described to me what was going through his head as he was being beaten.

"The newly-commissioned officers who kept striking me—blow after blow—did not know I had my loaded pistol holstered under the extra-long Army jacket I was wearing. I could have pulled the gun out and blasted Fadhul at any time. I desperately wanted to kill him but I knew if I did, my entire family, including my wife and children would be killed in retaliation.

I promise you, if I had been a single man without a family to worry about, I would have shot him dead on the spot!"

But the seasoned commandos eventually rallied to his defense and saved him from a bloody death. From that moment on though, he knew Amin's new guard could never be trusted.

Allichema had been viciously assaulted but could not fight back. He had the power to kill his attackers but restrained himself to protect his family—hardly a satisfying response to the madness swirling around him. He did what he had to do to survive. But when Allichema spoke of the incident after all these years, it was apparent he wasn't proud of his passivity—he was deeply ashamed. Perhaps he felt ashamed he had readily joined in the beating of others, or hadn't anticipated his own beating, or hadn't found a better response than helpless submission to the pummeling. The truth is there was nothing more he could have done. Even a trained soldier—with a loaded gun—was helpless that horrific day.

A fellow survivor, I shared his guilt and shame. What could I, a teenager thousands of miles away, have done to prevent my father's murder? The painful, unsatisfactory truth was: Nothing.

This discussion between us, two grown men—victims of the same massacre—who survived with wounded pride and shattered senses of self-determination, was comforting to both of us, I believe. We were men who had learned we could never have all the answers, never fully protect our loved ones, or win every battle against our foes.

Sometimes the very best you can do is survive.

What began as a massacre in the morning, turned into a mutiny by afternoon—500 lives later. The seasoned soldiers stopped following the orders of Amin's loyalists and began chasing them away. After Amin's cronies were run out of the camp, the Army intelligence officers who remained began supervising collection of the hundreds of corpses. The bodies were loaded onto trucks and dumped along the road between the towns of Mbarara and Masaka.

To be sure, I had already heard about this massive dumping of cadavers from Tibihika and the other soldiers I interviewed in Mbarara. But as Allichema again recited the violence to me, I had a startling realization.

For the first time it occurred to me that when my father and Stroh arrived a few weeks after the June 22nd massacre—in early July—many of these hundreds of bodies *would have still been visible*. Not a single body had been buried.

Did my father and Stroh see piles of flesh rotting on shattered bones? Each man had brought a camera. Did they photograph the dead? What did they feel when the saw the decaying remains of so many bludgeoned soldiers? Even if they had been told hundreds had been killed, they still probably wouldn't have been prepared to see all the bodies exposed. The reality of the massacre must have been far more gruesome than they anticipated.

Then more astonishing pieces to this puzzle suddenly started to fall into place in my mind:

Newsweek's Andrew Jaffe had written within weeks of the disappearances, on August 2, 1971, that after hearing reports of hundreds of officers and men massacred at the barracks, Stroh and my father headed for the Mbarara barracks, a three hours' drive from the capital. "By nightfall, he (Stroh) had managed to meet secretly with soldiers who told him they had seen bodies carted away by trucks following a mass execution. Stroh now had another big story. But this time he had done his job too well and learned too much."

According to *Newsweek*, in the days following the disappearances as U.S. Embassy officials in Kampala vainly sought to discover what had befallen the two men, Jaffe reportedly traveled to Mbarara and succeeded in tracing their movements.

The article went on to state that after a meeting with U.S. Ambassador Clyde Ferguson, Amin agreed to fly to Mbarara with a U.S. consular officer for an on-scene investigation into the disappearances.

Yet transcripts of the Commission hearings months later stated the reason Stroh and my father drove to Mbarara and went to the barracks was *unclear*. Whether *anyone* had been killed at the barracks before their arrival was *unknown*. Perhaps Stroh was interested in reports of fighting along the Uganda-Tanzania border, or an "alleged massacre" in the Barracks.

Jones stated in the Commission of Inquiry Report that he did not know the motives anyone in Mbarara might have had to kill my father and Stroh.

Of course, Jones *knew exactly* what my father and Stroh had "stumbled onto" before the Inquiry even began—it was reported in *Newsweek* within days! In addition to the trip Amin and a U.S consular officer made to Mbarara for an investigation immediately following the disappearances, Jones himself had toured the barracks nine months later—when many of the 500 bodies presumably would still have been visible. American officials, with whom Jones was secretly in constant contact, were also fully aware of the massacre.

Tibihika *never once* mentioned any massacre in his affidavit.

Not *one word* in the Commission of Inquiry Report about 500 murders and 500 rotting bodies!

Had Jones not strategically "overlooked" the 500 bodies, the motives for my father and Stroh's visit to the barracks would have been obvious, as would the motives of the murderers.

How do you investigate the murder of two men without mentioning they disappeared while investigating the murder of 500 others? Yet that's precisely what Jones, the Americans and the Commission of Inquiry were forced to do. They could not openly accuse Amin—the sovereign—of any murder he had committed within the country.

Major Allichema went on to say that around 5 p.m. on the day of the massacre Amin arrived in Mbarara by helicopter from Kampala. News of the massacre and mutiny had reached him in Kampala and he had come to restore order. He apologized to the remaining seasoned soldiers at the barracks and assured them his only intention had been to have his newly commissioned officers trained at the barracks, not to have them destabilize the situation. The massacre had been a stupid mistake, Amin admitted. In the years to come many, many more people would be killed "by mistake" according to Amin and his cronies, including Allichema's own brother, he told me.

Amin did not stay long in Mbarara—he sensed he was not safe there. The surviving soldiers had lost confidence in him and his newly commissioned officers. Amin could neither control the remaining soldiers nor could the soldiers control Amin. The soldiers knew their new leader's incompetence would cost many more lives. Sometime after the massacre, all the newly commissioned officers, including Fadhul, were transferred to Kampala by Amin for a crash course and later sent to Israel for training.

Allichema then began to speak of my father and Stroh. When Stroh came to the garrison on the morning of July 9th, he was taken to the Orderly Room to meet with Major Juma. Juma had an angry exchange of words with Stroh and ordered him to be locked-up in the Quarter Guard. Stroh must have been beaten nearby in the morning because when he was next seen at lunch time his clothes were already muddied as two military policemen forced him to run with his hands above his head toward the Orderly Room and into Juma's office. When he was beaten in the morning, Stroh must have warned his attackers that he had not come alone to Mbarara—his travelling companion back at the Rest house would be a witness against them.

Allichema was the first person I interviewed who claimed to know my father had been brought to the barracks from the Rest House and placed in the same cell with Stroh in the lower level of the building. The lower-level cells, he explained, were out-of-view from the main road leading into the garrison. Routine disciplinary problems were housed upstairs in the lock-up—audible, if not fully visible, from the road. The two were held in the single cell together for three or four days.

Allichema's account conflicted with Tibihika's claim the two men were kept in separate cells and killed shortly after imprisonment, but was consistent with my own intuition and beliefs. Allichema's information came, he said, from a Karamojong tribesman—a military policeman who was guarding the two men daily. This guard, Sergeant Jacko, would confide to Allichema each evening when they met for dinner in the Officers' Mess that he did not agree with the treatment my father and Stroh were receiving. The two white men were being beaten with clubs and iron bars but would not have been cut in the cell for fear their blood would be found. My father and Stroh were denied food. Allichema solemnly observed one of the worst punishments you can inflict on a man who is used to eating two or three meals a day is to deny him food.

The bodies of the two men were found by road workers, partially buried under a pile of dirt used to build a road near an airfield outside of Mbarara, who in turn reported the finding to the Army.

Allichema, like Tibihika, incongruously maintained Ali Fadhul was not responsible for the killings even though—if the two men were held several days in the Quarter Guard lock-up, as Allichema claimed—Fadhul must at least have been aware of and permitted the torture to continue, as well as been present at the barracks when the final order to kill was issued. Both Allichema and Tibihika blamed Major Juma who was conveniently, now dead.

Allichema said the Orderly Room personnel, under Juma's direction, took the bodies of the two men 60 miles away and burned them. When I brought to his attention that his account of events conflicted with Tibihika who told me he collected the bodies and then burned them behind the Officer's Mess, Allichema said it would have made no sense for officers who were attempting a cover-up to bring the bodies back to the barracks to burn them. Bringing the bodies back for burning would have been riskier than leaving them where they were. I agreed.

And that was all Allichema knew about my father and Stroh's murder.

He went on to tell me that he and other seasoned soldiers in Mbarara at the time were regularly feeding information to David Martin, a London Observer reporter who later published a book about Amin in 1974 entitled, General Amin detailing the scale and nature of the atrocities committed since Amin overthrew Obote in early 1971. He praised Martin for the accuracy of his reporting and then laughed as he observed that since Martin's information had come directly from the soldiers, it should have been accurate. Allichema said that because of his frequent interviews with Martin, he was comfortable being interviewed by me.

Nevertheless, in his book, Martin's account of the Mbarara massacre differs in many respects from what I learned from Allichema. Martin wrote members of the Acholi and Langi tribes were separated from other troops on the square and then were herded into lorries and driven to a nearby ranch where their throats were cut. Martin's report differs as to the location where the killings took place and the method of killing. His account of the killing of my father and Stroh is based upon what Tibihika told him: the two men were killed the same day they were captured—when Ali Fadhul was away.

Allichema did not have the power to stop Amin's evil; nevertheless, he had not blindly, silently followed orders. He gave incriminating information to the international press and, at great personal risk to himself and his family, told the world the truth about what was happening in Uganda. The international community did not respond to Ugandan voices crying out for help and Amin continued in power, killing hundreds of thousands over time. But Allichema had done all he could.

I had a copy of the Commission of Inquiry report spread open on the table as we talked, referring to it on occasion. Toward the end of the interview, Allichema asked to look over the document as he had never seen it before. Upon closer examination, he noticed Tibihika had stated a Motor Transport Sergeant Major Bindwa had been one of three men who accompanied him on the journey to destroy Stroh's car. Allichema said Bindwa was an old friend and next-door neighbor at the time of the massacre. He had no idea Bindwa had been involved in destroying Stroh's car and was surprised Bindwa had never mentioned it to him. As he reflected further, he suspected Bindwa had tried to save his life by hinting he should not go to the parade grounds when he arrived at his home in Mbarara on the morning of June 22nd. Allichema realized Bindwa had likely been privy to lots of information he had not. If Bindwa were still alive, Allichema would be able to learn more from him about the probable location of my father and Stroh's remains. But, as he thought more about Bindwa's whereabouts, he recalled Bindwa, like many of the soldiers closely associated with Amin, had been involved in border fighting and might be dead or a fugitive.

I walked Allichema out the main entrance of the Sheraton and handed him some money, I said, for a taxi home. But I suspected he would find a better use for the money—perhaps he would use it to buy a nice dinner for his ailing wife and family.

I never asked Allichema about his own actions that day in Mbarara as he stood on the parade grounds and the names of soldiers to be killed were shouted out. How many men had he clubbed to death before he was beaten? I don't judge him for what he may have done. How do you blame someone who, in the middle of a bloodbath, terrified, does what he believes he has to do—what he is told he must do—to survive?

For a few hours on a Sunday afternoon—his day off—Allichema shared with me, exclusively for my benefit, memories of the Mbarara massacre and mutiny he had witnessed, participated in and been a victim of, which were still painful for him to recount. I was grateful to him.

Whatever guilt he may have had for his actions on June 22, 1971, if any, was between him and his God.

CHAPTER 28

INTERVIEW WITH A MURDERER

I t was my last day in Uganda.

General Muntu had arranged for me to meet with the Commissioner of Prisons in the morning, and then, with an escort from his office, to go on to interview Lt. Col. Ali Fadhul at Luzira Maximum Security Prison where he had been held on Death Row for the past twenty years.

Fadhul claimed to be of the Muslim faith which, General Muntu had warned me at our earlier meeting, was probably not helpful to my cause.

"Christians are often 'saved,' or repent in prison," he explained. "Muslims seldom do because they do not have such a concept in their religion. If you are Muslim, you are 'chosen' and do not need saving."

The General's statement intrigued me. Since I knew little of the Islamic faith, despite my mother's religious heritage, I asked him to elaborate.

"The notion of original sin and salvation are vastly different in Christianity and Islam. In Islam, humans are born free of sin. They are on earth as a result of Adam and Eve, but this does not mean that all their children bear the burden of their mistakes. In Christianity, there is the belief that the incarnation and death of Jesus is the only path to salvation. For God to forgive our sins, there must be sacrifice. Someone must pay for the sin—God cannot simply forgive us. In Islam, everyone is born in a state of purity but sins committed during their lifetimes may corrupt them. Sins have consequences, but they are not inherited. Muslims are in this world as a result of Adam and Eve's eating from the tree, but are not burdened by their original sin."

Notions of "original sin" aside, it was well-known Fadhul had engaged in sinful acts countless times during his lifetime. He had been sitting on Death Row for decades, convicted of only one of the many murders he had ordered or committed with his own hands. In Islam, murder is a major sin but sincere repentance—called "tauba" or "tawbah"—can wipe away a person's sins, forever and completely. It involves showing genuine remorse, praying for God's mercy and forgiveness, and avoiding that sin in the future.

Lastly, mentioned Muntu, "Under Islamic law, victims of crime have a say in how the perpetrator is to be punished. While Islamic law generally calls for murderers to face the death penalty, the victim's heirs may choose to excuse the murderer from the death penalty in exchange for monetary damages. The murderer will still be sentenced by a judge, possibly to a lengthy prison term, but the death penalty will not be imposed. This principle, known as "diyyah," or "blood money" in English, is more appropriately referred to as "victim's compensation" and is most commonly associated with death penalty cases."

In the final analysis, it didn't seem Muntu's observations about the differences between Christianity and Islam regarding sin—if true—made it more or less likely murderers of either faith would seek to repent or ask forgiveness. So, there was still a faint hope Fadhul would show remorse, seize this opportunity for repentance for the numerous gory murders he had either committed, was vicariously responsible for (as the commanding officer under principles of military law) or, at a minimum, covered-up.

Albert, now looking like an Army Major smartly dressed in his uniform picked me up at the Sheraton. We first met with the Commissioner of Prisons, a soft-spoken, thoughtful older man who was in no hurry to send us on our way. He took the time to tell me he recalled hearing about my father's murder and was very sorry for my loss. He lamented that period in the history of Uganda when torture and murder were commonplace. What a weighty, dark body of knowledge this man must possess, I thought. His job was to know the whereabouts and status of tens of thousands of Ugandan prisoners living in hellish conditions. Worse still, given his age, I assumed he must have been knowledgeable about happenings in Uganda's prisons over the decades since independence. What nightmares he must have every night! The Commissioner knew Fadhul personally and said Fadhul would be suspicious, possibly wary talking to me. The Commissioner assigned one of his senior officers to accompany us to the prison.

As we passed through Luzira's gates, I was surprised to see the prison was in far better structural condition than the soldiers' barracks at Mbarara. Unlike the barracks, it seemed someone was maintaining these premises— perhaps the prisoners themselves—and there was no indication of past bombings or shootings. While, from outside, it looked like the prisoners were living in better facilities than the Ugandan Army and their families, the warden complained the prison population was far greater than the prison was designed to hold. There were often more than 40 inmates crammed into bare, windowless concrete cells measuring just 26 by 26 feet, he said.

It was suggested I meet Fadhul with only the warden present—excluding the Army and Prisons officers—to increase the likelihood he would believe whatever he told me would not result in further official action against him. The warden mentioned Fadhul had requested an interpreter because he did not speak English well and was more comfortable speaking in Swahili. The warden sat at his desk and I sat in one of the three chairs in front of it.

Fadhul was a large man, slightly overweight in face and belly with small, beady closely-set bloodshot eyes. He removed his slippers before he entered the warden's office. He was confident as he leisurely strolled through the doorway barefoot. Despite having spent decades helplessly locked away, he acted as if he was in control of his fate—like he owned the place. He appeared to be physically powerful but not muscular. Arduous physical labor was not required of him at the prison, it seemed. He wore a yellow, short-sleeve cotton shirt, matching pants and a close-fitting Muslim prayer cap, or "taqiyah."

"As-salamu alaikum," I said greeting him in traditional Muslim fashion, to which he responded, "Wa alaikum assalaam." I immediately tried to establish a rapport with him by explaining my mother was Muslim and that my Muslim name was Ahmed Khan. He coldly commented mine was an Indian Muslim name. In that moment I realized that my Indian Muslim heritage was not going to be helpful in talking to him given the animosity that existed between African and Indian Muslims in Uganda.

While Fadhul seemed to understand and speak English well, after I explained who I was and what I wanted to talk about, he requested the interpreter join us, given, he said, the important nature of our discussion. A young interpreter was asked to come into the room.

Wily Fadhul needed no interpreter.

In fact, he spoke English better than the interpreter and periodically corrected the interpreter's translation of his Swahili. He also reminded the interpreter to speak to me in English, not Swahili, when the interpreter got confused. Fadhul soon realized I spoke enough Swahili to potentially eliminate any buffer or delay he might have hoped the interposition of an interpreter would create. I too corrected the interpreter, letting it be known I spoke Swahili. The superfluous interpreter quickly receded into the background as Fadhul and I spoke to each other directly in English.

Fadhul began his account by saying he was not at the barracks at the time the killings took place. He said he was far away in Kampala at the time. (The Commission of Inquiry had concluded he was in Masaka on the 7th and 8th of July at a conference.) When he returned to the barracks, he was told three journalists had been imprisoned and subsequently handed into the custody of a team from Amin's State Research Bureau that had been sent from Kampala with appropriate documentation.

I had read plenty of official reports about the State Research Bureau (SRB) established by Amin immediately after the coup with initial technical assistance from Israel. Its responsibilities were to gather military intelligence and conduct counterintelligence.

Together with the Public Safety Unit (PSU), the SRB terrorized local populations. Over time the SRB and PSU expanded to include about 15,000 people, many of whom acted as informers on fellow citizens.

In early 1972, Amin ejected Israeli technicians from Uganda and agents from the Soviet Union were brought in to replace them. They subsequently instructed SRB personnel in the methods of the KGB and many were sent to the Soviet Union for specialized training. In 1978, Amin announced to the world he had invited the Palestinian Liberation Organization to help him organize the SRB.

"They are even better trained than the CIA or congressmen," Amin boasted. "Their work will be very important and if they are needed by other countries, I will lend them. This group is going to be headed by me directly. It will be known as the SSS-Amin Operation."

Empowered by a sweeping decree which gave state agents wide latitude, the SRB tortured and executed many suspected dissidents over the Amin years, provoking international outrage. For its role in state repression and killings, the SRB came to be known in Uganda as the "State Research Butchery."

Fadhul said that was all he knew of what happened to the two men. The notoriously cruel and highly secretive State Research Bureau took them away. If Fadhul was telling the truth, then presumably the Israelis—who were still advising the SRB throughout 1971, as well as sharing information with American officials—would have known the whereabouts and fate of the two men and told American officials. None of the declassified records I reviewed indicated such but, then again, most of the records were not provided to me by the Department of State or the CIA and remain classified for national security reasons even today.

There was a grain of truth in Fadhul's account—as mentioned earlier, Amin's intelligence unit had reportedly been closely monitoring Stroh for espionage quite some time.

When I asked who the third journalist was, Fadhul did not have a clear answer. All I could gather was the third person may have been African. Had there been a third man who was a journalist? An anonymous African whose disappearance had never been noted or investigated—possibly to protect him?

The Commission on Inquiry had established that while Fadhul was not at the barracks when Stroh first went to see him on July 7, by his own admission he was at the barracks all day July 9. Had the killings taken place that day, Fadhul would have had to know since the barracks were not that large—unless the killings happened during the lunch hour and Fadhul had gone home for lunch. By afternoon, Justice Jones reasoned, Fadhul certainly had learned of the killings inasmuch as he chastised Major Juma for driving Stroh's car in plain view.

At a minimum, the Justice concluded, Fadhul clearly took charge of the botched cover-up operation.

I told Fadhul of my prior meeting with Tibihika in Mbarara and that he had told me Fadhul would have answers to my questions about my father and Stroh. Fadhul seemed mildly annoyed at Tibihika for suggesting he knew more about the killings but said the two were close friends. He had, in fact, helped Tibihika flee to Tanzania, he said.

Why would Fadhul, an Amin loyalist (and distant relative), have helped Tibihika desert from the Ugandan Army, only to then testify against Amin and the Army in the Inquiry, I wondered? Why would Fadhul tell the Commission that even though Tibihika had deserted, Fadhul still considered him an officer in the Ugandan Army?

Still, Tibihika had testified Fadhul was not involved in the killings and Fadhul displayed no animosity toward Tibihika. It seemed the two had decades earlier agreed to support one another. Fadhul said the only person who would know exactly what happened was Sergeant Jacko, the Karamojong tribesman who had supervised the incarceration of the two men in the Quarter Guard. I should also contact Major Juma, said Fadhul.

But the Commission of Inquiry had concluded all the men who had been guarding my father and Stroh had been killed within weeks of the murders by Amin loyalists—killings Fadhul must have known about and probably personally ordered.

"Major Juma is dead," I said, "I'm told he died about a year ago."

"Really? I hadn't heard that. But I've been in this prison for so many years I don't know what happened to many of the people I once knew."

For a brief moment I almost felt sorry for him being isolated in prison for so long. But then I didn't believe he truly was. He was really more like an organized crime boss who, even in prison, seemed to have his ugly tentacles stretched out into the community. He had no fear of prison guards or the warden and they all seemed to respect him. It was well known he had made multiple pleas to the Museveni government for clemency and no one was ruling out the possibility.

Fadhul then tried to appeal to me or perhaps the warden who was listening to our conversation.

"I too am a father," he said. "I would help you if I could but I really don't know anything more. Believe me."

I was annoyed, tired and near the end of my journey—I would be leaving Uganda in a few hours.

Declassified telegrams I obtained from the U.S. Department of State raised additional questions about Fadhul and his role in the murders.

Initially, Justice Jones and Ambassador Ferguson were convinced Fadhul, who was loyal to Amin and had already killed thousands of hostile tribesmen on Amin's orders following the coup, would be protected by Amin under any circumstances. Fadhul's defiant attitude toward the Commission indicated he believed he was beyond its reach. But, as the Inquiry progressed over time, Jones told Ferguson he believed "Amin was preparing let full responsibility fall on Ali if that is what evidence calls for."

"A marked change has taken place in Col. Ali Fadhul," said Jones at one point. "He now appears to be genuinely frightened instead of his usual arrogant self. This may be because, for reasons unrelated to the Inquiry, General Amin is prepared to throw Ali Fadhul to the wolves."

What "reasons unrelated to the Inquiry" may have made Amin willing or eager to place blame on Fadhul? At one point in time American intelligence had concluded:

> "Amin was furious with his officers because they assured him last summer that all evidence relating to the killings had been disposed of and there was no possibility of an inquiry turning anything up. The officers are in turn angry that they are being blamed by Amin for having botched the job."

According to other declassified State Department telegrams, three Ugandan Army colonels had reportedly called on Amin and urged him to have Fadhul "take the rap" for the murders. "These colonels are themselves guilty of innumerable murders in the past year and hope Ali Fadhul can be made to assume blame for everyone," said agency officials.

On the other hand, a different group of colonels were rumored to be supporting Fadhul and advising him to "tell all," i.e., to put the blame on Amin. Supposedly there had been a telephone call from Amin to Fadhul "telling him to 'do away' with the two Americans who had been pestering Simba battalion."

Justice Jones said "the finger pointed more at Major Juma than Col. Ali Fadhul." Nevertheless, he planned to discredit Fadhul in the hearings to such an extent that a number of people who had important testimony would be encouraged to come forward and testify before the Commission without fear of reprisal by Juma or Fadhul. Jones believed other residents of Mbarara who could "wrap up the case" would come forward—if and when Fadhul and Juma were "thrown to the dogs."

Ali Fadhul, for whatever reasons, never was "thrown to the wolves" or "the dogs" by Amin or the three Army colonels—at least not for my father and Stroh's murders—and he never did admit Amin had, at a minimum, ordered the murders. However, declassified documents reveal there were plenty of powerful people who wanted to put the blame on him for murders he committed (whether or not ordered by Amin), as well as others he may not have committed. Sixteen years later, in 1987—at age 48—his bloodthirstiness caught up with him and he landed in prison for a brazen murder he committed in public view.

This day at Luzira Prison in 1997—26 years after the murders—Fadhul had beaten me in his own pathetic way. I could not force him to tell me the truth. These freedoms he still had—to lie to me, to defy me—even on death row in maximum security. I was unable to conclusively establish whether he or Amin ordered the killings, or that he or Amin had actually committed the murders. But, as the Commanding Officer he had overall responsibility for whatever happened in Simba Battalion, including the responsibility to report the killings to the Commander-in-Chief, Amin—which he supposedly never did. Fadhul also clearly ordered the disposal and burning of the bodies and Stroh's car.

Whether he had committed and gotten away with the murders of my father and Stroh was unclear, yet he sat before me having already spent decades behind bars wasting away—fated to spend the rest of his life in this hellhole. This mass murderer with a well-deserved reputation for brutality, was helpless.

I, on the other hand, was not.

While I couldn't force Fadhul to admit anything, I had every reason to believe I could avenge my father's murder by having him killed in the prison—this very day. It would have been so... very... easy... to arrange.

But, as I said, knowing you can kill someone and walk away without consequences is very different from actually doing it.

I seriously considered killing Fadhul that day, but didn't. And my father, who strongly opposed capital punishment, wouldn't have wanted me to kill Fadhul or anyone else responsible for his murder. As far as I am concerned, Fadhul deserved to die and as the son of one of his murder victims, I had the right to kill him. Thankfully, I chose not to.

After applying for a presidential pardon on three separate occasions over the 22 long years he spent on death row in Luzira, Fadhul was finally pardoned by President Museveni and released from the prison in 2009, at age 70.

Asked by a reporter how life had been in Luzira, Fadhul replied, "there is no good prison in the world."

A free man, he had nowhere to go. He reportedly returned to his dilapidated, long-abandoned home to find it had been systematically vandalized. All the windows and doors of the house had been stolen over the years and only a brick wall surrounding the house remained delineating the estate that had once been. He was suffering from skin cancer, diabetes and ulcers—so poor he had to turn one of the windowless rooms in his house into his home. By 2010, a year after his release, he could no longer sit, eat, or walk on his own. He had to receive regular treatments by Nsambya Hospital and doctors hired by his family. Yet the elderly former soldier still had a few local supporters and family members who congratulated him for escaping the hangman's noose.

Idi Amin went into exile, first in Libya, then Iraq, and finally in Saudi Arabia following his overthrow at the hands of Tanzanian troops and Ugandan rebels in 1979. He died in 2003 at the age of 78, in Saudi Arabia where he had lived for years.

During the nearly quarter-century of his "soft" exile, no nation tried to bring Amin to justice. Human Rights Watch did once bring up Amin's case to the United Nations Commission on Human Rights, but to no avail. Under international law, any nation—including Saudi Arabia—could have and should have prosecuted him.

As Reed Brody, special counsel for prosecutions at Human Rights Watch, said, "If you kill one person, you go to jail; if you kill 20, you go to an institution for the insane; if you kill 20,000, you get political asylum." In 1999, when an Italian journalist asked Amin whether he felt remorse he replied, "No, only nostalgia."

Despite all of his atrocities, Amin was not killed but died from natural causes—kidney failure. Prior to his death, the family reportedly begged the Ugandan President to allow him to return to the country to spend the rest of his life there, but Yoweri Museveni declined the request saying Amin would be made to answer for his crimes of human rights abuses the moment he came back to Uganda. He was buried in Ruwais Cemetery in a simple grave, without any fanfare.

I walked freely out of the shadows of Luzira Prison that day in 1997, into the brilliant, nourishing sunlight. I had my personal freedom, my health, my wealth, my youth—a future before me where anything was possible.

Like the young Ugandan soldier handed a gun for his own use by Amin, I had everything I needed to go after—and take—whatever I wanted in life.

EPILOGUE

None of the clear-cut external goals I set for myself at the outset of my journey to Uganda were accomplished. I did not solve the mystery of my father's murder, definitively determining where, when, why, how or by whose hands he was killed. I was unable to locate and retrieve his remains.

But grieving the brutal murder of a parent is an internal, emotional process—as well as external—not defined by concrete goals. Complex bereavement, I have learned, is not linear but circular. Each time I revisit the murder of my father, no longer as a child but as an aging adult with a growing capacity to sort through factual evidence, analyze legal and diplomatic matters, as well as my emotions—including recalling painful memories—I grow in strength. I reconnect with and reclaim pieces of my past, redefining who I am and what the future may hold for me.

Every sojourn back to the time of the killings paves the way for, and in my experience, seemingly guarantees future growth.

My journey back to Uganda was not about exacting revenge. Justice Jones had warned the unnamed murderers decades ago that "Nemesis," the god of retribution from whom there is no escape, would "one day claim her pound of flesh." However, it is unclear whether justice had ever been dispensed by the goddess, or by mortal hands. Given the opportunity to retaliate, I had chosen not to take the lives of the perpetrators and no other individual touched by their evil had taken lethal action.

My journey was not necessarily about solving the mystery and, most certainly, not about forgiving the murderers. It was about remembering who

I was when the murders were committed, who my father was—honoring our father-son relationship, gaining a deeper understanding of my father's life work, his final days and hours of unimaginable suffering and how his and Stroh's murder impacted others and how it impacted me.

The sudden, unexpected disappearance of a loved one in a remote, unsettled region of the world; international military, judicial and intelligence investigations that went on for approximately two years exposing horrendous, grisly details but never identifying and prosecuting those responsible; bodies and remains that were never found; ties to the past obliterated—these were all profound injuries in need of healing.

It was a healing journey 26 years after the murders, undertaken by an accomplished adult, emotionally and professionally prepared and assisted by governments, military and intelligence communities. As an adult I was able to see that living in Uganda under Amin was far more dangerous than I could possibly comprehend at ages fifteen to seventeen. Time and again, hitchhiking, riding on a pikipiki motorcycle through the busy streets of the city of Kampala and on safari in the bush, I had been lucky.

Days after his 46th birthday and less than a week before he was scheduled to return to the United States, my father's luck had run out.

Returning showed me that after I left, Uganda had changed dramatically and for the worse. The entire country had descended into chaos. My father and I were not the only ones who suffered. No one was spared—millions of lives were ended or traumatically disrupted. As I had observed in my earlier conversation with General Muntu (and the General agreed), it seemed virtually every Ugandan was a victim, a perpetrator, or both, of the abominations that occurred.

Neither my father nor I could have possibly foreseen what was to come. It was a worst-case scenario no one could have imagined or prepared for. The massacre of hundreds and then hundreds of thousands was unthinkable. I needed to forgive my father for being in harm's way and myself for not preventing his murder—to accept that we were both blameless.

The greatest surprise came when I stood in our old apartment home at Makerere University and realized that all these years, deep in my heart, I had never let go of him. Never having the chance to say goodbye, I believed he was still there in the same place, like the loyal little toy dog and tin soldier in Eugene Field's poem *Little Boy Blue*, "gathering dust" awaiting his son's return. My father was still there for me, I believed.

And in a sense, he has always been and will always be. As a father now, I know that even in death, my love for my children will not ever end. If they need me, I will be there for them because they will always be in my heart, and I hope—trust—I will always be in theirs.

This journey had been my chance to reconnect and say goodbye, not only to my father, but to the life I once lived—my family, home and first seventeen years. Nothing was the same after my father's murder and never would be again.

And while I had expected the thousands of pages of declassified documents I reviewed to reveal incompetence and disregard for my welfare and the Stroh family, that's not what I found. Rather, the career Central Intelligence Agency and Department of State officials had actually been thoughtful and careful as they juggled the multiple factual, legal, financial and diplomatic issues involved. The level of vigilance and professionalism was impressive.

I tell myself, and have reason to believe, I am the very best at what I do—forensically investigating the incredibly complex world of international pensions and institutional investing involving trillions of dollars. The U.S. Government officials who represented my interests after the murder of my father were equally exceptional. Revisiting my father's murder as a mature, stronger survivor allowed me to see that even as an orphaned, penniless teenager, there were good people in the world—in both America and Uganda—looking out for me.

I was also reassured to learn that the Stroh family, for all its riches at that time, was not treated measurably better than my family by the U.S.

Government. I and my family benefitted from some of the resources the Stroh's brought to bear—especially Nicholas's connections in the worldwide press—and the Stroh family benefitted from intelligence provided by Ugandan contacts, friends of my father. In my opinion, the United States Government treated both families fairly. Neither family was disadvantaged for the benefit of the other.

Likewise, the international press's relentless pursuit of justice ensured Amin's Commission of Inquiry—which everyone, including the presiding judge himself, predicted would be a "whitewash"—was able to place responsibility for the murders squarely with the Ugandan Army. The massacre my father and Stroh went to Mbarara to investigate was not once mentioned in the Inquiry, soldiers responsible for the killings were never named and the fact Amin himself ordered the killings was never publicly acknowledged. But Amin's brutality was exposed and the international community never forgot. The international press had done its duty—speaking truth to power.

My journey back to Uganda gave me the opportunity to see the Simba Battalion barracks, the parade grounds, the government Rest House where my father spent his last night as a free man and the Guard House where he was imprisoned, beaten, tortured and after several agonizing days, possibly killed. The broader circumstances surrounding my father's killing—a massacre of over 500 Acholi and Langi soldiers, beaten to death by their colleagues and their bodies cold-bloodedly disposed—were finally described in detail to me. I sat face-to-face with the men whose names had long been associated with my father's murder and were burnt into my memory—Tibihika, the key testifying witness and Ali Fadhul, Amin's treacherous henchman. The murderers were desperate people, I now knew, whose worst instincts were unleashed at a time of widespread brutality and chaos. Not merely given a license to kill, they were ordered to kill.

I hadn't uncovered all the facts, but I had collected enough additional information on this journey to envision and comprehend much of what had happened. The pain of my father's murder would never go away, I knew, but now I had finally done all I could for the father I loved. I went back to find him, and in so doing, found myself transformed.

In my mind, this macabre riddle best summarizes my learning:

Q: *What's worse than mourning the brutal murder of a loved one?*

A: *Believing you caused, contributed to, or could have prevented the killing.*

To grieve, you must stop blaming yourself.

Now that I am much, much older with the majority of my life behind me, I have come to believe we all have important journeys we are destined to take—adventures that define who we are and what it means to be human. If you are called to such a journey, I encourage you to not resist but embrace the dreaded uncertainty. As much as you can, prepare for success but recognize that life's most profound odysseys can never be carefully mapped out. So much of where your path will lead will be unknown at the outset. But the remarkable feature of life-affirming journeys, I have found, is that you always encounter others who recognize the importance of what you're doing and will want to help you—as if the universe wants you to succeed and comes to your aid. You may feel yourself uplifted then passed over countless heads, floating on a sea of helping hands.

And if, when you were very young, something truly awful happened to you—an impossible situation not of your own making and beyond your control—you may feel compelled to journey back as an adult once you can do what you needed to care for yourself when you were a child, but couldn't.

Hopefully, you will be one of the blessed who survive to return.

Robert Louis Siedle
July 3, 1925- July ? 1971